A Journey, Remembered…

Isaac B. McDonald

Parson's Porch Books
www.parsonsporchbooks.com

A Journey, Remembered…
ISBN: Softcover 978-0-692-32776-0
Copyright © 2018 by Isaac B. McDonald

All rights reserved. No part of this book may be reproduced or transmitted in any form or by any means, electronic or mechanical, including photocopying, recording, or by any information storage and retrieval system, without permission in writing from the publisher.

A Journey, Remembered…

Contents

Acknowledgments 7
Introduction 9
Chapter 1 12
   Family History And Birth
Chapter 2 25
   Early Years
Chapter 3 36
   Early Years In Lake City, Florida
Chapter 4 46
   Early High School Years
Chapter 5 56
   Late High School Years
Chapter 6 66
   The College Years
Chapter 7 79
   Early Seminary Years
Chapter 8 91
   Late Seminary Years
Chapter 9 102
   Full-Time Ministry-Early Years
Chapter 10 112
   Paducah: The Early Years
Chapter 11 124
   Paducah: The Later Years
Chapter 12 147
   The Early Alabama Years
Chapter 13 159
   The Later Alabama Years
Chapter 14 178
   Early Hodgenville Years

Chapter 15 193
    Late Hodgenville Years

Chapter 16 205
    Hodgenville: Concluding Months

Chapter 17 219
    Unemployed: What Every Minister Fears

Chapter 18 232
    Interim Pastorates: The New Adventure

Chapter 19 248
    Interim Pastorates: A Continuing Saga

Chapter 20 256
    Going Strong, But Counting Down

Acknowledgments

The writing of this book has not been without encouragement from both family and friends. It cannot go to print without a word of thanks to those who have assisted, advised, encouraged and even prodded this author along the way.

As indicated elsewhere, my wife, JoAnn, was the first to suggest that I tell my story. She has been a source of encouragement and support throughout this endeavor. Further, with her computer skills, she has rescued me from a multitude of my inabilities and frustrations at the keyboard. The truth is that this volume would still be in the making if it were not for her patience and help. My everlasting thanks goes to her.

Our oldest son, Paul, a published writer, read my first manuscript telling me it was a good read, but tactfully added that it needed more work. Referring back to it today, I find his suggestion to be right on target. Thanks, Paul!

My cousin, Joan Lemke Stine, of Orlando, Florida, is more like a sister than a cousin. She learned that I had a manuscript ready for an editor. She gently suggested her granddaughter, Erin Fish. It was a stroke of good fortune. Thanks, Joan, for a timely suggestion.

Erin Fish was beginning a career in editing. She has an encouraging touch with those who aspire to be wordsmiths. Patiently, she worked her way through three different manuscripts. Finally, she said my work was ready for a publisher. For all her efforts, I offer my heartfelt thanks.

A host of friends and authors offered suggestions and support. Among those were Charles Chandler, Glen Mollette, John Killinger, George Ferree, just to name a few. My gratitude is not enough for their kind suggestions but thanks a heap!

An everlasting word of thanks to Almighty God, who called me to labor in His vineyard and gave me the gifts that I have used to minister in His name. May He be praised forever!

Introduction

"Each of us is a book waiting to be written, and that book, if written, results in a person explained."

~Thomas M. Cirignano

A Journey Remembered contains the partial story of my life. I have written it in response to the suggestions of family and friends who have heard portions of the story over time and have suggested repeatedly that a written record be made. Family history appears in genealogy and stories told to me by older family members who were more than willing to share. Though some accounts may have been slightly exaggerated, they are part of the family story. Having listened carefully to what my elders have shared with me, I may be the sole repository of family lore. Also, I have been assured that children, grandchildren, friends and other associates might find what I have written to be interesting and worth reading.

So I have put in print what I know and remember. The importance of this exercise was brought home to me in a comment by my wife, JoAnn. She stated quite simply that I ought to write what I could remember before something happened, and I would no longer be able to remember clearly. That statement caused me to begin writing what you are about to read. It is a record of my memory of a lifelong journey. I began writing in early June 2004. I was at that time 73 years old. Surprisingly, it has taken longer to write what you are about to read than I first anticipated. To those of you who read this record, I offer my thanks for taking the time to read an old man's account of his life and experiences. May you find the record informative and interesting.

George Meredith said, "Memoirs are the backstairs of history." That being true, we must not hesitate to share them. A memoir is exactly what this book is meant to be. It is the story, as I recall, of my life. Hopefully it is noteworthy. It tells of an unfolding, lifelong journey, of the following of a divine call to a way of life far different from anything I had dared to imagine in my early teenage years. It is the story of a quest, a searching, a striving to excel and to be the best possible in a calling that came to me during my middle teenage years and carried me forward as I sought to fulfill and answer the call of God for a special vocation.

Did I aspire to be a minister? No, I did not. Left to my own choices, I would have gone in another direction. Early in my seminary years, I considered leaving the ministry to go into medicine. I believe to this day that I would have been a good medical doctor, but I never could feel that I would be doing what God had called me to do if I left the ministry. Later I will tell of personal struggles and questionings during which God repeatedly assured me that He had called me and that He wanted me to continue in the ministry. Even now, in the twilight years of my life, that assurance remains with me.

I confess, without apology, that my life is not one filled with the heroics or accomplishments of the great leaders of our nation or of those who shaped the religious foundations that we cherish. However, I am proud to take my small place in the line of those who have loved this nation as well as those who have sought to contribute to its spiritual life, growth, and foundations through the efforts of a people long known as Baptists. The line of Baptists out of which I have come had their beginnings in England and Europe before coming to Colonial America. With Bible in hand, they came to this new land to carve out a place where they could be free to make a life for themselves and practice their faith without interference from those who believed differently.

I was blessed to live in a time when a good education was available to those willing to seek it. Further, I arrived at a time when Southern Baptists were reaching their zenith in terms of growth and national unity. But that time quickly passed. While I was able to complete college and seminary and move into an active ministry, the denomination which had birthed and nurtured me was about to rupture and slowly begin to lose its sense of direction and witness. To me, it was and is as if a terrible curse descended upon Baptists. I confess that I still grieve over the loss of denominational fellowship as well as a declining witness in our lost world.

Appearing at various times are incidents of misunderstanding and conflict. I confess that I never enjoyed either, but it seems that my life was blessed with a liberal measure of each. I was often surprised by these events while others were anticipated or seen approaching. I still wish that I had been blessed with the gift of avoiding such experiences rather than living through them.

As I tell of these events, I have concealed the identity of those whose actions may appear less than commendable. Most of those persons involved have now gone to their eternal reward, but they have descendants who do not deserve to be embarrassed or offended; therefore, I have made use of some fictitious names.

Having done that, I am reminded of the words of Anne Lamont who said, "You own everything that happened to you. Tell your stories. If people wanted you to write warmly about them, they should have behaved better." I confess that her words bring a smile to my face.

It is the middle of June 2017 as I complete this writing. More than a decade has been consumed with this endeavor. Every chapter has been edited and rewritten more than once. Where I had some sort of record, I made certain that the story was accurate. This is especially true of events in which there was conflict and efforts were being made to resolve differences. When persons are identified, it is because they were a part of the story whatever the circumstances. Experience has taught me that when persons differ in opinions, everyone believes that they are right. My effort here is to tell the story without assigning fault whenever possible. But, where differences exist, I still believe I was right.

And life goes on, continuing to move forward. This is a part of my story. I hope it is as readable as it was and continues to be livable. I have tried to share it warts and all. May you be able to rejoice in the good and profit from any of my visible missteps!

> "The Lord has promised good to me,
> His word my hope secures;
> He will my shield and portion be
> As long as life endures."
> From "Amazing Grace
> by
> John Newton, 1725-1807

Chapter 1

Family History and Birth

Everyone comes from at least two families. Often there are family heritages that reach back to grandparents, great-grandparents and beyond. In that respect, I am no different. My mother was a Young and my father was a McDonald, but there is more family history than just the names.

Both of my mother's parents had family that had settled in South Carolina and Georgia before the American Revolution. The Young family arrived in Charleston, South Carolina in 1732 in the persons of three brothers, Sam, Luther, and Oliver. Another brother, John William Young Jr., arrived in Charleston in 1735. These brothers were the sons of John William Young Sr., a native of Scotland who lived on a sheep ranch in the River Clyde Valley in Scotland. The family of John William Young Sr. had emigrated from Ireland in 1658, a year before he was born. Family records passed on to me from my mother which she had received from her father indicate that John Sr. died in 1740 at age eighty-one.

John William Young Jr. was twenty years old when he arrived in South Carolina in 1735. He lived on a farm in Level Land, South Carolina. The records that I have indicate that he died in 1815, which would have made him about one hundred years old. There appears to be some gaps in the records that have been passed on to me (I have my doubts that John William Young Jr. fathered a son at the age of ninety-seven). The next listed descendant of John William Young, Jr. is probably his grandson, William Lytle Young, born February 22, 1812. William and his wife, Mary Burgess, had fourteen children, seven sons and seven daughters. The family continued to live on the family farm in Level Land. William was a man of many gifts. He was a farmer, carpenter, blacksmith, and shoemaker. He is buried at Little River Baptist Church, Level Land, South Carolina.

The oldest son of William Lytle Young was James Pickens Young Sr., who is my great-grandfather. He and his wife, Sara Frances Calaham (born July 24, 1860, in Abbeville County, South Carolina; died June 11, 1938), had eleven children, seven sons and four daughters. Both of these great-grandparents are buried at Neal Creek Baptist Church, Anderson, South Carolina.

William Pickens Young Sr. was the oldest son of James Pickens and Sara Frances Young. He was my mother's father. He was born on January 15, 1884, in Abbeville County, South Carolina. On August 1, 1906, he married my grandmother, Anzonetta "Nettie" Anderson. My grandfather was a farmer and rural mail carrier in Lavonia, Georgia. He later went into the grocery business, but a bout with typhoid fever (some in the family insist that it was rheumatic fever which later brought on his heart disease) forced him to give that up. While recovering from the ravages of this illness, he began to study insurance and went into that line of work. He moved his family to Florida in 1926 and continued working in insurance until his death on May 28, 1945. He was a lifelong Baptist, serving his church as a deacon and Sunday School Superintendent. He was also a Republican, the first one that I ever knew personally. Though I never heard him speak of his political beliefs, I did hear him speak of his spiritual beliefs. He was the best man that I ever knew. My cousin William Y. Harrell once said that our "Grandpa was the glue that held the family together." Looking back at the changes that took place in our family after his death, I can only conclude that my cousin was right.

My grandfather's only son was named William Pickens Young Jr. When his only son was born, my uncle's wife decided to give him a name she thought was not commonly used in the Young family. She named my cousin John William Young. It was not until much later that we discovered that our Scottish ancestor and his son who later came to this country both bore that name. Solomon was right when he said, "There is nothing new under the sun."

When I was in my late teens, my mother received a phone call early one Sunday morning. I learned that the call came from a cousin, Edna Anderson Manning from Barnwell, South Carolina. She was doing genealogical research on the Anderson family. Edna was in town with her husband, W. H. Manning Jr. She wanted to visit with my mother to verify some information on the family and gather any other information that my mother had. She had come to the right place. My mother had an excellent memory and she had quietly been gathering as much information on both sides of the family as was available to her.

This event introduces the source from which I have been able to learn much of what I know about my paternal grandmother's Anderson family. Edna and her husband did a thorough job of researching both of their families. In early 1959, they published a 1600-page volume entitled, "Our Kin", which was the product of all their research and travels. I am in possession of my mother's copy of that book.

The principal seat of the Anderson family was West Airderbreck in Scotland. A branch of the family settled in Fermoy in County Cork, Ireland. Sir James Anderson, Lord Provost of Aberdeen, is said to have used the same coat of arms with a few minor changes. The Andersons appear to have been a most prominent family in Scotland.

Edna Manning writes that "the name Anderson means 'the son of Andrew' and is the ninth most popular name in Scotland. The clan Aindreas, 'Sons of Andrew', came under the head of the Clan Ross, the progenitor of the old Earls of Ross being the eldest son of Gilleoin nah-Airde, the ancestor of Anrias. The plaid of the Andersons,

Andrews, and Ross is an attractive one, having a bright red background with green and blue stripes." The plaid that she describes is that of the clan Ross. My research reveals the Anderson plaid to be on a turquoise green background which changes to various shades of green with red and green stripes. Both plaids are striking in beauty.

Numerous immigrants bearing the name Anderson came to America and settled both in the North and South. One of the earliest Andersons who settled in Virginia was Thomas. He came from Northumberland, England, on the border of Scotland. It appears that three groups of Andersons came to Virginia and settled there. A William Anderson, born in Scotland in 1693, came to America in disguise because he is alleged to have participated in the uprising of 1715 led by the Pretender Prince James, son of James II. It is believed that he received financial help from his family back in Scotland. They apparently had the resources to help him begin his new life in America. He was a man of means, buying and selling several plantations in Prince George County, Maryland. He died at age 104 in 1797. He had four children, two sons and two daughters.

The oldest son of the above-mentioned William Anderson was Thomas Anderson. Thomas' wife was Mary Bruce, also of Scottish descent. On December 3, 1776, a deed was recorded in Lincolnton, Lincoln County, North Carolina (see Deed Book 2, page 382), stating that Thomas Anderson Sr. and his wife, Mary, sold to Thomas Anderson Jr., of Tryon, North Carolina, one hundred acres of land including houses and timber. This said parcel of land had been granted to Thomas Anderson Sr., on April 10, 1761. From this information, we can assume that the Thomas Anderson family had moved south from Maryland to Virginia and on to North Carolina and established themselves there. This seems to confirm the later word passed down through the family that the Andersons had moved to Georgia from Burke County, North Carolina. While no traceable link between the William Anderson who first settled in Maryland and our Anderson family has been established, it is believed that our branch of the Anderson family descended from him.

Since there has been no record found of the name of the wife of Thomas Anderson Jr., Edna Manning suggests that he probably married a lady from one of the several Farmer families in the area. Thus, the name of their only child of whom we have record is Thomas Farmer Anderson. The reason for a lack of family records given by Edna Manning is the fact that General William Sherman and his troops burned the town of Morganton, Burke County, North Carolina, during the Civil War and the records perished in the fire. Edna was not happy with Sherman's actions.

General Thomas Farmer Anderson was born in October 1779 in North Carolina. He died in Banks County, Georgia, on March 17, 1875, at the age of ninety-seven. He is buried in the Anderson Cemetery between Homer and Maysville, Georgia. He was active in the Georgia State Militia. He organized a company of men and served with

Andrew Jackson during the War of 1812. Returning to Georgia after the War of 1812, he continued his service in the State Militia of Georgia, rising to the rank of Brigadier General. He did not retire from the State Militia of Georgia until age seventy-seven. He also served multiple terms in the Georgia State Legislature in the House of Representatives and the Senate. He was an active member of the Grove Level Baptist Church. He was looked upon with respect as a family man, businessman, farmer, military man, and a political leader in his community and state.

The second son of General Thomas Farmer Anderson was James Anderson, born November 18, 1809. He was the father of twelve children and husband to Martha Arrowood. He died in Atlanta sometime around 1890. His wife, who was born in 1814, died in Hartwell, Georgia on January 11, 1894. They were the parents of my great-grandfather, Harvey Reese Anderson, who was most likely named after his uncle, Dr. Harvey Reese Anderson. James Anderson lost his eyesight as the result of a farming accident in about 1870. The family left the farm and went to the city where the children could find work to help support the family. Four of James Anderson's sons served with the Confederacy during the Civil War. Thomas D. Anderson, born in 1834, was killed in the war. John L. and Harvey Reese Anderson, identical twin sons, were both severely wounded in battle. With the family moving from the old homestead along with the ravages of war and poor health, contact was lost, and little is known about most of the family. It is believed that most of the sons went west, but no one seemed to know where.

My grandmother's father was Harvey Reese Anderson, one of the twin sons of the above-mentioned James Anderson. Born in 1840, he would have been about twenty-one years old when the Civil War began in April 1861. My grandmother's story was that he and his brother were sixteen years old and that they ran away and joined the Confederate Army, but that appears to be a family exaggeration. He and his twin brother, John L. Anderson, were said to be identical twins. Most people could not tell them apart until after the war. John lost a leg in the war and Harvey was wounded in the upper chest and right shoulder, losing use of his right arm and hand. Harvey served in the 24th Regiment of the Georgia Infantry during the Civil War. He was wounded at Crampton's Gap in 1862. Word passed down through the family is that he lay wounded for three days before aid came to him. My grandmother often told the story of a Yankee soldier passing by him as he lay wounded. Harvey was said to have had bright, curly red hair. The Yankee soldier stopped, took out a knife, cut off a lock of hair, and departed, leaving Harvey with a canteen of water and a blanket. When the Yankee soldier first took out his knife to cut the lock of hair, Harvey said he was afraid that he was going to cut his throat and finish him off. Granny also told me that often his daily ration of food while serving in the Confederate Army was a handful of parched or roasted corn.

After the Civil War, Harvey sold his property in Banks County, Georgia, moving to Hartwell to live. He served several terms as Tax Collector for Hart County, Georgia. My grandmother told me that he was a scribe because of his beautiful and legible handwriting. After the War, he taught himself to write again with his left hand having lost the use of his right hand as a result of his war wounds. On October 11, 1883, he married Nancy Ann McConnell (b. Oct 27, 1860, d. September 5, 1931). They had five children, one son and four daughters, all of whom were born in Hartwell. Harvey Reese Anderson died as a result of the lingering effects of his military wounds. He was buried in Hartwell, Georgia, on April 22, 1896.

The second child of Harvey Reese and Nancy Ann Anderson was Anzonetta Anderson, known as "Nettie" born on December 14, 1886, in Hartwell, Georgia. On August 1, 1906, she married William Pickens Young, Sr. They became the parents of one son and four daughters. My mother, Meldred Anderson Young, was their oldest child, born May 3, 1907. It is my understanding that all of the children were born in Lavonia, Georgia, except the youngest, Mary Sue, who was born in Easley, South Carolina. The family lived on a farm, and "Will" as my grandfather was known, was a rural mail carrier. Following my mother's birth on May 3, 1907, came the birth of twins, Helen and Hallie, born on May 9, 1909. Two years later, my mother's only brother, William Pickens Young Jr., was born on July 17, 1911. On April 6, 1915, my grandmother delivered her last child, a daughter named Mary Sue.

With five children born over a period of eight years, my grandmother had her hands full as a mother and a wife. I do not know how much education she had, but she was an avid reader. She read the newspapers of her day. She read the sermons of prominent ministers which were printed in the newspapers on a weekly basis. She read the Bible and could quote it without hesitation. She was a woman of strong opinions and morals. She would often cite as poor examples members of both sides of the family who had fallen into sin and a wayward life, encouraging her grandchildren to stay close to the Lord and to run from Satan. She had countless quotes from the preachers of her day, the Bible, Benjamin Franklin, and many other sources which she was quick to share with her grandchildren. Most of the time, we did not want to hear what she had to say, but for some reason we can easily recall her words and instruction.

My mother's parents had a marriage that lasted thirty-nine years, ending with my grandfather's death. They were always together but were completely different in many ways. The marriage survived hard economic times, personal sickness and epidemics, moves away from close family relationships along with the trials and troubles of their maturing children. Two of their daughters had marriages that failed and resulted in divorce. Throughout their married life, my grandparents were faithful Christians and members of a local Baptist church.

A Journey, Remembered...

After my grandfather's death in 1945, my grandmother sold their home and small farm. She went to Panama City, Florida, to live with her youngest daughter, Mary Sue. Unfortunately, that arrangement did not prove to be satisfactory. She also tried living with her other daughters for brief periods of time, but the stress on them and their families proved to be too great. Finally, she came to live with my mother in Lake City, Florida. It was not a happy situation. My mother's marriage to Ralph Hardee Sr. already had its problems. This proved to be an additional stress. Though my mother never said that having her mother in the home caused the divorce that followed, both my brother and I feel that it was a major contributor to the failure of the marriage. However, Granny remained with my mother until her death on July 5, 1959.

My mother, Meldred Anderson Young, was the oldest child of William Pickens Young Sr. and Anzonetta "Nettie" Anderson Young. She was born in or near Lavonia, Georgia on May 3, 1907. She married Isaac B. McDonald Sr. on March 16, 1931. I was born nine months and two weeks later on December 30, 1931. After her divorce from my father, she married Ralph Simm Hardee Sr. on December 16, 1936. My only brother, Ralph Simm Hardee Jr., was born on December 14, 1937. My mother was an idealist, always trying to get things in the family and elsewhere as perfect as possible. She was intensely loyal to her family to the point of self-sacrifice. She could never understand why her sisters were not of the same mind. This became a source of conflict between them that intensified over the years and was never resolved.

My mother's second sister was Sarah Hallie, the first of a set of fraternal twins born on May 9, 1909. Sarah Hallie married Hiram W. Sperry of Apalachicola, Florida, on June 29, 1928. Their first daughter, Mary Hollie, was born on January 25, 1930. Their second daughter, Ann Murrow, was born on September 19, 1932. The family moved to Panama City where Uncle Hiram went into the construction business after World War II. He had a thriving business at the time of his death in the late 1960s. He became a Brigadier General in the Florida National Guard after the War. Mary Hollie retired from teaching in Atlanta, came back to Panama City, and cared for her mother and Aunt Mary Sue until their deaths. She then returned to Atlanta. Ann married B. G. "Buddy" Hair of Baton Rouge, Louisiana, and they reside in that area. During the years when we lived in Hardeetown, Florida, Aunt Hallie saw to it that Santa Claus always came to our house. We were poor, they had more, and they shared.

My mother's third sister, a twin to Hallie, was Helen Ann. She was the smaller of the twins and a delightful person. Her first marriage was to Perry Harrell. Their son, William Y. Harrell, whom we called Billy, was the oldest grandchild. He was born August 25, 1930. Aunt Helen's marriage to Perry ended in divorce. My grandparents took Billy and cared for him as if he were their own child until Grandpa's untimely death on May 28, 1945. My records on Aunt Helen's marriage to Julian Fralick are inaccurate, but I know they married around 1940. They never had children. Billy lived with them after Grandpa died. Uncle Julian was a carpenter, gifted with his hands, and was a creative builder. He was a very patient and kind. He dearly loved my Aunt Helen.

My mother's only brother was William Pickens "Dub" Young Jr. He was born July 11, 1911. He married Mary Virginia Winderweedle on October 12, 1934. They had three children: Luanna, born March 8, 1938; Wilma Frances, born July 18, 1939; and John William, born October 24, 1941. Uncle Dub was the first of my mother's siblings to die. He passed away on September 20, 1946, at the age of 35. His death was another untimely and tragic blow to the family.

My mother's youngest sister was Mary Sue, born on April 6, 1915. She received a lion's share of love and attention from the family. She told me that Granny was so protective of her that she refused to let her go to school until she was in the fourth grade. Granny home schooled her before home schooling was the vogue. When I asked Aunt Mary about the curriculum that Granny used, she said that Granny taught her from Uncle Dub's school books and had her do his lessons until she entered fourth grade. Aunt Mary was a tall, classy lady. She was attractive, charming, and always had men friends, but chose never to marry. I remained very close to her throughout her life.

My father, Isaac Burkhalter McDonald Sr., was born in Ray City, Berrien County, Georgia, on September 3, 1912. He married my mother on March 16, 1931. While both of my parents loved each other, their marriage did not last. My mother, who was my father's second wife, was older than my father and had much different goals for the marriage. My father was younger and was struggling to keep a steady job during the Great Depression years. His immaturity was obvious in the failure of his three marriages. He was single at the time of his death on January 9, 1945.

For much of my early life, I assumed that my father left my mother and me because he did not love us. My mother had said as much on several occasions. However, something happened after I was married and had children of my own. In a conversation with my mother, I stated that had he loved us, he would not have left us. My mother quietly got up, went to a trunk in which she kept things, took a package of yellowed letters out of it, and gave them to me. They were letters that my father had written to her during their marriage breakup and divorce proceedings. I still have those letters today. In them, my father told of his frustrations about keeping a steady job and about not having any money to support a family. Poverty was a reality, and the legal demands put on him by my mother and the court system seemed to have overwhelmed him. However, he continued to insist that he loved me and my mother. I gained from those letters a perspective and insight into our family breakup that changed many things for me.

It was obvious from my father's letters that my mother had placed on him the responsibility for keeping the family together. It is also obvious that he was hardly more than a kid of about nineteen to twenty years old. He was a happy-go-lucky person, a kind of free spirit. When it came to women, he loved the chase and could not seem to find a way to give it up. On the other hand, my mother was not about to put up with a man who would not be true to her. She also expected, and rightly so, that he would do his best to keep his end of the financial bargain. The clash that followed brought the family relationship to an end. They divorced when I was about two years old.

In my mother's heartbreak and disappointment, I am almost positive that she told him that she never wanted to see him again. I am certain such language was not easy for him to hear or accept. He did continue to visit, but he soon moved away to northwest Georgia and the visits ended. My mother and I moved from Chipley in west Florida to Chiefland, Florida, about three years later. All contact with my father and his family ceased. We had no contact with him or any of his family until early April 1945, when one of my father's sisters contacted my mother's father and shared with him the news of my father's death on January 9, 1945, in a military plane crash in Biak, New Guinea. My grandfather came to me that evening and shared the sad news.

This brings my story to the McDonald side of my family. As of August 2015, we have been able to go back only as far as my great-great-grandfather, Angus McDonald. He was born in about 1806. On September 10, 1835, he married Nancy Williamson in Jones County, Georgia. Her date of birth is estimated to be sometime in 1816. The 1850 census shows them living in Crawford County, Georgia, where Angus was employed as an overseer. The 1860 census shows them to be still living in Crawford County, and Angus is listed as a farmer. They appear to have been the parents of six children, five boys and one girl. The boys were John, born about 1837; James A., born July 27, 1841; Robert L., born about 1843; William F., born about 1847; and Neal J., born about 1849. The one daughter was Margaret A., born about 1839. Visit the Clan MacDonald web site, www.macdonald.com, and enter the name Angus McDonald. You will find scores of persons in Scottish history with that name. Thus far, we have been unable to make any McDonald connection beyond Angus who was born in or about 1806.

My great-grandfather was James A. McDonald. According to the 1910 census, he was born in 1841 in Monroe County, Georgia. He died at age ninety on March 12, 1931 and is buried in the Confederate Cemetery at Bethany Church in Cochran, Georgia. On March 4, 1862, he had enlisted in the Henderson Rangers from Houston County, Georgia. The Houston Rangers were in Company H, 45th Regiment, Georgia Volunteer Infantry, Army of Northern Virginia. He was a private and fought at Gettysburg. He was severely wounded when, according to my Uncle Talmadge, a cannon ball exploded near him. His pelvis was fractured, and he lost his left arm. Of course, he was captured. He received the medical treatment that was available and luckily survived. He told Uncle Tal that two women cared for him while he recovered. Food was so scarce that they ate rats, but he survived. Late in the War he was paroled and returned home. He walked all the way back to Georgia. It is a long way from Gettysburg, Pennsylvania, to Cochran, Georgia.

Sometime after arriving home in Cochran or Empire, Georgia, James A. McDonald married Frances C. "Fannie" Davidson. She was the daughter of Joseph Davidson and Delila Buckner. She was born May 4, 1839, and died March 18, 1923, in Bleckley County, Georgia. She appears to have been previously married to a man named Joiner who was killed in the Civil War. She had one daughter by that marriage named Fannie. The 1870 census lists this daughter as Fannie Joiner, age nine, a child from her mother's previous marriage.

Family members tell that Fannie's first husband and James were good friends. When they joined the Confederate Army, James had promised his friend that if anything happened to him, he would look after his family. True to his word he did. Five children were born into their family, two sons and three daughters, including Fannie's daughter by her first marriage. My grandfather was their fourth child and the first son. The youngest child was also a son named James Edward McDonald. Some of his family still live in Cochran, Georgia. His daughter, Eula McDonald Williams, was still alive in May 2000. She lived in Cochran across the road from the old home place of James A. McDonald which was still standing at that time.

My great-grandfather appears to have never lost his Southern sympathies, indicated by the fact that he named his first son, who was my grandfather, Robert Lee McDonald. Further, my grandfather named one of his sons, Fitzhugh Lee McDonald. Fitzhugh Lee was a Confederate General with whom my great-grandfather served during the Civil War. James A. McDonald is alleged to have served as a personal aide, a valet, to General Lee and was with him until James was wounded in the Battle of Gettysburg. I have no way of verifying this story but am sharing it as part of our family verbal history.

After hearing the story of James A. McDonald serving with General Fitzhugh Lee, I did some research and learned that General Lee was a nephew of General Robert E. Lee. He was born in Virginia on November 19, 1835. He attended the US Military Academy at West Point and graduated in 1856. He resigned his commission in the US Military to accept a commission as first lieutenant in the Confederate Army in May 1861. On July 24, 1862, he became a brigadier general and on August 3, 1862, he became a major general. He led a cavalry brigade in several Civil War battles including the Battle of Gettysburg. So the family story may be more truth than fiction.

According to the 1880 census, James A. McDonald and Fannie Davidson McDonald had six children: Fannie, Ida, Ella, Robert Lee, Annie, and James Edward. Their ages then ranged from seventeen years to about three years. Since James A. lost an arm in the Civil War and was unable to do manual labor, he became a school teacher. Family tradition says that he taught the children of sawmill workers. The following is a bit of verbal family history shared with me by my uncle Talmadge McDonald. He called James A., who was apparently small in stature, "The Little Professor." Uncle Tal also said that James A. kept a good supply of turkey feathers nearby. He would trim the end of the feather with a small knife, split it, thus making a quill to use for writing.

Robert Lee McDonald Sr. was born on August 14, 1873, in Telfair County, Georgia. He died in 1953 at the age of eighty and was buried in Valdosta, Georgia. He married Lilla Marie Woodson on December 26, 1891, in Dodge County, Georgia. She was born in Telfair County, Georgia, on December 10, 1876. She was the daughter of Fred Barfield Woodson and was the oldest of five children. Her brothers were Ovid, Fred, and John. She had one sister named Minnie. From 1893 until 1914 she gave birth to twelve children, seven boys and five girls. Their names in order of their births are: James Frederick, Robert Fulton, Mittie Virginia (Aunt Mary), Fitzhugh Lee, Allie Lillian, Annie Vivian, John Wesley, Eunice Irene, William Talmadge, Lemuel Candler, Isaac Burkhalter, and Lois Alberta. Two of the girls, Lillian and Vivian, were twins. My father, Isaac B. McDonald Sr., was Lilla' youngest son. She died on November 14, 1924, from breast cancer. She is buried in Ray City, Berrien County, Georgia, where the family was living at that time. At the writing of this document in August 2015, I have no other information on my grandmother's family.

The 1910 census listed Robert Lee McDonald as a sawyer, meaning that he was employed at "sawing wood in a lumber camp or a sawmill." His principal employment for most of his working life was at or around a sawmill. He ran a sawmill for Isaac Burkhalter, a prominent land owner and timber baron in south central Georgia. In fact, my father was named for him. The story that Robert Lee McDonald told my mother was that Isaac Burkhalter complained to him that his wife would not name any of their children after him. Knowing that Robert Lee's wife expecting, Isaac said to my grandfather, "Mac, if your next child is a boy and you name him after me, I will give you that red brood sow over there. And I will have my doctor son deliver the child free of charge."

Grandpa Mac took the offer. The sow later delivered thirteen pigs. My father got the name, but the young doctor was not present for my father's birth. He was all the way across the county delivering another child. My grandmother delivered my father with the help of a midwife. According to Grandpa Mac, my grandmother cut the umbilical cord herself. She had a lot of grit. When I was born, my mother named me after my father, a fact that I did not learn until I was about nine years old. Until that time, I thought my name was simply "Ikie."

Isaac Burkhalter owned several sawmills. According to family members, my grandfather was one of his more responsible employees often overseeing the operation of those sawmills. In those days, the railroad could be persuaded to build a spur out to the location of a sawmill if the location was reasonably permanent. Mr. Burkhalter later bought his own steam locomotive, thus making it possible to move the newly cut lumber to the main railroad line for shipment without having to wait for the railroad employees to move it.

Because of my grandfather's employment with Isaac Burkhalter, three of his sons learned to operate a locomotive and became railroad engineers. Fred, Fitzhugh, and Talmadge all went to work for the railroad as engineers and followed that profession their entire lives. Talmadge was nineteen years old when he went to work for the railroad. Family members said that he was the youngest railroad engineer in world at that time. Lemuel also went to work for the railroad as a conductor. My father learned to drive the big semi-trucks that hauled the logs and the cut timber. Later, he became a trucker.

While serving as Pastor of Lone Oak First Baptist Church in Paducah, Kentucky, from 1963 until 1971, I met a retired railroad engineer who had worked with my uncles in Georgia. He was a close friend of my Uncle Fred. He recalled that my Uncle Fitzhugh had the smoothest touch on the locomotive throttle that he had ever seen. He said that "Fitzhugh could start a train moving and you would not know it was moving until you looked out the window and realized that it was going about ten miles per hour." He jokingly said Uncle Fred was not quite that smooth.

After my grandmother Lilla's death, my grandfather married again. His second wife's name was Belle. All the family called her "Aunt Belle." She was several years younger than my grandfather and much less refined than Lilla. They had one son whom she named Robert Lee McDonald Jr. He died of a heart attack while in his mid-forties. I had little contact with him or his family and know almost nothing about them.

I had one brief visit with my grandfather, Robert Lee, and his wife, Belle. LaVerne Blue Jr., the youngest son of my Aunt Mary, and I went to visit with these grandparents in Valdosta, Georgia. It was a pleasant weekend visit and we returned home. The next week, a letter arrived from Aunt Lillian saying that Aunt Belle had written that their Social Security check should have arrived while we were visiting them, and that Aunt Belle thought we had taken it. She told my mother that if that was the case and if we would return the check, all would be forgiven.

My mother was astounded and angered. She read the letter to me and I told her the truth. Neither LaVerne nor I knew anything about the check. We did not even see any mail while we were there. Since we had visited over the weekend, it turned out that the mail was late. The check came the next week, but an apology from Aunt Belle never arrived. LaVerne and I were kids in our early teens. Neither of us knew how to steal a check, sign it, or cash it. The accusation was preposterous and unwarranted. My displeasure over the accusation caused me to vow that I would never again have anything to do with my grandfather or his wife and I never did.

Chapter 2
Early Years

One of my natural gifts is that of a retentive memory. I recall events, people, and the ordinary things of life that many people do not retain. My mother may have had the same gift because she often told me things that had happened earlier in her life. I do not remember everything that has occurred, but I recall a great deal. Much of what you will read in these pages comes from the deep recesses of my memory. Having said that, I would remind my readers that I did not keep a dairy nor did any member of my family keep any sort of diary. This is probably why my wife kept insisting that I write this document while my memory was still clear.

My parent's marriage was already in trouble by the time of my birth. I was born at the home of my maternal grandparents, who were living in Live Oak, Florida, at that time. My mother told me that I was born on Wednesday, December 30, 1931, at 6:30 p.m. While writing this I consulted a 1931 calendar and a copy of my birth certificate. They revealed that I was born exactly as my mother stated. Dr. H. M. Strickland delivered me but apparently did not file a record of my birth until sometime later in January 1932. He filled out the birth certificate on January 8, 1932, but listed my birth as December 30, 1932, at 6:40 p.m., which is a ten-minute time difference between his notes and my mother's memory. The mistake about the year I was born was discovered and corrected on February 1, 1946, when my mother was in the process of filing for a minor's pension as the result of my father's death during World War II.

I do not know how long my mother and I lived with my grandparents in Live Oak, but my first memory of any place that we lived was in Chipley, Florida. My mother had completed all but three months of nurses training and had been able to go to work for a physician in Chipley. She rented an apartment in someone's home. During the day, my mother left me with either one of two families named Scott and McRae. I recall that our apartment was either in one of their homes or we lived next door to them. Both families had several teenage children, so I was never lacking for someone to look after me.

My second birthday was celebrated with a party. I remember receiving an alarm clock with the image Mickey Mouse on the face. Mickey's arms were the hands of the clock. His head would move with each tick tock of the clock. It was like he was nodding yes as the clock ticked. That clock lasted into my teenage years. I wish I had saved it.

One of the vivid memories from those years in Chipley was a visit from my father. He was a truck driver, delivering beer to various establishments. I remember him driving a big white truck to our house. It was about the size of a Coca Cola or Pepsi truck used today for city delivery. As darkness was falling my mother and I sat in the truck and talked with my father. I was fascinated with the colored outside lights that were on the cab of the truck. I kept playing with them turning them on and off. Finally, my father said, "Don't do that, son. You will run my battery down." As the visit continued, I recall that my mother's voice began to sound angry and frustrated. I do not know how the visited ended, but I do not recall my father visiting us again.

There was a strong storm, possibly a hurricane, while we lived in Chipley. I seem to have vague memories of it, but what I remember most is the aftermath. The weather was beautiful after the storm, but there were tree limbs down everywhere. Houses had damage. The roof on a neighbor's porch had been blown partly away. Much of the conversation of people for several days centered around that storm.

My mother's only brother married while we were living in Chipley. We rode the train to Live Oak for the wedding. My uncle William P. Young, Jr. married Mary Virginia Winderweedle, the only daughter, of a Live Oak merchant. They had a mom and pop store next to their house in Live Oak. My uncle and aunt ran that store for several years before they sold it and moved to Lake City, Florida.

While we lived in Chipley, we attended the First Baptist Church. I do not know how old I was when my mother stopped leaving me in the church nursery and began taking me with her into the worship service. She told me that one Sunday morning during the offertory prayer, I got away from her and wandered down front near the Lord's Supper Table. After I got there, I began to crow like a rooster. The crowing was a little trick that the Scott and McRae teenagers had taught me. The incident amused the congregation and embarrassed my mother.

I did not attend school in Chipley, but I did attend a kindergarten. I don't know who sponsored or ran it, but I remember attending and being with other children near my own age.

Sometime after my fourth birthday, my mother and I moved to Hardeetown, Florida, a small village about a mile away from Chiefland, Florida, in Levy County. My mother's parents were living there, and we moved to be with them. It seems that my mother's job with the physician in Chipley had ended. I think he closed his practice and moved to another town. These were the years of the Great Depression, and the economic effects of that era lingered in the South much longer than in other parts of the country. In fact, the South did not recover from the effects of the Civil War and the Great Depression until World War II came along.

One of my first memories of Hardeetown were of the butterflies that congregated around the mud puddles and other accumulations of ground water. I remember seeing more butterflies than I had ever seen before. They were beautiful and fascinating to watch. I was also introduced to an outdoor toilet. It seemed to me that the entire outhouse was filled with spiders, and I was terribly afraid of them. Their presence made going to the toilet a terrifying venture!

We entered into the social activities of the community, which consisted mostly of attending church at the Hardeetown Baptist Church. My first memory of being in a Sunday School class was at that church. I also noticed a man who sang in the choir who paid some attention to me and a lot of attention to my mother. I understood that because I thought she was the prettiest woman that I had ever seen. That impression lasted well up into my teens. My mother was a very attractive woman. She had brown eyes, jet black hair, fair skin, pleasant features, and a warm and friendly personality.

The man in the choir was Ralph Simm Hardee. The Hardee family had migrated from South Carolina into Georgia and settled in Florida. Hardeetown was a small village named for the Hardee family. There is a Hardee County in south central Florida, and there was a former governor named Cary Hardee from Live Oak, Florida. Hardeetown has since been assimilated into what is now greater Chiefland.

My mother began dating Ralph Hardee, and on December 16, 1936, they were married. Following their marriage, my mother and I moved with my stepfather into the old plantation home that Isaac P. Hardee had built when he first came to Florida around 1860. His son Emmett R. Hardee had inherited the home along with four sections of land. Emmett was the father of Ralph. Ralph's mother was the former Laura Beauchamp. When we moved into the old plantation home to live with them, they appeared to accept us with open arms. I called Emmett "Grandpa Hardee" and Laura "Grandma Hardee".

The Hardee plantation home was a two-story wood frame house with a porch all the way across the front of the house on both stories. It was the first plank house built in that part of Florida. Isaac P. Hardee had the timber cut and the planks hand-planed and shipped via the Suwannee River to Clay's Landing near Manatee Springs. The lumber was then hauled about seven miles to the home site. The home was located in a clearing that faced a large grove of towering live oak trees. There was a road approaching the front of the home that wound its way through the trees to the house. The house could be seen some distance before one arrived. There was a family cemetery located on the south side of the house. Most of the Hardee family and some slaves have been buried there. When I lived there, I often helped with cleaning up and keeping the cemetery grounds in good repair. I was amazed as a child to see the graves of so many babies and children. The old childhood diseases of measles, whooping cough, diphtheria, and pneumonia took their toll on families. The Hardee plantation home, which is still standing, was until recently owned and occupied by a member of the family.

The first Christmas that I can recall took place just after Mama and I went to live with my stepfather in the Hardee plantation home. A large Christmas tree was placed in the family living room. It was brightly decorated, and gifts were placed under the tree. One evening before Christmas, most of the Hardee family gathered for the exchange and opening of gifts. It was a happy occasion.

A large Christmas tree was also placed in the sanctuary of Hardeetown Baptist Church where we attended. I was particularly impressed with the glory and beauty of the Christmas music. I could not read at the time, but my mother helped me learn the words. I sang the Christmas carols with great joy. On the night that we had our Christmas program, Santa came and gave gifts to all the children. Though I was only six years old, I did not think he looked much like the pictures that I had seen of Santa.

Sometime during the first year of their marriage, my mother and stepfather moved into the old pharmacy building that Emmett Hardee owned in Hardeetown. Emmett had attended Columbia College in Lake City and had become a licensed pharmacist. However, he had closed the pharmacy by the time we came on the scene. The old pharmacy building was a large structure about twenty-five feet by thirty-five feet with no partitions. My parents set up various areas for a family room, bedroom, kitchen and the like. I don't think we had electricity or running water. I don't recall anything about the toilet. The building was on the main street that ran through the town. Wesley Arrington had a general store almost directly across the street.

The Atlantic Coast Line had a railroad track that ran north and south right by our house and through the middle of Hardeetown. The railroad station was on the main street just across the railroad tracks toward Chiefland. There was quite a bit of traffic on the railroad. There was a local freight and passenger train, with more freight than passengers, that ran morning and evening. We called the train "Sunny Jim." There was a fast passenger train that ran from Chicago to Tampa and St. Petersburg late each day. It came south at almost midnight and returned north at about daybreak. It was called "The Southland." Only on rare occasions was I awake when it passed, but I saw Sunny Jim both times it passed each day. The engineer, fireman, and brakeman would all greet us with a wave as they passed by and we waved back. Trains were special in those days.

When the 1937-38 school year began, I entered the first grade at Chiefland. Since my birthday came before January 1, I was permitted to enroll even though I was only five years old. My teacher was a lady named Gertrude Sapp from the small town of Bell in Gilchrist County. She was an old maid school teacher. I found her to be patient, kind, and helpful. I sent her an invitation to my graduation from the University of Florida. I felt she should know that her efforts on my behalf had not been in vain.

Though I enjoyed school and liked most of my teachers, the social experience at school was entirely different from anything I had ever experienced. The Levy County social structure was agricultural, mostly anti-education, and highly clannish. I soon learned that the Hardee family did not consider me one of their own. I was not "blood kin" to them. When I got to school, I realized that I was on my own.

Further, there was a pecking order in the community. Since I was an outsider, I was at the bottom of the pecking order. I was fair game for anyone who had a grudge, a gripe, or the need to pick on someone. This was something that I had never experienced before because previously I had been in the company of family or friends. I had no siblings and had never experienced conflict or fighting with any of my cousins. You can imagine the shock that came when I was thrust into a competitive society dominated by children from large, aggressive families. Most of the boys wore bib overhauls to school and went barefooted until after the first frost. My mother insisted that I wear short pants and shoes, which set me apart and caused my peers to make fun of my appearance and heap continual abuse on me. Without family or friends to insist that such behavior stop, I became a constant target of those who chose to make life miserable for others. Also, my mother, idealist that she was, had taught me not to fight, and I really did not know how to stand up for myself.

Several events from these years stand out in my memory. The first took place sometime during the first grade. Many of the students brought their lunch to school. Lunch would be a couple of biscuit sandwiches wrapped in newspaper. Occasionally a student would stuff the newspaper in the air vents of the foundation of the school building. One day I saw some brightly colored matches that a boy had brought to school. I traded him a pencil for the matches. During recess, I went into the corner of the building to get away from the wind and began to strike the matches. One of the air vents which contained the discarded lunch newspaper was in that corner of the building. A teacher looked out the window and shouted loudly, "Ikie, stop trying to set the school on fire!" I was so frightened that I dropped the burning match and it is alleged to have set some of the newspaper under the building on fire. However, I never saw evidence of any kind of fire.

The assistant principal came on the scene. I was taken to the office where I was questioned about what I was doing. I told them that I was striking the matches that I had gotten from another student. They insisted that I was trying to set the school on fire. I denied their charge and said that I was only playing with matches. They told me that I could be sent to the state reform school in Marianna for what I did. After trying everything they could do to intimidate me and getting no confession out of me, they sent me back to my class. But the word was out. I was the boy to tried to set the school on fire. To this day, there are those, some of whom are members of my family, who repeat that story. I have been told that some of the newspaper did catch on fire, but the building did not. I still insist that I did not try to set the school on fire. That is my story and I am sticking to it.

Reflecting on this event, I am caused to ask some questions. What kind of people were these who accused a six-year-old boy in the first grade of trying to set the school on fire? This was 1938 at the latest. Innocent children living in rural Florida were not doing things like this. Or if they did, I was not aware of it. Why would school authorities question, threaten and try to intimidate a child of this age with such serious accusations? A strong, negative impression about the faculty and the administration of the school remains with me to this day.

Another event took place in the fourth grade. I was sitting in class with the other students when the principal came into my classroom and asked in a loud voice, "Ikie, why did you call that girl a damn liar?" I replied that I did not know what he was talking about. He questioned several students in the classroom, all of whom stated that I was guilty of calling one of my classmates "a damn liar." I was shocked and could hardly believe that such a thing was happening. It appeared that for some reason a group within the class made up the story, reported it to the teacher, who in turn called in the principal. I received a strong tongue lashing and a rebuke before my peers, but I insisted that I was innocent of the accusation. The pecking order was at work. I was the outsider with no one to defend me, plead my case, or believe my word.

That same year when Christmas arrived, another traumatic event took place. The class drew names for the annual exchange of Christmas gifts. The limit for spending on a gift was ten cents. Times were very hard, and all I could scrape up was five cents. I took my five cents, bought a gift, and placed it under the tree. When the gifts were passed out, the boy whose name I had drawn threw a fit in front of the entire class saying that he had spent ten cents on the gift he gave and only got a five-cent gift in return. My teacher turned to me and asked how much I spent. I told her that I had spent five cents because that was all I had. By that time, I was in tears. I took the gift that I had received, gave it to the boy who had thrown the fit, left the class and walked home. No one tried to stop me as I left. I think the teacher was so surprised that she was at a loss as to how to intervene in or mediate the clash. Later that afternoon two boys from my class rode up to my house on their bicycles and brought me a gift. They told me to come on back to school the next day and forget the incident. Though I have forgiven everyone involved in the event, I do not think I will ever forget what happened, nor will I forget the unexpected kindness of those two classmates.

My second grade teacher was a young, single lady named Jesse White, a big change from Gertrude Sapp, the middle-aged spinster who taught me in first grade. Miss White married a farmer during the school year. She arranged with their parents to take two of her pupils' home for an overnight stay each week until all the class had spent the night in her home. I remember that they had no electricity. Kerosene lamps provided the light, and they heated the weathered, unpainted farm house with a fireplace. Her husband shelled peanuts by hand after supper in preparation for planting the next spring.

Miss White divided our class into two reading groups; one slow and the other fast. It was a big day for me when I moved up to the fast reading group. She was a person of strong religious beliefs. Though she never let us know her own denominational preference, she was devout. On a morning when two men had been executed at Florida's Raiford State Prison, she called for a moment of silent prayer for the families of those men. Also, she read Bible stories to the class. I recall that she read a portion of the Exodus story each day. I waited anxiously each day to learn if the Israelites were going to get out of Egypt.

Other teachers were a Mrs. Hague, Mrs. Walker, and Vivian Harper. Mrs. Harper was a neighbor. Her sister was the teacher under whom I later did my practice teaching when I was a student at the University of Florida.

On December 14, 1937, during my first school year, my brother was born. I did not know that my mother was pregnant and would not have understood had I known. I still thought the stork brought babies. Ralph Junior, as we called my brother, was born in the early morning hours of December 14th. That was also my Grandmother Young's birthday. I had spent the night with a neighbor family named Campbell. Early the next morning, Mrs. Campbell woke me and told me that it was time for me to go home. It was barely daylight and there was a frost on the ground. I recall that I had a hard time waking up. Mrs. Campbell kept telling me to hurry as we walked the quarter of a mile from her house to mine. When I got in the house, my mother called me to her bed, lifted the covers, and there lay my brother next to her. She had been telling me that I might get a baby brother. She said, "This is your brother." My response was, "I knew I would get one."

We continued to live in the old Hardee pharmacy building for some months after my brother's birth. I came down with chicken pox just before Christmas and spent most of the Christmas holidays inside. We had a lot of company as people kept coming by to see the new baby. Since this was my stepfather's first child, his family and friends visited bringing gifts of baby clothing, fruit, nuts, and candy. It was a joyous time. When they came by after dark, we would shoot firecrackers in front of the house.

Sometime within the next few months, my mother decided to get into her own home. Some conflict had arisen with the Hardee parents. Daddy, as I called my stepfather, had been running the farm operation at their farm. Most of his married brothers and sisters had moved away. Not being married until he was thirty years old, he had remained at home and cared for their farm. In fact, he had been the one who had stayed at home, worked the farm, and made most of the living for his aging parents. However, not being one of the favorite children, he did not enjoy much of the fruit of his labor. The farm income was often spread around among two or three of the favorite children. My mother felt that he was not getting a fair deal from the family and he agreed, but there was not much other work available at the time. It seemed that it was almost impossible to make much of a living or get ahead. He did find other work temporarily, but nothing permanent.

Daddy's problem with alcohol began to surface again. Mama knew that he had previously had a drinking problem, but he had promised her that he would quit if she would marry him. Mama, ever the idealist, took him at his word and married him. In a few months, the drinking began to come back into his life and ours. It would remain that way for their entire marriage. In fact, his problems with alcohol proved to be a lifelong struggle. He often became violent when he was drinking. Both my mother and I became the objects of his anger when he was drunk. He beat my mother on several occasions, and twice I witnessed him threaten to kill her.

There were many times that his anger was directed toward me when he was drunk. My mother made a point to stay between us, and I made a point to stay out of his way. When I became a teenager and grew to manhood, there were several times when he was drinking that he tried to bait me into physical conflict. I never took the challenge because I knew that one of us would kill the other one before it was over. The sad thing about this is that my stepfather was a good and likeable person when he was sober. He was intelligent, humorous, easy to get along with, and a hard worker. However, there was a deep anger, frustration, and hurt in his life that he was unable to resolve. He turned to alcohol for comfort and it began to rule his life. Had he been able to deal with these problems, he could have enjoyed a much better life.

In the late summer before we moved out of the old Hardee pharmacy building, I came home one day to hear Grandpa and my parents discussing some events that were happening in Europe. I could tell that they were all concerned and upset. I learned that Hitler was leading Nazi Germany to be very aggressive in Europe. Both Grandpa and Daddy said that they thought fighting would break out within ninety days. And sure enough, it did. The tone of that conversation made me feel insecure and uneasy.

We attended the Hardeetown Baptist Church the entire time we lived in the Hardeetown area. We were regular in our attendance. The church had Sunday School every Sunday and preaching on two Sundays a month. The pastor was Rev. Knight. He and his family lived in a house that was across the street from the church. We had a revival when I was about eight years old. The evangelist was a Rev. Peterson. We had morning and evening services. Near the end of the week, the crowds began to increase, and many decisions were being made. I really liked the singing and would sit with my Grandpa during the service. One night several of my peers went down front and professed faith in Christ. The next night another group did the same thing. On the last night of the revival when more of my peers went down front, I told Grandpa that I wanted to go also. He stepped out of the pew allowing me to go to the front and talk with the preacher.

Looking back, I know I was under conviction and needed spiritual counsel and guidance. When I got to the front to talk with Rev. Knight, he asked me several questions related to believing in Jesus and wanting my sins to be forgiven. All the questions could be answered with a "yes." That was the answer I gave. When I shared with my family what I had done, they all seemed to be happy for me, but no one made any effort to explain to me what it meant for a person to accept Christ as Savior and Lord. They did tell me that I would have to quit using bad words. That I already knew. Later, I was baptized with a large group of believers into the fellowship of Hardeetown Baptist Church. The baptism was at Manatee Springs. I did not know it then, but I was not saved. I would not come to know Christ as my Lord and Savior for several years, but I was on my way towards making that decision.

I do not know how she did it, but my mother bought a twenty-acre plot of land on the edge of Hardeetown. Grandpa and Uncle Julian, my Aunt Helen's husband, began to build a house on the land which would become our home. The inside of the house was typical construction, a two-by-four frame with a tongue-in-groove board walls and ceiling. The outside was pine logs cut from timber standing on that land. The logs were arranged vertically rather than horizontally. We had no electricity or running water. We had a well from which we drew water with a hand pump, a wood burning stove for heat, and a wood stove for cooking. We had an outdoor toilet.

When we moved into this house, Daddy and Mama separated. He chose not to move with us. The first winter that we lived there was one of the coldest on record in Florida. The temperature got down into the teens several times, the lowest being about thirteen or fourteen degrees. I walked over our land picking up pine knots in a bucket to use for fuel in our small wood heater. I would also walk up and down the railroad track that ran back of our house. Occasionally, coal would fall off the train and it was great for heat. I often walked to school, nearly barefoot on frozen ground wearing short pants. That was all that I had to wear. Times were very hard, and we were poor.

That winter I developed double pneumonia. I will never forget how sick I became. This was before we had any of the modern antibiotics that we use today. A person's immune system either had to fight off the disease or they died.

Our family doctor was Dr. Young. I remember several visits that he made to our house while I was sick. On one of the last of those visits, he stopped at the door and talked briefly with my mother. I heard him say, "Meldred, you boy is very sick. It is now about 8 p.m.; if he lives until midnight, his fever should break. If not, you may lose him." I woke up the next morning with my fever gone and feeling much better, but I was so weak that I could hardly walk. Dr. Young came back by our house that day and saw that I was better. He left saying, "I don't think you will need me again anytime soon." I was glad.

If we had not had some neighbors who were generous, we would not have had food or heat during much of that winter. I know that it is not wise to get in the crossfire of family disputes, but none of the Hardee family lifted a finger to help us during this time. I know that Mama and Daddy were separated, but one of the children in the house was his only son. All of the Hardees had food to eat and wood to burn for heat. While we may not have been their direct responsibility, we were family. They left us to fend for ourselves as best we could in very difficult circumstances. I do not remember any of them coming to our house or checking to see if we needed anything.

One night during the marriage separation, Daddy showed up at our house obviously drunk. Mama would not let him in the house. He tried to force the door, but with no success. Mama had a shotgun and she told him that she was going to shoot if he did not leave. He kept beating on the door. She pointed the gun out a window away from him and fired a round. He shouted, "You missed me." Of course, she had no intention of hitting him, but she fired off another round as a warning. In about ten minutes, Ray Hardee, Daddy's older brother, drove up and talked him into leaving. That is the only time any of the Hardees became openly involved in the dispute between Mama and Daddy. I have always thought that the only reason that Ray came to our house that night was that he was afraid that Mama might actually shoot Daddy.

One of the jobs that Daddy had was working on a farm that some wealthy Germans were developing in Levy County. They came in, bought large tract of undeveloped land, built a house and outbuildings, and were in the process of clearing the land for a farming operation. They paid ten dollars for a work week that was five and a half days. It was good work and good pay at the time. This work was interrupted when the Germans who were developing the farm suddenly departed. They were later arrested by the FBI as they were en route to New York City. It turned out that they were spies and were working undercover for the Nazi government. In the summer months when he was not working on the farm, Daddy would pack watermelons in boxcars for shipment to the markets up north. It was temporary work, but the pay was good.

With the country facing the threat of war in late 1939 and early 1940 and with military preparation beginning, various types of factories began to start up. Daddy got a job in nearby Archer, Florida, in a factory that manufactured shell casings for ammunition. After having worked at the factory for a few weeks, he came to our house one Saturday night in a small Chevrolet coupe and asked my mother if she would go for a ride. He was drinking, but not drunk. My mother refused to go for a ride but allowed him to come in and spend the night. It was obvious to me the next morning that their separation was ended.

The next few months were filled with the mundane events of going to school, observing holidays, preparing and working a summer garden, learning to whistle so that the sound could be heard for a long distance, and learning to ride a bicycle. I got a used bicycle for Christmas, but I enjoyed it as much as if it had been brand new.

On December 8, 1941, I went to school and was greeted with the news that the Japanese had bombed Pearl Harbor. We did not have a radio, nor did we take a paper. I was astounded when a classmate told me that we were at war. Little did I realize how the War would change my life and the lives of all Americans. I was half way through the sixth grade, but I would not finish the school year in Levy County. Our move to Lake City, Florida, would begin a whole new chapter of my life, most of which would be good and exciting.

Chapter 3
Early Years in Lake City, Florida

With the first years of World War II upon us, dramatic changes began to take place in our lives. The military draft was in place. Men in their late teens and into their early forties were being called up for military training and duty. Military bases were being built everywhere. Camp Blanding near Starke, Florida, was being carved out of virgin pine forests; the Naval Air Station in Jacksonville was being expanded; and a Naval Air Base in Lake City was being built. My uncle Hiram W. Sperry, a Captain in the Florida National Guard in Panama City, was called to active duty with his company of engineers for the purpose of building Camp Blanding. He later went to Texas and then on to Alaska where he spent the remainder of the War working on the Alaskan Highway and military bases in that area.

My mother had been employed sporadically in various WPA programs. These programs were part of the New Deal brought into existence during the first years of Franklin D. Roosevelt's presidential administration. My stepfather had continued to work on the Hardee family farm and at any other odd jobs that he might find. But all this was changing.

When the Rural Electrification Administration began to finance the power line construction that would bring electricity to the rural areas of Florida, my stepfather tried to get a job with one of the construction companies, but his application arrived too late and he missed out on that opportunity. He heard about the TVA dam construction up in Tennessee, but that was too far to go without some definite assurance of employment. However, our country was beginning to prepare in the face of the threat of war. And soon, war was no longer a threat, it was a reality.

Just before the United States entered the War, my stepfather got a job in an ammunition plant in Archer, Florida. My mother heard of job opportunities at the Naval Air Base in Lake City. She applied for work there and was soon employed. As we prepared to move to Lake City, I was overjoyed. My mother's parents lived in Lake City as did her only brother and his family. Another aunt and uncle also resided there from time to time. Also, there was a slightly older first cousin, Billy Harrell, who lived with my grandparents. Billy and I were as close as brothers. I looked forward to living near him.

The move meant several things. We would be leaving our log home on the twenty acres that my mother had purchased. We would be leaving Levy County, Hardeetown, and Chiefland, places and a social atmosphere in which I had never felt at home. We would be moving closer to family who had always loved and nurtured me. We would be moving into temporary living quarters and would have electricity, running water, an indoor bathroom, and gas heat. My mother would no longer have to cook on a wood stove. Most of the streets in Lake City were paved, whereas most of the streets in Chiefland and Hardeetown were dirt or crushed limestone. Schools were bigger and newer, and the people were friendlier and more accepting of outsiders. It was like dying and going to heaven.

But there were adjustments. My mother would be working longer hours and my brother, six years my junior, would often be left in my care. My stepfather did not have a job in Lake City, so he remained in Levy County commuting to his job in Archer. The family was divided again. It would be several months before my stepfather would get a job on the paint crew at the Naval Air Base in Lake City. He did come to Lake City, but I do not think he ever really enjoyed living there. Things went well for several months, but his drinking problem began to surface again, and with it, the level of tension and friction between my mother and stepfather continued to increase.

When we lived in Levy County, I had gone by the name Ikie Hardee as I attended the public schools. But when we moved to Lake City, I began to use the McDonald name. Part of this change was because the Hardee family never accepted me as one of their own. I was not one of them. Then my mother shared with me the story of my name which was Isaac Burkhalter McDonald, Jr. Though I was nicknamed "Ikie", I was really Isaac and I was definitely a McDonald.

We moved twice early in our stay in Lake City. The second move put us closer to the Naval Air Base where my mother worked. Convenient transportation was a necessity throughout the War years. I finished the sixth grade in the city schools. When my stepfather came to live with us, we moved four miles west of town on US 90, which was about a mile west of where my grandparents lived. We were almost directly across the highway from the Shady Grove School, where I attended the seventh grade.

The Shady Grove School had about forty students enrolled in grades one through eight. The main school building was located on the south side of US 90. It contained one large classroom and two smaller rooms that were used for storage. It was heated in the winter with a wood stove. There was a porch all the way across the front of the building. The lunchroom was a separate building about thirty yards east of the main school building. Outhouse-type toilets were located in the southeast and southwest corners of the school property, one for boys and one for girls. There was a reasonable amount of playground space south of the main school building.

The sole faculty member was a lady named Irma Walters. She was the wife of our bi-vocational pastor, Hugh Walters. Mrs. Walters was not thought to be in good health. She was alleged to have miscarried, ending a pregnancy, at least once during the school year. She probably did not feel like dealing with thirty to forty children of various ages each day. She was a petite lady but very strong willed. I do not remember much about her teaching abilities. Each day she seemed to go through the motions of trying to get students to work their way through the materials which she had assigned.

I do not know how I came to get on her bad side, but our personalities clashed, and I was the loser in the battle. In those days teachers could apply corporal punishment. The fear of getting a whipping kept most students under control. My infraction was talking back when I should have remained silent. I was called to the front of the class, told to take off my coat and stand there while she whipped me with a large six-foot-long switch as my classmates watched. The switch was still green but strong enough for the task. I was wearing a cotton tee shirt, a cotton sweat shirt, and a cotton flannel shirt. She whipped me across the back until the switch had broken off to less than three feet in length. I never cried or whimpered. But when I took my clothes off for bed that night my tee shirt was caked to several large stripes where the skin had broken, and I had bled from the beating. I said nothing to my mother about this incident until about a week later when she saw my back as I was taking my weekly bath. This was the worst beating I ever had in school. Had it happened today, the teacher would have been arrested, fired, and probably sent to jail. In retrospect, since she had a switch that had recently been cut and brought to the classroom, I am almost certain that she had planned the event. It was not a spontaneous act.

Before the next school year began, my parents had arranged to buy a house three miles closer to town. It was a big improvement over the house in which we had been living. It would have electricity, running water, an indoor bathroom, and propane gas for cooking and heating. Also, we were back in the city school district. However, the house was not finished. We began touching up the drywall, painting, finishing the carpentry, and drilling the well for our water supply. In those days you could hit a good well at about forty feet. Ours came in at about forty-eight feet. It was an exciting time.

Many things influence young people as they are growing up. Though I was unaware of it then, my parent's divorce and my mother's remarriage had a lasting effect on me. Combine that with the war atmosphere, changing economic conditions, moving from one place to another, changing schools, getting to know new people, seeing the family in conflict, struggling to grow through the teenage years, and trying to establish a sense of personal identity, I had a lot to process emotionally.

I had often heard people say that the eighth grade in school was one of the most difficult. I found that to be true. Unfortunately, I also made some friends who were rebellious and not interested in being good students. Their influence on me was not positive. I did my assigned work occasionally, but I did not produce consistent efforts toward learning. At the end of the year, I was told that the only way I could move on to the ninth grade would be to attend summer school. This requirement would be costly because my parents would have to pay the tuition for the summer classes. They did this, and I did the class work. This moved me on to grade nine. However, hindsight has made me aware that I was woefully unprepared for this step.

Poor academic achievement, associating with the wrong crowd, continuing family conflict, and common teenage problems all combined to keep my personal life in turmoil. I did not like my stepfather. We had a poor relationship. He would tolerate a great deal of rebellion on my part until I pushed him over the edge and then he would give me a severe beating. The beatings were intense enough to leave marks and bruises on my body. All of this would simply increase the tension between us. I ran away from home for an entire weekend once. The family did not know where I was, and after a couple of days on the run dodging them and not knowing what to do next, I came back home.

One of the things that I enjoyed most about living in Lake City was the three movie theaters. They were the Lake, the DeSoto, and the Columbia. There had been no theaters in Chiefland. My grandparents were moviegoers as were my cousins. Admission was nine cents if you were under twelve years of age and twelve cents if you were twelve years or older. We went every Saturday. I loved the cowboy movies, the weekly serials, the cartoons, the war movies, and the newsreels.

While I did not realize it at the time, I was becoming a news addict. I would listen to our radio at home each morning, and I never failed to listen to the news at twelve noon each day when not in school. Additionally, reading the daily newspaper and seeing the movie newsreels kept me informed as to what was happening in the world. When school was in session, we had "The Weekly Reader" in our history or social studies class. Reading it was usually followed by a test over the subject matter. I always scored well because I paid attention to the news. This habit has followed me throughout my entire life.

During the War years, it was not unusual to see a convoy of military vehicles slowly driving by our home on US 90. Troops would be transported in the large trucks with the canvas tops and siding. These convoys always traveled at thirty-five miles per hour, which was the legal wartime speed for all motorized traffic. Gasoline was rationed to the general public; the amount one was allotted depended on the kind of employment or business activity in which one might be involved. Other items that were rationed were meat, sugar, coffee, various canned goods, clothing, shoes, and building materials. I am certain that the list of rationed items was larger than this, but these are the items that I remember. Since my mother worked at the Naval Air Station in Lake City, she could get the enlisted military personnel to buy shirts, dungarees, and shoes that I would wear. I never cared for these military issue items, but they were good clothes and I wore them.

It was during the eighth grade that I began to notice girls and they began to notice me. I was one of a few new kids in the class, and several of the girls were very friendly. Of course, I loved the attention and I loved the girls. The tradition of the McDonald family was that the men loved all the ladies, and I did my best to keep that tradition alive. My classmates and I would get together for parties on the weekends at someone's home. Most of the games we played were kissing games such as "Post Office" and "Spin the Bottle." All of this was fun. It helped us in learning how to socialize and relate to each other in an acceptable way. I had several girlfriends and seemed to be "in love" with someone all of the time. If I had a fault, it was that I tended to get too deeply attached to one girl instead of paying attention to more than one. I soon learned to spread my attention around which was more fun.

During the eighth grade school year of 1944-1945, I became aware of death and its impact upon human life. One of my classmates, a boy named Billy Joiner, died during the school year. He was a happy, cheerful person, but we all knew that he was sick. He had some kind of cancer and the treatment had caused some of his hair to fall out. Suddenly, he was absent from school and then the word came that he had died. We were all sad.

With the War being fought in the Pacific and Europe, there seemed to be a steady stream of death messages that came to our small community. My friend Morris Williams informed me that between sixteen and twenty young men from Lake City and/or Columbia County died during the War. Further, there were plane crashes occasionally at the local Naval Air Base and in Jacksonville. Every time a plane went down, there were several deaths. We heard about death every day.

The intensity of World War II became stronger each day. Questions about who was in the military and where they were serving often arose. I overheard one of my aunts who lived in Panama City, Florida, telling my mother that she had seen my father in an Army Air Corp uniform in that city. She had not been able to talk to him, but she had definitely seen him. Hearing her share that information with my mother, I took the initiative and wrote the War Department and obtained his address. I wrote him three letters, two of which he received, but the third was returned because of his death. Fearing that my mother or stepfather would get the mail first, I had asked him to reply to me at a neighbor's address. But he did not reply to either of my letters. I know that he received them because his personal records, sent to me after his death, revealed that he had completed a form shortly before his death, giving direction to the military to award his military medals to me should he not live to receive them himself. He had listed my name as a minor son. I am convinced that he would not have done this had he not received my letters. I have wished many times that I had simply given my father my return address and said nothing about the possibility of my mother not wanting him to contact me, but that is hindsight.

I have mentally gone through all kinds of reasons as to why my father did not answer my letters. My best analysis of the situation goes back to the breakup of the marriage between my parents and the bitterness that must have developed during and after their divorce. While my mother never said unkind or harsh things about my father to me, she did indicate that he did not love us enough to stay with us. She did tell me that he asked her repeatedly to forgive his infidelity, to take him back and give the marriage another try, but she refused.

In her bitterness along with the fact that his older brother, Fred, had accused my mother of trapping my father into the marriage just seemed to snowball into something bigger than she was able to tolerate. It is likely that she told my father that she never wanted to see him again. If that is the case, he may have decided to stay out of her life, and therefore my life, forever.

However, as my mother gathered the records of my father's other marriages and divorces while applying for a survivors' pension for me, the records of their marriage and my birth all showed that my uncle's charges were false and groundless, a fact that she said was the truth until her dying day! In fact, she told me that she never had sex with my father until they were married.

My father's twin sisters, Vivian and Lillian, both told us that my father had indicated that he wanted to find me before he went overseas. Why he did not is a mystery to me. They said that he did not know my mother's married name and thus did not know where to look. He had several friends in Lake City where we lived. My grandparents and uncle, all of whom he knew, lived in Lake City. He was often in town visiting friends, a fact that I learned after his death. In fact, I am positive that I saw him in the bus station with one of his friends just before he shipped out overseas. I still think my father could have found me, but I think the lingering memory of his conflict with my mother may have caused him to neglect trying. Add to that the fact that young people often do not believe that they are going to die. He may have talked about dying to his family, but deep within himself he may have kept believing that he would go overseas, complete his tour of duty, and come back home. I can go through all of this, and I have done it many of times, but the truth is that I will never know in this life why he neglected to find me. I may get to ask him why when I get to heaven, but it will not matter then. However, this fact is inescapable; had my father been responsible in his personal life and had he made a reasonable effort to find me, none of this frustration and uncertainty would be lingering today. And I would have been spared a great deal of emotional pain and sorrow.

My father's death occurred on January 9, 1945. My uncle Fred McDonald was notified by telegram on or around January 21, and an official letter of notification was dated January 28, 1945. I did not receive the news until early April. My Aunt Lillian contacted my mother's father at an insurance office in Jacksonville, where he occasionally worked, sharing the news with him. She and her twin sister, Vivian, realized that their brother Fred had no intention of carrying out my father's instructions to "take care of my boy" with the share of the insurance payment that was entrusted in his care. Having found us, they filed a request for payment of the gratuity pay in my name as my father's minor son. They did this to keep Uncle Fred from getting the money. They knew that if he got it, I would never see a cent of it. This is when he is alleged to have protested to the government that I was not a legitimate child of my father. My mother despised him for this until the day she died. And she proved him to be a liar.

When my grandfather came to our house with the news of my father's death, he did not come inside. It was early evening, nearly dark, and he stood in the yard next to our front porch. Our front porch light was on. He called me out of the house and told me that my father's sister, Lillian, had come to his office and told him of my father's death in early January. I stood on the porch looking down at him as he appeared to read from a slip of paper. I do not remember if I said anything to him, but I do remember turning, walking the length of the house, going out the back door, and sitting down on the back steps. I sat there and cried. My mother came out and tried to comfort me. I do not remember what she said. I just remember her being there. She was the only person who tried to comfort me that night. I do not remember much of anything that happened for the next few days. I do remember going to school the next day and sharing the sad news with my friends and teachers. It was the end of a dream of being reunited with my father and of being able to share some of our lives together.

The actual details of my father's death were shared with me by one of his friends who served with him and claimed to have been an eye witness to the plane crash that took his life in Biak, New Guinea. He said that my father had completed his combat missions and had gone to a military base on the mainland waiting for transportation home. This military base was also where new aircrafts were delivered before being put into service and where used aircrafts were repaired before being returned to service.

While my father was waiting for transportation back home, a person who was to be a crew member for ferrying a new plane to its assignment became ill. My father was asked to replace that crewman since his transportation would not be available until later. When my father learned that the new plane was being sent to the base where he had just been serving, he agreed to be a crew member if the plane could also carry food and drink not normally available to those at the base. Having secured that treat for his friends, they delivered the new plane and the food. On the return takeoff, the plane, scheduled for repairs, lost either a wing or part of a wing at about two-hundred-feet altitude. The plane crashed, and all the crew was lost.

Another account of the above story came to me through Talmadge McDonald, my father's older brother, who lived in Macon, Georgia. He had a friend in Macon who had served with my father in New Guinea. That friend had shared with my Uncle Tal an account of my father's death that was nearly identical to the one I have recorded above. He said that he had witnessed the crash and had seen my father's body after it had been recovered from the wreckage.

Several significant deaths took place during 1945 and 1946. Grief is a natural part of the loss one faces when someone to whom they feel close dies. I am in my ninth decade of life as I write these words, and I confess that I still struggle with the pain of losing a person to whom I have felt a close attachment. I feel the pain of not having really known my father. It is something that is always just beneath the surface, and it surfaces unexpectedly in ways that are difficult to describe. It seems to be a grief for a loss that I have never been able to lay to rest. I do not have the same kind of grief over the loss of my mother. I had her for over sixty years, and I grieved as I watched her mental and physical decline before her death. I still miss her, but the grief that I still have over the loss of my father is a pain that will not go away. I have often thought that if we had held a memorial service it might have helped. Then I have thought that if I could visit his grave in the Philippines it might help. But I am not sure. There are times that I am still brought to tears over the loss. I know of no way to make the pain of this loss go away. I pray about it and get some relief, but later the pain returns. This is one of life's strange mysteries to me. I do not have an answer for it, and I may never find an answer.

The significant deaths just mentioned were those of my father, Isaac B. McDonald Sr.; my grandfather, William P. Young Sr.; my mother's only brother, William P. Young Jr.; and the U.S. President, Franklin D. Roosevelt. While President Roosevelt was not a family member, he was deeply loved by many Americans, my family included.

With the death of President Franklin D. Roosevelt on April 12, 1945, the entire nation went into mourning. In fact, the entire world went into mourning! It was almost as though the world had come to an end. I followed all the news about President Roosevelt's death and funeral with great interest. Many feared that we would not be able to win the War either in Europe or in the Pacific without his leadership. However, the new president, Harry S. Truman, assured us that the victory was ours for the taking, and so we looked to the future. I recall my mother crying more over Roosevelt's death than she did my father's death. But our entire nation wept when President Roosevelt died. Everyone was in tears.

Our country had hardly finished with the funeral of President Roosevelt, when my grandfather William Pickens Young Sr. died suddenly from a heart attack. His death occurred in the early morning hours of Monday, May 28, 1945. My mother's brother had visited with Grandpa on Sunday evening. They had a good visit, laughing and talking until my uncle had gone home. Then, just before daylight, my cousin and grandmother were awakened by noises that Grandpa was making as he struggled to breathe. It appeared to be a massive heart attack because he was dead in a few minutes. They lived four miles from town, without a telephone, and by the time they summoned help from neighbors, Grandpa was dead. It was a terrible shock to our entire family.

Grandpa's funeral was on Memorial Day, May 30, 1945. He had observed his sixty-first birthday in January. He had served the Mt. Carmel Baptist Church near Lake City, Florida, as a deacon, Sunday School Superintendent, and teacher. He and my grandmother were faithful members of the church and had been instrumental in leading the church to begin having worship services with preaching every Sunday instead of just two Sundays a month. Grandpa was either the second or third person to be buried in the new cemetery adjoining the church. Later, my grandmother and four of their children were buried in the family plot.

My grandfather's death left a large leadership vacuum in the church family. It also left a large hole in our family, one that has never been filled. I have often said that he was the best man I ever knew, and I really think he was. He had a good mind and was not afraid of work whether it was mental or physical. He loved to joke and tell funny stories. He always chose to do what was right. He never spoke harshly in my presence about other people. I never heard him use profanity. He loved his wife, his children, his grandchildren, his extended family, and his friends. He was always willing to go out of his way to help other people. I did not realize then what a profound effect his death would have on our entire family. The family was never again as close as it had been. This is something that I regret and would like to change but have been unable to do so. While I remained on good terms with my aunts, uncles and cousins, there were fractures in the family fellowship which have grown deeper with time. But to my knowledge, I am on good terms with all my cousins on the Young side of the family.

This was not the case with my mother and her siblings. They all loved each other, but the sibling rivalry, encouraged from early childhood by my grandmother, made it difficult for them to be together for very long without getting into a heated argument. They were loyal to each other, but my mother and Aunt Hallie were always striving for the leadership position in the family. Neither of them would give ground and neither of them realized what the rivalry was doing to them personally or to the family. When they were in their seventies, they began avoiding each other to the point that there was little if any communication between them. I find these circumstances to be sad, but it is one of those family things that was and is a reality.

I began this chapter telling about the beginning of World War II and our family's move to Lake City, Florida. In 1945, World War II was rapidly coming to an end. The Germans surrendered on May 7, 1945, and the Japanese surrendered on September 2. The Japanese surrender came only after we Americans had dropped atomic bombs on two Japanese cities. The first, on August 6, destroyed Hiroshima. The second, on August 9, destroyed Nagasaki. There are various estimates of the death toll of these two atomic bombs, but the best that I can find say that the first bomb killed 100,000 with 110,000 more injured. This action was justified with the rationale that many more lives, both Japanese and American, would have been lost had we been forced to invade the Japanese mainland. While this is probably true, the loss of life in these two cities was tragic. The Japanese asked for surrender terms on August 10, but the actual signing of the terms of surrender came on September 2, 1945. There were demonstrations of joy in the streets of every city in America with the word that the War was over.

Most of my July and early August of 1945 had been spent working in the tobacco warehouses in Lake City. There were at least three large warehouses where farmers brought their tobacco and had it auctioned to the highest bidder. I was thirteen years old, had just received my Social Security card, and was hired as a common laborer in Strickland's Warehouse. My pay was $0.40 per hour which was the minimum wage at that time. I was not large, but I worked hard because I wanted to earn what I could before school started.

On my lunch break at the tobacco warehouse, I would often walk the four or five blocks over to Uncle Dub's house to get a sandwich and listen to the noon news. I was at his house when I learned of the use of the atomic bombs and of Japan's willingness to consider terms for surrender. My feeling at the time was that whatever happened to the Japanese was what they deserved. I was quite bitter over my father's death and the deaths of others that I had known. But I was both happy and relieved when the news came of the Japanese surrender.

With the month of August coming to an end, I found myself looking forward to the beginning of school. I was going to be in the ninth grade. I planned to be on the football team. I was optimistic about the future. Little did I realize the changes that were about to take place. It was going to be a time of great adjustment. Our family would be caught up in these changing times. Some of it would be for the better and other parts would be very difficult, but I was optimistic about the future.

Chapter 4
Early High School Years

My high school years covered the last half of the 1940s. This included the end of World War II and the years in which the United States was coming off a wartime economy and trying to make adjustments for the world being at peace. We all had hopes for the entire world to be at peace, but that dream was not to be realized. The Soviet Union and Communist China would keep the world on edge wondering where hostilities would break out again.

While the international world was filled with the uncertainty that comes with the daily threat of more war, our domestic scene was flooded with tremendous changes that were going on all around us. With World War II being over, much of the wartime economy was winding down and returning to a peacetime time economy. The American workforce faced great uncertainty. Men and women were returning from military service seeking to find employment in a shrinking economy. Previously, our nation had come out of the Great Depression to go on a wartime economic footing. Now, great effort was being made not to return to our former depressed peacetime economy.

As this was taking place, my mother and stepfather were facing the prospect of being laid off from work at the Naval Air Base in Lake City, Florida. Military bases throughout the country were being closed. Also, my mother was in the lengthy process of gathering for the government all the legal information for obtaining a minor child's survivor's pension for me. With the problems of rearing a rebellious teenager, having an alcoholic husband, and facing an uncertain and shrinking domestic economy, my mother had an almost perfect recipe for stress. I am certain that she knew she was stressed, but I did not.

An additional change came from my father's family. There had been no contact with them since my parents divorced in the early 1930s. After my father's death in early January 1945, the family began to reach out to us and a happy family relationship developed. There were twelve children in my father's family, seven boys and five girls. I became acquainted with two of his brothers and four of his sisters. The twin sisters, Vivian and Lillian, took the initiative. Aunt Vivian contacted my mother and arranged a visit in late April 1945. With her on this visit was her daughter, Monteen Clements Tomberlin, and son-in-law, Philip Tomberlin. Phil was recently discharged from the U.S. Marine Corps and was in the process of buying a farm east of Lake City. "Teenie," as we called Monteen, was employed by a prominent Jewish family in Jacksonville named Wolfson. The Wolfson family had become quite wealthy during World War II and were expanding a financial empire that previously had been a salvage company. Aunt Vivian and the Tomberlins would continue to live in

Jacksonville. They were always loving and supportive family members. Aunt Vivian had a second daughter named Lawana, who was one of the most beautiful women that I had ever seen.

As I visited the family in Jacksonville, I met Aunt Lillian and her children. She had two daughters, Wynette and Mary, and one son, Pat. Pat had recently been discharged from the military. Later, he would attend the University of Florida earning a degree in engineering. When I enrolled at the University of Florida in 1950, Pat was still there. We became close and remained so until his death in 2015. Aunt Lillian had previously divorced the father of her children.

My father's oldest sister was Mary Johnson. She was the mother of LaVerne Blue Jr. who was my age. He was killed at age seventeen in a tragic automobile accident. Her oldest son was Fred Lemke Jr. who was slightly younger than my father. Fred and his wife, Isobel, had one daughter, Joan. I was about three years older than Joan and we developed a brother and sister relationship that has lasted all of our lives. My father had another older sister named Eunice Smith. She had four sons, but only the youngest, Kenneth Smith, is still living. Ken and his family reside in Alaska.

In late August 1945, the Columbia High School football team began its fall practice and I worked out with the team every day. Our coach was Jim Melton, who was one of the finest men I ever met. He was from a leading family in Lake City and had been an outstanding athlete in high school and college. I never heard him use profanity or raise his voice in anger or frustration with any of our team members. He was an excellent coach and a positive influence on all the team members. Physically, I was never a big person. I was about five feet seven inches tall and weighed about one hundred fifteen pounds soaking wet, but I had quickness and speed in my favor. I paid careful attention to the coaching that I received, and Coach Melton encouraged me stating that I could become a good ball player.

A problem arose with my mother, who hated football and any kind of contact sports. In early childhood I had a severe case of measles. The doctor caring for me during that time is alleged to have suggested to her that she should never allow me to participate in athletic activities. She began to insist that I give up any effort to play football. It became apparent that I would have no peace at home until I left the team. After a month into the season, I explained to Coach Melton the problem and turned in my gear.

My mother did not realize that athletics would have taken me out of the circle of friends who were a negative influence on me. I do not want to be too critical of her. She was highly protective of me and thought she was doing what was best, but I still believe she was misguided. Later, when I went out for the team again, she was much more supportive. Hindsight tells me that I lost a great opportunity to learn, grow, and develop as a person under Coach Melton. That could have turned my troubled young life in the right direction much earlier.

When I registered for school in the ninth grade, I chose subjects that would not demand a great deal of work. I was looking for an easy path through school and I continued to associate with a group that had no academic ambition. They were rebellious and constantly in trouble. There were times that I skipped school simply because I did not want to be there. I began to smoke thinking it would make me appear more mature. Tobacco was easy to get then, even for a minor.

My mother was aware of my behavior. She sought help from the school faculty and received some cooperation but did not find the help that she wanted or needed. She began to blame the school and the faculty for some of the problems. It may have been true that some of the faculty had failed to be helpful and may not have belonged in the profession. We seemed to have had a parade of faculty who made their way through the school system during the war years and shortly thereafter. They were here today and gone tomorrow. But there were some excellent teachers at Columbia High School. While my mother should have received more and better help, the school system was not entirely to blame for our problems.

Near the beginning of my first year in high school, I made a major life decision. An overzealous religious person made a prediction that the world would end about two weeks later at four o'clock in the afternoon. I knew the Bible said that no one knew when the world would end. But this prediction produced quite a bit of news publicity and much discussion among my school classmates and me.

Many passed this prediction off as the act of a religious fanatic. However, on the day that the event was supposed to occur, discussion increased especially in our school classes. In my general science class, taught by Daniel P. Folsom, the subject came up. Mr. Folsom let us discuss the issue and participated in the discussion himself. The class ended with our being reminded that the Bible said no human knew when the world would end.

The school day ended at three o'clock and I got off the school bus at home about fifteen minutes later. The more I thought about the prediction, the more uneasy I became about my readiness to meet God should the world end that day or any day. I sent my brother off to play with the neighbor children while I went in the house, got my mother's Bible, and returned to the front porch. Her Bible had an index with a question and answer section in the back. I looked up the Second Coming of Christ and read all the references listed. The more I read the more anxious I became. I looked in the back of the Bible again and found a listing on How to Be Saved. It was approaching four o'clock as I began to read. I read the third chapter of John's Gospel and went to the fifth chapter. I read John 5:24 which says, "Truly, truly, I say to you, he who hears my word and believes in him who sent me, has eternal life; he does not come into judgment, but has passed from death to life."

As I read those words, I closed the Bible, walked over to the edge of the porch and began to pray. I told God that I knew that He loved me. I told Him that I wanted to be forgiven of my sins and I wanted to be His child. I thanked Him for what Jesus did for me when He went to the Cross. As I prayed, a peace began to come over me like I had never known. The fear that I would not be ready to meet God should Jesus return disappeared. I sensed that everything was right between God and me. What I did not realize at the time was that I had just been saved. It was so simple and easy, but I felt that all was well. Though this was life's most meaningful decision, I was unable to identify it as that for many years. I had crossed the line from being lost to being saved in one short moment.

Through the years I have been privileged to make many friends. I have found friendship to be one of the truly great blessings of life. Some friendships have turned out better than others. The friendships that have lasted are difficult to define, but they bring a blessing to life without which we would be very poor. Friendships that go sour are disappointing, but there is nothing that can lift one's spirit like the support that comes from a friend who knows us and loves us still. I have indicated that I made some poor choices in friends when I first came to Lake City. That is true, but during these high school years, I made friends who have remained faithful and true through the years that followed. It is true that when we visit with old friends, even though much time may have passed since our last visit, we are able to pick up and share again as though the time in between was just a day.

The three boys in the Joiner family were Jim, Kenny, and Wallace. Their mother was a widow, and they had a younger sister. Jim, being the oldest, had a dominant personality, but was paranoid and aggressive. I still do not know what the attraction of our friendship was, but we were able to communicate and share our feelings. We became friends in the eighth grade. Jim was not interested in being a good student, though he had a good mind. He resisted the authority of the teachers and refused to learn or take any instruction. He was pleasant to be around when he was not angry, but his anger could flare up and spill over quickly. He quit school when he was sixteen and went to work. By the time he was in his early twenties he was already on the wrong side of the law. Later, he committed a robbery and was sent to prison. He died of a heart attack when he was about fifty years of age. Wallace, being the youngest, was delightfully humorous and was the most even-tempered of the boys.

Both Kenny and Wallace were good students. Kenny and I were in the same high school class, and Wallace was a year or two behind us. Kenny had a good mind and work ethic. He excelled in school and insisted that he wanted to become a pharmacist. Both Kenny and Wallace worked after school in the Seminole Drug Store on North

Marion Street in Lake City. When it was necessary for them to take time off from work, they helped me get the job filling in for them. We worked behind the soda fountain, would assist with other customers, and would sweep up each night before the store closed. We were paid six dollars a week for after school and Saturday work. A fringe benefit was that we could consume a reasonable amount of ice cream and milkshakes without charge. We also developed the practice of "knocking down" a little extra change if we got into a financial bind, but we kept this to a minimum lest we lose the job!

Kenny and I graduated from high school together. He joined the U.S. Army and was seriously injured in a jeep accident while serving overseas. He returned home, went to work for the Florida Department of Transportation, later retired, and died in late 2003 or early 2004. Wallace suffered a heart attack and died while in his mid-fifties. By the time I went to college these relationships had waned to speaking to each when we met, exchanging a little bit of good-natured kidding, and then going our separate ways.

I tell this story about the Joiner brothers because Wallace loaned me his bicycle to ride home one night in early December 1945. I was to ride the bicycle to school the next morning and return it to him. However, on the way to school the next morning, I had the misfortune of being hit by a car on U.S. 90 less than a quarter of a mile from my home. The car struck the back of the bicycle and I was thrown as though I had been shot out of a catapult about one hundred feet down the highway. I hit the blacktop on the left side of my head. The flesh, starting behind my left ear all the way around to the left side of my nose, was scraped across the highway. The knuckles and back of my left hand got the same treatment. Fortunately, I had on jeans and a heavy winter jacket, but my face and hand were pretty well torn up. The driver of the car was a recently returned army veteran from Falmouth, Florida. He stopped, put me in the car, and following my directions, took me to the local hospital emergency room. They patched me up and called my mother who came and took me to a friend's house for the rest of the day until she got off work. Friends at school later told me that when Kenny heard of the accident, he gave Wallace fits all day for loaning me the bicycle like it was all his fault.

That night I went to sleep and did not awaken fully for nearly forty-eight hours. My mother stayed close by checking on me every three or four hours. She believed that I had suffered a severe concussion. When I became fully awake, I saw that my mother had placed the cigarettes which had been in my pocket on the table by my bed. She had also supplied matches and an ash tray. I had never smoked in front of her and could not bring myself to do so. I gave the cigarettes to my stepfather and I quit smoking. This may support the belief that some good can come out of bad events.

A Journey, Remembered…

It was about a week before I had recovered enough to return to school. However, the real recovery took much longer. The flesh on my face and hand began to fill in, but it was transparent for several weeks. I had headaches and struggled at times to keep my balance. I think my inner ear on the left side of my head was severely bruised and may never have recovered completely. In time I was back to being my old, feisty self, and for that I was grateful. Fortunately, time and healing left me with few noticeable scars. The real cause of this accident was my poor judgment. I had heard the car approaching behind me as I rode in the right lane. I had looked back to see how far away it was and judged it to be more than a quarter of a mile away. There was another car meeting us in the left lane. When that car passed me, I swerved to the left lane to be out of the way of the car behind me, but the car behind me had also moved to that lane and was speeding up to pass me. When I moved to that lane, I moved right in front of him. He applied his brakes just as he hit the bicycle. I was fortunate not to have been more seriously injured or killed.

Christmas came shortly after my bicycle accident and was followed by my fourteenth birthday. On the evening of December 30, 1945, a friend and I were walking to the Magnolia Barbeque on the east side of Lake City. A service station was located on the corner just before arriving at the Mag. Walking past the service station, I noticed a car by the gas pumps; it was Phil Tomberlin's car and standing by it was my cousin Fred Lemke. We enjoyed a brief greeting as I told family members about my accident which explained the bandages that were still on my hand and face. Then I shared with them that I was on my way to the Mag to celebrate my birthday. Shaking hands with Fred on leaving, I felt something folded in his hand. It was my first five-dollar handshake. In January 2005, when I conducted Fred's funeral, I told that story.

My memory for the remainder of the school year is pretty much a blank. I finished the school year and passed every subject. I think in some cases my teachers passed me just to get rid of me. I was not a trouble maker, but I did face some consequences for skipping school. My mother continued to be unhappy with the school system. and she began to look for alternative solutions.

The Millard Roberts family were our neighbors. Their oldest daughter, Gwendolyn, was in my class at school. They too were unhappy with the school system. When Mom shared her feelings with them, they told her about Dasher Bible School, a Christian boarding school just south of Valdosta, Georgia. They informed her that Gwendolyn was going there the next year. Mom investigated the school, took me on a visit, and before I knew it, I was enrolled there for the next school year. Financially, I was able to attend this school because we had obtained the gratuity pay from my father's death and my survivor's pension was about to start.

Our neighbor Mr. Roberts was in the construction business. I later learned that he was also a Church of Christ minister. Further, Dasher Bible School was a Church of

Christ school. Academically, the school was good. I was not hurt by going there. Attending the school helped me mature, but most of the students, teachers, and administrators at the school were members of the Church of Christ. They were quite aggressive in their efforts to convert me. However, my family and I were Baptists. Much of the Church of Christ doctrine clashed with Baptist teaching which I knew and believed. While I did not know the Bible as well as they did, I was well grounded in my faith. I went to their church three times a week as required, but I did not become a convert.

School had been in session nearly a month when one of the teachers came to my room and told me that my Uncle Dub had died. I was aware that he was sick but did not realize he was near death. My mother had warned me earlier that such an event could happen, but I had not taken her words seriously. It was a tragic event and a shock to our entire family. In the space of twenty-one months, our family had experienced three deaths. My father's death was difficult only for me and my mother, but the death of my grandfather and uncle touched the lives of the entire family.

Shortly after my grandfather's death, I learned that family problems were alleged to exist between my mother's only brother and his wife, Mary Virginia. I heard the family speak in hushed conversations that my uncle had a drinking problem. We took him to out of town hospitals for treatment, but to no avail. When he died, I thought that he drank himself to death, but my mother and her sisters insisted otherwise. Various stories began to circulate among the sisters. I do not recall hearing my grandmother say anything.

Hindsight causes me to see and understand several things. One aunt told that Grandpa's heart attack and death had been triggered by my uncle coming to see him the night before he died telling him that he and Mary Virginia were filing for divorce. Then there were stories of infidelity on both sides, none of which have proved to be true. Grief produces anger, and the sisters were angry. They turned on Mary Virginia like a pack of wild animals. They claimed, "It was all her fault! She poisoned him! She wanted him dead!" And the cause of death has remained in dispute.

My mother with her nursing background said that my uncle had all the symptoms of pancreatic cancer. She said she discussed this possibility with my uncle's doctor who agreed. However, my mother said that the doctor explained that my uncle's wife had insisted that the cause of death on my uncle's death certificate be listed as "acute alcoholism." This enraged the sisters even more. Since I have never seen a copy of my uncle's death certificate, I do not know the full truth of this matter. I do not believe my mother would knowingly lie about something this serious. My uncle's death further split our fractured family. Some family members demonized his wife and it remained that way until her death.

My uncle's wife, Mary V., as we called her, was an elementary school teacher in Lake City. She was a graduate of Florida Southern College when it was not easy to send a child to an expensive private college. My mother stayed on good terms with her after my uncle's death because of my uncle's three children. I seldom went to their house but remained on friendly speaking terms with the family. Mary V. took a teaching job in St. Petersburg in the Fall of 1949 and moved the family there. This greatly improved her financial position which I later learned had been only $125.00 per month in the Columbia County School System.

However, with this move, our contact with them was almost completely severed. We seldom saw or heard from them unless there was a death in the family. In recent years, I have reached out to my cousins and they have been cordial. However, I feel that we lost a great deal when my mother and her sisters allowed their grief to make them so angry. I do not believe any of the negative accusations concerning Mary V. were true. It would have been better for everyone to have put the bitterness to rest and to have nurtured healthy family relationships. Mary V. was an excellent mother to her children, sending each one of them through high school and college. They all turned out well. She never married again.

I continued attending Dasher Bible School through the next spring. I did not have any close friends at the school but got along with all the students there. Some wanted to debate church doctrine with me, but it was never intense. I became more focused as a student and did better than average in my studies. I did some intramural boxing and tried to play basketball. I did not understand basketball and the coaches did not try to teach any of the fundamentals. Add to that the fact that I began to have back problems which may have been related to my bicycle accident. I went to several chiropractors and got some relief, but for the rest of the year, I struggled when participating in sports.

While at Dasher, I would go home at least twice a month to visit and get my laundry done. I would hitchhike home, but Mom would put me on a bus for the return trip. I always caught a ride home when I needed one and always arrived safely. Twice, I rode with men who were either homosexuals or pedophiles. They invited me to go on to other cities with them, but neither of them got violent or tried to abduct me.

My unhappiness at Dasher continued to increase. Every time I went home I had intense discussions with my mother about coming home. She wanted me to stay until the end of the year, but I did not want to stay. I think I must have finally worn her down with my continuing demands to return home. At the end of March or in early April, she relented and gave me permission to make the transfer. That proved to have been a mistake. The Georgia school system was different from that in Florida. I was taking more courses in Georgia. Some of those courses would not be not available in the Florida system should I transfer back home. My mother may not have realized this, or she may not have been informed. I did transfer most of my credits back to Columbia High School but lost some credits in the move. The assistant principal explained this to me after I had enrolled again at Columbia High School.

Returning to Columbia High School, I discovered an entirely different atmosphere there. We had several new faculty members. Further, I was approaching school with more commitment to being a good student. I was still not living up to my potential, but I was doing much better. My biology teacher was a native of Live Oak, Florida. She asked me if my father was Ike McDonald. I replied that he was my father, but that he had been killed in the War. She said that she knew he was dead, and she had known him. He had dated her sister at one time. She was always very nice to me.

When school ended I began looking for summer work. I was not yet sixteen years old and was forced to pick up work with farmers who ran small truck farms raising produce. The work involved picking the produce when it was ready for harvest, and the pay was both small and irregular.

The property on which our home was located was about one full acre, allowing us to have a garden and a small enclosed pen for our cow. We bought the cow shortly after we moved to this property. The space for the cow and garden were fenced to keep unwanted animals out. I helped care for the garden and cared for the cow. I would put her in her pen, feed, and water her at night, and milk her twice a day. We had an open range in Florida allowing livestock the freedom to graze wherever they chose.

The threat of polio was a reality during these years because the vaccine had not yet been discovered. There were epidemics in various parts of the country and the news constantly reminded us of every new case that was discovered. It kept a lot of social activity for children and teenagers curtailed during the summer months. We were warned to stay out of crowds and to stay away from swimming pools and most social gatherings of teenagers. We were not certain as to how the polio virus was carried or caught, but the consequences could be life threatening and life changing. This put a damper on a lot of summer activity for teenagers, but I still got together with my friends.

Near mid-summer I developed a bad sinus infection. Antibiotics were new, and the older doctors were reluctant to prescribe them. I suffered most of the summer with this infection and was weakened physically by it. When fall football practice began in late August, I was in no shape to even practice, but I made the effort. Coach Hill later told my mother that it was evident that I had been sick and was in no condition to participate.

At this point, half of my high school career was complete. Much of this journey had been interesting. I had not been the best student, but improvement was being made.

My circle of friends was changing, and I was making much better decisions. My focus on life was becoming more mature. I was beginning to grow up, but I had a long way to go. My mother would joke about the problems she was having getting me over "fool's hill." She insisted that every time she thought she had me over the hump, I would turn around and run back for more. She said she thought I enjoyed finding all the problems that I could possibly discover. I did not enjoy the problems, but I did find my share of them. Many more interesting things were to come!

Chapter 5
Late High School Years

All of 1947 continued to be a time of change. Some of it slipped past me, but I was aware that the Lake City Naval Air Station was in the process of closing, which meant my parents would soon be out of work. My mother considered trying to stay with a civil service job, but that meant transferring to another city unless she could get a job at the VA Hospital in Lake City. The same was true for my stepfather. As in many things, political connections ruled, and my folks seemed unaware of how to play that game. They were both out of a job before the year was over. My stepfather began to work as an independent painting contractor, and my mother became a housewife again.

Our economic situation would not have become so uncertain had my stepfather not had a drinking problem. Further, he had developed a strong dislike for paying taxes. His solution to this problem was that he would work until he made just enough money not to have any tax liability, then he would do little or nothing the rest of the year. This put our lifestyle in a serious situation. My mother began to do some part time work and my survivor's pension helped, but we were still not living as well as we had when they both had jobs. The national economy was less vigorous than it had been during the War, but for the most part, our country was adjusting well to the post-War economic conditions.

As I said before, I decided to go out for football again. My mother was still unhappy with my decision, but we had less conflict over it than when I went out for the team in the ninth grade. Practice began in late August, about three weeks before classes were to start. I was still suffering from the results of the sinus infection I had developed during the summer, but I enjoyed getting up, running, and going through the exercises and drills that came with practice.

We had a new head coach, O'Neal Hill, who was recently out of the Marine Corps. Coach Hill came from a prominent local family and was a University of Florida graduate. His assistant coaches were Hollis Evans, a graduate of Centre College in Kentucky; Tommy Terry, a Lake City native and a graduate of Florida Southern College; Ted Tucker, an Ohio native and a Marine Corps veteran; and William Sullivan, a Kentuckian and a graduate of East Tennessee State University. These men had superb credentials but lacked coaching experience. Tommy Terry was the B Team coach; Ted Tucker worked with him and served as head coach for basketball and baseball.

About two weeks into the school term, I learned that the team was going to be cut to a certain number of players, which was a new experience for our school. Previously, if a person went out for football and stayed with it, they got a uniform, were assigned to a position, ranked in that position, and remained on the team until the end of the season. The list of players making the team was posted on a Friday. I missed school that day, but I called Coach Terry to learn the results and he told me that I was not on the list. I was devastated. I asked him to talk with Coach Hill and see if there was a mistake. He said he had already discussed this with Coach Hill and that there was no mistake. I begged him to go back and intervene on my behalf, but he said he had already done that and there was nothing more he could do. He said that he was sorry, but he encouraged me to stay in shape and to try again next year. It was a great disappointment because I really did want to be a part of the football team. I learned later that Coach Hill was aware that I had been sick during the summer and was not fully recovered. My best efforts on the field could not disguise this fact.

In spite of my disappointment, life went on. I was taking English, Algebra, American History, Study Hall, Chemistry, and Physical Education which had been linked to the football program. I was doing surprisingly well in all my courses except English. Previously, my English teachers had not demanded much of me and I did not have a good foundation in the subject. Madge Hutcherson was the teacher for junior English. Early in the first semester we focused on literature, reading and memorizing both poetry and prose. Later we got into grammar, the diagramming of sentences and writing. I immediately began to protest that I could not do the work and refused to make any effort.

The teacher, "Old Madge," as we called her, did not accept my excuses. She refused to let me get away with being lazy and doing nothing. I never saw her lay a hand on a student, but that was never necessary for her. Her tongue lashings were enough to get anyone's attention and she got mine. She told me in front of the entire class that I had a good mind and that I could do the work. She was adamant in stating that she was not going to put up with failure on my part. I had never had a teacher like this. She would chew me out in front of the class when I did not make an effort and praise me in front of the class when I did good work. I went to work trying to do the best that I could. I had experienced all of her tongue lashings I could tolerate.

I barely passed that first semester in English. I had numerous conferences with Miss Hutcherson as I struggled in her class. She knew that I was trying, but we both knew that I had a long way to go. My English class met during fifth period. She had another section of the same class during sixth period. She asked what I was doing sixth period. I replied that since I was not on the football team, I usually went to the library or study hall. She said that if I would get permission to attend her sixth period class, she would work with me and see if I could get caught up so I could do better in my regular fifth period class. We did that for the rest of the year and I improved enough the second semester to have a passing grade for the entire year. The next year as a senior I maintained good grades in English the entire year.

It is in social settings both structured and informal that we get to know people and friendships are formed. Being an outgoing person, I made both casual and close friendships. It is true that our friends influence us both positively and negatively. As I look back, I realize that I had a wide circle of casual friends with whom I was not close, but with whom I maintained positive relationships. Then there were the close friends with whom I would hang out before school, during lunch, and at social activities. As I matured, I was careful to form positive friendships.

For some time, Alvin Yanke and I were close friends. Alvin was the adopted son of a couple that had no other children. I do not think his father was from Lake City, but his mother was. Mr. Yanke had a taxi business which he ran during and after the War. He and his wife apparently could not have children, so they adopted Alvin when he was a baby. Alvin was a good student, and we enjoyed each other's company. I spent the night at his home on occasions and we were both in the Boy Scouts. He became an Eagle Scout. On occasions after we had gone to a movie, we would go by his father's taxi stand and his father would give me a ride home. It was about a mile and a half to my house. The taxi fee was fifty cents. Sometimes I would pay him, but there were times that he would not take my money. Alvin and I were both members of First Baptist Church where we attended Sunday School and church, sang in the youth choir, and participated in other youth activities.

Though we drifted apart, we both attended the University of Florida. Alvin would occasionally ride from Gainesville to Lake City with me because I had a car and he did not. He married a local girl, went into the Air Force, and retired as a colonel. After he retired and returned to Lake City, he made a point of coming to hear me preach whenever I was in Lake City and was filling the pulpit as a guest minister. He died from lung cancer a few years after he retired. I regret his untimely death; he was a good friend.

Sometime during my junior year in high school, I formed a friendship with Tommy Ramsey. We were the same age, but I was a year ahead of him in school. He was the adopted son of Sam and Mellie Ramsey. Sam Ramsey worked for the Florida Alcohol Tobacco and Firearms Bureau. He was a World War I veteran whose health had been severely affected by being gassed in France. Mellie was a registered nurse who worked at the VA Hospital. Their marriage was filled with conflict. They had adopted Tommy hoping that having him would make things better. They both loved Tommy, but their marriage relationship did not improve.

Tommy and I became very close friends. We did just about everything together. We went on double dates, went to parties, bought suits that were just alike, and participated in all our church activities together. In the summer after my junior year, we both went to the commander of the National Guard Unit in Lake City, misrepresented our age, and joined the Guard. We went to National Guard Summer

Camp together. During my senior year we played on the high school football team. We were closer than brothers. When I became involved in a heavy romance during my senior year and decided to answer the call to the ministry, our lives began to go in separate directions. I do not think either of us wanted this to happen, but it did.

Tommy had a great senior year as the quarterback of our Columbia High School's football team. He attended one year at the University of Florida and then joined the Navy. We lost track of each other when he went into the Navy and did not reconnect until about 1980 when I called him after learning that he had become a vice president with the Bank of America. It has been a long and rewarding friendship. We still visit and renew our friendship whenever I am in Lake City.

George Ferree and his family moved to Lake City right after World War II. I believe he arrived as we were beginning the ninth grade. His mother was a teacher and his father was a World War II veteran employed by the Florida Power and Light Company. George was a friendly, relaxed person with whom it was easy to become acquainted. Our friendship began to develop when we were in the eleventh grade. Becoming better acquainted, we found it easy to laugh, joke, and share our thoughts. We would spend the night with each other, do our studies, and go to the school dances together. George was a great dancer. He and his high school sweetheart would put on a jitterbugging show at nearly every dance. He was also an excellent athlete playing football and baseball.

George had a good mind, excelled as a student, and became the valedictorian of our class. His school teacher mother had taught him good study habits. As we began to study together for tests, I learned a great deal from him about how to study and use the material we covered in our classes. He was a very positive academic influence on me. His influence carried over into our college life when we were at the University of Florida.

Late in our junior year of school, both George and I experienced the call to ministry. We were not alone; about twelve young men in our school had the same calling. As with everything, George launched into preaching with all of his energy. While I was feeling my way along, he encouraged me, taught me how to outline and prepare a sermon, and took the leadership for the group of young men who began going to the county jail each Sunday afternoon to preach and witness to the prisoners. Since the white and black prisoners were segregated on separate floors, he would often preach to one group while I would preach to the other. I only had two or three sermons, but the crowd changed almost weekly. I could alternate the messages and not be repeating myself to those who heard me. We made these weekly visits to the jail our high school junior and senior years.

Just before George's last year in college, he married his high school sweetheart, Barbara Norsworthy. Upon graduation from the University of Florida, he became pastor of the Methodist Church in Baldwin, Florida. Their first child was born while he served there and completed his master's in education at the University of Florida. He became unhappy with many things in the Methodist Church, leaving to take a teaching position in Sarasota, Florida. He never returned to the ministry. He earned a doctorate from Tufts University and taught at Tufts, the University of Missouri, and Michigan State University.

My wife and I visited with George and Barbara and their three children when they lived in Columbia, Missouri. Later, I learned through Morris Williams that they had separated and were getting a divorce. I tried to contact George but failed to do so. I did stay in touch with Barbara for several years. George remarried and went to teach at Michigan State University. He was still teaching there twenty years later when at the insistence of his mother I gave him a phone call. He was surprised, but we soon began to visit when he traveled through my area between school sessions and his southern residence. Since that time, we have remained in touch and often visit together. Though our lives have taken different paths, we have remained close friends.

Morris Williams was the youngest son of an older couple in Lake City. His father was an educator having come to Kentucky to attend what later became Western Kentucky University. When his father returned to Lake City, he taught school and later served as Superintendent of Schools for Columbia County. Morris had siblings from his father's first marriage that were old enough to be his parents.

Morris was a year behind me in school. He went to the Methodist Church and was in their Boy Scout program. We did many things together but did not become close friends until we were in college. He was one of a group of young men who were greatly influenced by a city-wide revival that we had in Lake City. He was not alone; several young men, including myself and George Ferree, experienced the call to the ministry and began preaching as a result of that revival. Morris often went with us to preach at the county jail when we held services on Sunday afternoon. He later turned his life to the vocation of public education and had an outstanding career. Our friendship has grown over the years. We keep in touch and visit whenever I am in Lake City.

These friendships were formed during my high school years. They have endured the changes and tests of time. I have been blessed by these friends. There is not a one of them with whom I cannot be open and honest. To this day we hug when we greet each other, and we part by affirming our love for each other. This kind of friendship is one of life's best blessings!

The big life event in the latter part of my junior year was my call to preach, which I have previously mentioned. It was a mystical calling which completely changed my life. It came to me at night in the form of a dream while I was asleep.

In the dream, I looked toward heaven and told God that I knew He had something He wanted me to do. I stated that if He would tell me what it was, I would do it. To my surprise, God answered, and I listened. I knew it was God who was speaking to me and I was terrified. I awoke from my sleep and went to my mother's bedroom. As I stood by her bed, she awoke and asked me what was wrong. I told her that I had just had a disturbing dream. I asked her if I could stay with her. She motioned me to the other side of the bed and I lay down and soon went back to sleep. The next morning, she asked about the dream and I told her I would tell her about it later.

The next few weeks were difficult for me. I struggled with the call that I felt must be to the ministry. I thought at first that God wanted me to go to the mission field, but to me that was the same as the ministry. I protested to God that I was not qualified nor gifted toward the ministry. Furthermore, I did not want to be a preacher. Looking back, I see God at work in my life and I feel that He was calling me earlier, but I was not inclined to listen. Perhaps the kind of experience that took place was necessary to get my attention. After much protesting to God and resisting the call, I decided that I had to do what God wanted me to do. I went to my pastor, J. T. Mashburn, and shared with him what had happened. His counsel was that if God was calling me, I should do His bidding. I had a long discussion with my mother. Later, I decided to give God a positive answer. I had no idea as to how this was going to change my life. The choice of one's life vocation is one of the most important decisions that a person ever makes.

The school year ended, and I was able to get a summer job working at McDuffie's Gulf Service Station on North Marion Street near the middle of town. I enjoyed serving the customers, many of whom were traveling from up north to various parts of Florida. I learned how to fill a car with gas, check the oil and tire pressure, fill the radiator, clean the windshield, and sweep out the floorboards. I learned the distance from Lake City to most of the towns north and south of our location. Tourists constantly asked for information that would guide them to their destination. Further, I learned the best routes to take to other places. It was a great summer job.

As I stated earlier, Tommy Ramsey and I had enlisted in the local National Guard unit. We were looking for adventure and we got it. Our unit was filled with World War II veterans. They had been around the world, seen combat and many other things. We were green kids, but they tolerated us and gave us some valuable guidance. Our summer camp took place at Ft. Jackson, South Carolina. It was the second time I had been to that state and I loved it. The Lake City business community was gracious about giving National Guard members time away from their jobs for summer camp.

Our National Guard Company was a Heavy Tank Unit. The tanks we had were those which had been available for use early in World War II. They were armed with fifty-caliber machine guns and 75mm cannons. The U.S. developed better tanks with bigger guns later in the war, but most of those were still in service and not available to us. In addition to learning the fundamentals of military life, we had to learn to shoot and care for our weapons. Tank crews were armed with .45-caliber Army Colt pistols. I learned how to dismantle, clean, and reassemble my pistol. On the firing range, I proved to be an excellent shot. As a gunner in a tank, I had to learn how to sight the gun and fire it. We had classes for all of this and I soon had a grasp of what they were teaching. When we went to the firing range to shoot the tank cannon, I found the sighting completely wrong when I prepared to fire the gun. I asked for permission to adjust the sight and having done so, I hit the target dead center. I was one of a few that was accurate that day.

While we were at Fort Jackson, the Russians set up their blockade on Berlin. It was a tense time and rumors began to circulate that President Truman was going to call up the National Guard. Should that happen, I would not be able to go home, and I would not get to finish high school the next year. Happily, that proved to be only a rumor and we went home on time. But for a day or two I was really wanting to see my mother.

We traveled on a passenger train going to and from Fort Jackson. We left Lake City near the end of the day, spent the night on the train, and arrived at our destination early the next day. Most of the cars were Pullman sleeper cars with beds prepared for us so we could sleep. It was not a bad way to travel. Returning from Fort Jackson to Lake City, we arrived home at about eleven o'clock on Sunday morning. Once the train stopped, it took very little time for us to make our exit and fall into formation. Our Company Commander, Captain Henry Cochran, decided to march us right through the middle of town on North Marion Street. Marion Street was the main street and was also U.S. 41 and 441. We marched about ten blocks through the middle of town until we came to the turn which would take us about two blocks west to the Armory. We did not meet a single automobile the entire way, nor did any drive up behind us. I had chill bumps all the way.

While at Ft. Jackson I received a letter from Carolyn Bearden, a nice young lady who went to our church. She had been dating one of my high school friends who was also in the Guard. The letter was an obvious overture for my attention. I answered the letter and when I got home, she had my full attention. She was the youngest daughter of a widow. Her family had moved to Lake City from Mississippi before World War II. Her father had died unexpectedly. Carolyn and her mother were very gracious to me and a long romance developed.

Though Carolyn was two grades behind me in school, we soon decided that we cared enough for each other to marry. However, we were both aware that we needed a college education. We dated through my high school senior year and my first two years of college. The romance was filled with highs, lows, and conflict. As I was beginning my third year in college, she stated that she still loved me and intended to marry me, but she wanted to date other people. We had some discussions about that over the next few weeks. Then I wrote her a letter telling her that I did not feel that I could continue under the conditions she had laid out. I returned several things that she had given me, asked for my football letter which was attached to my athletic sweater, and told her that I would not be back.

She removed the letter from the sweater, kept the sweater, and returned the letter. She wrote me two letters after that, but never offered to come to my terms for continuing our relationship. She was married within a year. Ending this relationship was one of the hardest things I ever had to do. It took me two years to get over the emotional loss. She was my first love, though she would not be the last. First love always seems to hold a special place in a person's life. Given the roller coaster nature of our relationship, I am convinced that had we married, the marriage may not have lasted.

The summer of 1948 was ending, and school was about to begin. Late August brought on the beginning of football practice. I was determined to make the team this year. I worked hard, ran the drills, and never missed a practice. The coaches had me playing the left end position. The previous year had not been a good one for the team and the coaching staff knew that they were under pressure to produce. We had good material for a team, but as it turned out, Coach Hill did not possess coaching skills.

Since I was small and inexperienced, I dressed for the varsity games, but only got to play on the B Team. Tommy Terry was the B Team coach. He was patient, encouraging, and thorough. We played an eight-game schedule winning six of our games. Tommy Ramsey was our quarterback. The Varsity offense used the old single wing formation, which the B team used part of the time because we had to scrimmage them in practice. However, the B Team began using various forms of the T formation. This was a new offense, but we did well with it. The Varsity was 1-8-1 for the season, which ended Coach Hill's tenure. At our fiftieth class reunion, I stood looking at the team photograph with fellow class member Marvin Coates. We both agreed that with the material we had on the team, we would have had much more success had we been given more effective coaching. The other coaches were hampered by the head coach's lack of ability.

During football season, Ted Tucker, the head basketball coach assisted Tommy Terry with B Team coaching duties. Coach Tucker encouraged me to try out for the basketball team. When basketball practice began I was there. Time came for the team to be cut, and Coach Tucker called me into his office. He thanked me for trying out, but said I was not going to make the team. When he listed those who had made the team, I protested that I was as good as at least two of the boys he was keeping on the team. He replied, "Ikie, that is true, but you are a senior and they are juniors. I will have them back next year and I have to go with the chance that they will be back and better next year." I saw his point, thanked him for giving me a chance, and for being honest with me about the outcome. Ted Tucker was a good man and an excellent coach.

In the early spring a problem developed for me in the National Guard. The master sergeant in our company decided that he wanted me to be the company clerk. He discussed this with me, and I told him that I had no interest in the position or promotion. He proceeded to place me in the position and I quit going to drills. In a very short time I received a letter from the company commander telling me that if I was not present for the next drill, he was sending the sheriff after me. My mother thought it was amusing.

I showed up for the drill in civilian clothes and was ordered to get into uniform and report to the commander's office. When I reported, the commander asked me to explain the reason for my behavior. I explained that I did not wish to be company clerk and had declined the position when the first sergeant had offered it. He asked if I would obey an order to serve in that capacity. I replied that I would, but I did not think I would do a good job. Then I told him I was planning on going to college and there was some question as to whether I would be able to be present for the monthly drills. I told him that it would be best if I could get out of the Guard. He told me that if I would attend all drills until early summer, he would give me an honorable discharge. I agreed to this, did what I agreed to do, and he gave me my discharge. He was a class act.

My senior year went quite well. I had a different attitude toward school and was making a genuine effort at being a good student. My grades were better than average. I do not recall any special problems during the school year. I was focused on my calling to the ministry and I was trying to decide where I should go to college. Stetson University was the Baptist College in the state and I applied there, was accepted, and assured of a ministerial scholarship which would cover my tuition costs. I was totally unaware of what the other costs would be.

During the summer of 1949, the local economy seemed to be much more fragile than it had been previously. The only job I could find was at the tobacco market and it did not last all summer. I made some money but had very little saved when it came time for me to depart for college. I was naive about the cost of school and about how to prepare to depart for school. But I was determined to go and committed to the fact that I wanted the education that college would afford me. Above all, I was filled with hope that I would make it through the process. It was going to be an adventure and I was ready for it.

Chapter 6

The College Years

In the fall of 1949, I entered my first year of college at Stetson University in De Land, Florida. If ever there was a person who was uninformed and unprepared for the college experience, it was me. I had met several Stetson students during the summer who were members of a youth evangelistic team that led a youth revival at my home church, First Baptist Church, Lake City. They had been gracious and were helpful, but as I look back, it is a miracle that I was able to complete the year. The proverb "ignorance is bliss" really applied to me.

When I announced my plans to go to college, my stepfather said nothing. I asked him if he would help me, but he said that he had his hands full providing for the family. I knew from that moment forward I could not depend on him for help or encouragement. In fact, he never came to hear me preach. It was not that he did not have the opportunity; for several years my preaching never took place more than forty miles from our home and some occurred in local churches. To this day, I do not understand his attitude toward what I decided to do with my life. True, he was an alcoholic, but he was not against religion. I suspect that his decision to be uninvolved in what I did arose out of the conflict that he had with my mother. Staying away from church and not being involved was another way of getting back at her. Also, he knew his drinking was unacceptable behavior in Southern Baptist circles.

On the Wednesday evening before I was to leave for school on Thursday, I went to the midweek prayer service at First Baptist Church. I spoke to the group briefly and asked them to pray for me that I would have success at college. When the prayer service began I did not even have enough money for bus fare to De Land. In fact, I had no money. As the crowd began to break up and depart several people came by and gave me gifts of five dollars or more. When I left the prayer service I had more than twenty-five dollars in hand. I was on my way.

I was aware that I would have to work at least part time in order to remain in school. I made a covenant with God, asking Him to help me find a job, telling Him that I would give Him fifteen percent of everything I made. During my first week on campus, an older student came to me with the proposition that I develop a dry-cleaning pickup for the two dormitories where I lived. He would take the clothes to the cleaner and bring them back to me. I would deliver them, collect for the service and we would share the profit. It worked, and I was never without folding money in my pocket the entire year. I kept my covenant with God and He took good care of me.

Many ministerial students, the football team, and law students lived in what had been the bachelor office quarters on the old Naval Air Station just outside of De Land on the Daytona Beach highway. The law school was housed in the administrative building of the former military base. We took our meals in what had been the mess hall. Since these facilities were four miles from town, we rode buses driven by older students to the main campus for our classes. The last bus ran at ten o'clock at night just as the library closed. Students were advised to catch it because it was four miles from the campus to their residence. Some students had cars, but many did not. It was not a convenient arrangement, but it worked. I lived there for the first two quarters of the school year.

I took a full academic load the first quarter. I did well in everything but English, which surprised me because I had done so well in English my last year in high school. My problem lay in my lack of writing skills since writing had not been greatly emphasized in high school. I had several conferences with my teacher about how to improve my grade. He was sympathetic and helpful, but he told me that I must work harder to get the job done. When the quarter was over, I made a C in English and B's in my other subjects.

Because of my ongoing romance with Carolyn Bearden, I did not spend my weekends at college. I hitchhiked home every Friday, spent the weekend in Lake City, rode the bus to Jacksonville late Sunday and caught a ride there with a group of young preachers who were headed back to De Land. My thumb served to get me a ride most of the time when I was coming home. My weekend trips home upset my mother; she wanted me to stay away from Carolyn as much as possible, and I wanted just the opposite.

An ongoing test of wills developed with my mother over control of the survivor's pension that came to me every month. Since I was still a minor and would be until I was twenty-one years old, she insisted on controlling these funds. In fact, she stated that the rules given her as my legal guardian made her responsible to the government for how every cent of the money was used. I wanted all of the money to go toward school, but she insisted that I was home enough to justify her spending some of the money on needs at home. She did my laundry every week and provided many other things for me. We did not resolve this question until I began attending the University of Florida the next year.

As the second quarter began in January 1950, I began to realize that much activity was taking place on the main campus. I was missing out on many things. Further, I believed the profit from my dry-cleaning job was not an equitable split. I negotiated with the student who was picking up the clothes and returning them to me for a better deal and got it. Later, I went to the housing office and arranged to get a room in the dormitory on campus. I asked for a job with grounds crew on the main campus and got that also.

At the beginning of the third quarter, I moved into the dormitory on the main campus, left my dry-cleaning pickup job, and began working each afternoon on the grounds crew. I also took a full academic load. This move freed up better than an hour each day that I spent traveling to and from the main campus. My new job paid well; the work was physical and outdoors, and I enjoyed the new arrangement.

In one of my English classes I read an essay entitled "Education for Freedom" by Robert M. Hutchins, the former president of the University of Chicago. He made a powerful case for a liberal arts education, which caused me to begin looking at my course of study at Stetson. Since I was on a ministerial scholarship, I was required to major in religion. In my mind, this was not a liberal arts curriculum. My plans were to go to seminary as soon as I completed college. I felt it would be a better use of my educational efforts to seek a liberal arts degree in college and pursue my theological studies in seminary. Such an educational path would give me a much broader education and better prepare me for the ministry.

After discussing this plan with several people, some of whom were Stetson faculty, I approached Dr. Lafayette Walker, Chairman of the Department of Religion, asking to change my major. He listened as I presented my case but denied my request. Once he denied my request, he told me the matter was closed. He stood and left the office with me still sitting there. I was both disappointed and furious. Reviewing this event later, I realized that I had actually asked Dr. Walker to allow me to pursue studies outside his department. That could have been taken as an insult, but I do not think he saw it as that. I was just an eighteen-year-old freshman and did not realize that my request could have a negative meaning.

When my request for a change in my college major was denied, I began looking for other options. I wrote the University of Florida and asked for the applications needed for transferring to that school. When they arrived, I completed them and sent them back. In less than two weeks I received word that I had been accepted at Florida. This transfer proved to be one of my better decisions. The Florida campus was located only forty miles from my home. Many rural churches in the area were open to having a student for a pastor. I would be closer to my home base, and student employment opportunities would be greater. I was eager to take advantage of every opportunity that came my way.

As I was completing my last quarter at Stetson, my financial obligations became a concern. John and Lucille Inman, members of my home church, had created a scholarship fund through the church in memory of her parents. Her father had been a prominent bi-vocational preacher in the area. I asked my mother to check on the availability of those funds for paying the last of my financial obligations at Stetson. Mom discussed this with the Inman's who agreed to let those funds go to my account. I left the school without owing anything. It was a blessing and a relief.

During my first year at Stetson, my pastor, J. T. Mashburn, resigned his position at my home church in Lake City and accepted a call to First Baptist Church, Pompano Beach, Florida. Shortly afterwards, my home church called Dr. Allen J. Freeman as pastor. Dr. Freeman had served in the military during World War II and had completed his doctorate at Southern Baptist Theological Seminary just prior to accepting the call to First Baptist Church Lake City.

When I arrived home for the summer, Dr. Freeman approached me about the possibility of my serving on staff as a summer associate at First Baptist. I was eager but inexperienced. My job was to visit and do whatever else he wanted me to do. Within two weeks, I became aware that accepting the position had been a mistake. However, there was little choice but to remain and make the best of a bad situation. No matter what I did, it was impossible to please Dr. Freeman. There was hardly a day that I was not called into his office and given a strong verbal reprimand for some alleged infraction. I am certain that I made some mistakes and errors in judgment, but I still think the treatment I received was totally unjustified. As I was concluding my service to return to school, Dr. Freeman asked me to come by his house saying that he had something for me. I went, stayed for about an hour, as we discussed various topics, and departed. He never mentioned having anything for me. It had been a miserable summer.

As the summer ended, I went to Gainesville and enrolled in the University of Florida. I have few memories of that first year. The total matriculation fee for one semester was only $50.00. Of course, I had to pay for housing, meals, books and school supplies, but it certainly was a different world than the one I had faced at Stetson University. My total cost for school that entire first year at the University of Florida was $630.00.

There were some nice dormitories on campus which were occupied by the female students. Male upperclassmen also had good accommodations, but most of the new male students lived in single-story, prefab structures that had been built during and after World War II. We had three students per room. My roommates were serious students. We did not have any problems living together.

The lecture classes at Florida were usually large with as many as three to four hundred students attending a single class. Tests were multiple choice questions so designed to be graded by machines. All students were enrolled in the University College, a general curriculum designed for the first two years of study. When a student completed these courses, they could transfer to the college offering their major provided they had an academic grade average of 2.0 on a 4.0 scale. I found the classes to be worthwhile for the most part, but I did have some trouble with the math courses.

My intention was to major in biology and secondary education. My plans were to go to the mission field and I believed that a degree in education would enhance my chances of gaining an appointment by the Foreign Mission Board. I had taken biology at Stetson and really loved the subject. However, the atmosphere in the biology department at the University of Florida was entirely different. The attitude I encountered was that Darwin's theory of evolution was much more sacred than scripture. Those who did not buy into that mindset were the object of condescending humor or outright scorn. Needless to say, I did not find a sympathetic home in that environment. I wanted to learn, but I resisted having something crammed down my throat. My plans for a biology major were soon abandoned.

One refreshing discovery I made was that there were many opportunities for preaching in rural churches in the Gainesville area. That had not been the case in De Land because many of the Stetson ministerial students were veterans, were more mature in their thinking and behavior, and had their own cars. The available churches were soon filled by those students. I was able to preach a total of only six times during my stay in De Land. When I enrolled at Florida, I was in my home territory and preaching opportunities came nearly every week.

In early November 1950, I began preaching at New Oak Grove Baptist Church, a church near both Alachua and High Springs. The church was east of U.S. 41 and was about twenty-five miles from both Gainesville and my home in Lake City. On December 3, 1950, they called me to be their pastor and I accepted. My responsibility was to preach twice each Sunday, lead prayer meeting on Wednesday and perform whatever other pastoral duties that were necessary. This included visiting, funerals, and weddings. I was still eighteen years old but would be nineteen on December 30. My weekly salary was $25.00.

Now that I had a church, I needed transportation. A leader in my home church was an automobile dealer who had been kind enough to loan me a car when I was filling pulpits in the area. He found a 1942 Dodge sedan that appeared to be in good condition. However, once I bought it, I had problems keeping it running, and repair bills were keeping me broke most of the time. When I went back to my dealer friend for some help, he was no longer available. I had learned my first lesson in the fine art of buying an automobile: be careful when doing business with church people.

Since I had not been ordained to the ministry, ordination became the next step for me. Ordination in Baptist churches takes place at the request of a church that has called as pastor a minister who has not been ordained. The candidate for ordination must declare that God has called him into the ministry. Further, a congregation must have called him to serve as their pastor. That church then usually requests the candidate's home church to ordain him. Among Baptists there are no educational requirements for ordination though both college and seminary education is recommended.

The request for my ordination was sent from New Oak Grove Baptist Church to First Baptist Church, Lake City. This meant that my home church would form a committee known as an ordaining council to question or examine me to be assured of my call and doctrinal acceptability. That committee would recommend that the ordination proceed or be denied.

I immediately began to study the Bible as well as Baptist doctrine to be prepared for questions from the ordination council. Since Dr. Freeman was pastor at my home church, he was elected chairman of that council. As he began the questioning, he put some complicated theological questions before me. However, other members of the council sensed what was happening and became my advocates, reinterpreting the questions and leading intense discussions that answered the questions. Of course, I had some input, but it was kept to a minimum. When they voted on recommending my ordination to the church, it was unanimous.

My ordination service took place at First Baptist Church, Lake City, Florida on January 17, 1951. This was eighteen days after I became nineteen years old. Looking back, I find myself amazed that a church would call an eighteen-year-old boy to be their pastor. I thought I was mature, but I had much to learn. I may have been smarter at that time than I ever have been in my entire life. But God was still working miracles and I was a work in progress.

The following is a description of my ordination service. I still have in my files the hand-written order of service that Dr. Freeman gave to me at the beginning of service. This was prior to the arrival of copying machines and computers. The order of worship was written by hand on a "JUST REMEMBER" note pad provided by the Presbyterian Minister's Fund. Several ministers took part in the service. Dr. Freeman presided and Hubert Barnes, pastor at Southside Baptist Church, brought the Ordination Sermon. It was entitled, "A Man Sent from God." His text came from John 1:6-8. William Tyre brought the Charge to the Church. His text was Hebrews 13:7 and 17. Hugh Walters gave the Charge to the Candidate using I Timothy 3:1-9 and Isaiah 6:1-8. Dr. Freeman presented me with a nice, leather-bound Bible as a gift from First Baptist Church. After the Laying on of Hands, the Benediction was pronounced, and the service was concluded. My mother came and stood with me as the congregation came by to offer their congratulations and best wishes. Carolyn and her mother were there, but they stayed in the background.

My first semester at the University of Florida was not over until the middle of January 1951. I was disappointed in my academic performance. I could excuse it by saying that I was working multiple part-time jobs, preaching at various churches, and dealing with conflict at home and with Carolyn. However, I must confess that school should have come first. I was working and have no regrets about that, but I let conflict within my family and with Carolyn dominate my thought processes. It kept me in a state of turmoil most of the time. The result was that I did poorly in school with my grade point average dropping below 2.0 which was not good. Sadly, second semester was not going to be any better. I concluded the year being on academic probation beginning first semester, 1951.

Once I assumed the pastorate of New Oak Grove, I told my mother that I was setting up a bank account through which to pay my expenses. I asked her to allow me to deposit my monthly survivor's pension into that account. I explained that I would pay her for any expenses that were mine at home. After a brief but heated discussion, she agreed to this arrangement. I gave her money from time to time, but she was always reluctant to take it. There were living expenses related to being in school and work expenses related to my duties at the church. Managing all of this was part of the maturing process.

We had a revival at New Oak Grove in the summer of 1951. There were numerous converts. I was privileged to baptize the entire J. L. Matthews family. They were Methodists and had been attending our church for several months. Mr. Matthews' life had not been exemplary. Even though he had made mistakes, he was now trying to live a better life. I felt he should be encouraged, and I encouraged him.

When it came time to baptize the new members, I learned that baptisms usually took place in the Santa Fe River. The site was a swimming hole near the bridge where I crossed the river each week on my way to the church. We gathered for that service on a Sunday afternoon. As I waded into the water, the teenage boys kept assuring me that the bottom of the river went out gradually. I should have known better. Just as I was getting to the depth where it would be comfortable to baptize, I stepped into a hole and was over my head in the river before I knew it. Fortunately, I could swim. There were sheepish smiles on a few faces as I swam back to the place where I could comfortably perform the baptisms.

Later in the summer, I was at the Matthews' home for Sunday dinner. That afternoon I shared with J. L. the problems I was having with my car. He took me to his garage and showed me a 1950 Mercury Club Coupe that he had just gotten in a trade from his sister. He said, "I I want you to drive this car and tell me what you think of it." I took it out for a short drive and told him that I thought it was an excellent vehicle. He said, "With all the responsibility you have taken on, you must have dependable car." We struck a deal of $1600.00 for a car that had sold for $2200.00 a year earlier.

It had 12,000 miles on it and still smelled like new. He gave me $400.00 in a trade for my car. I financed $900.00 and he carried the $300.00 balance at no interest. When one less generous church member criticized him for helping me, he replied, "Ike is doing a man's job and he ought to be driving a man's car. We are supposed to be helping people in this world. Ike needed some help. I am glad I could help him. You ought to be ashamed for not helping him yourself."

When I went to my bank seeking a loan for the car I bought from J. L. Matthews, the bank president, Earl Haltiwanger, told me that the bank could not loan me the money because I was not yet twenty-one years old. He told me that I could not even own an automobile in the state of Florida. He did not comment on the fact that I already owned a car or that I had a bank account with his bank out of which I was paying most of my expenses. When I asked for his advice, he told me to come by his house after five o'clock that afternoon. I went to his home and he explained that though the bank could not loan me the money, he could do it personally. He said that he would have the note for me to sign and the check for the money the next day. I signed the note, took the check and deposited it into my account, and wrote J. L. a check for $900.00. I never failed to make a payment to Mr. Haltiwanger until the note was repaid. It was not until later that I learned that the going interest rate for such a loan had been six percent. Mr. Haltiwanger, a deacon in First Baptist Church, had charged me eight percent. Again, I learned a lesson about loans: always negotiate the loan first. While it is true that Mr. Haltiwanger helped me with the loan, it is also true that he could have given me a better interest rate.

A year later, J. L. learned that I was considering dropping out of school because of money problems. He came to me and asked me if that was true. I replied that it was. He handed me his checkbook and asked, "How much do you need?" I said, "I need as much as I already owe you, $300.00." He said, "Write a check to yourself for that amount and I'll sign it." I said, "But I don't know when I will be able to repay you." He said, "We will worry about that later. Right now, we need to keep you in school." When I finished college, I went to him telling him that I had a job and a church. I offered to delay going to seminary for a year and repay the loan. His reply was, "I loaned you that money to help you. If I make you stop school to repay me, I will not be helping you. Go on to seminary and you can repay me when you finish. Remember, there is no interest on this loan." I did that and shortly after finishing seminary while I was pastor at Calhoun Baptist Church in Calhoun, Kentucky, I began sending him a check for $50.00 a month until I had repaid the debt. No matter how long I live or what I do, J. L. Matthews and his wife will share in the fruit of my ministry. I will forever be grateful for their investment in my life and ministry.

My second summer job after going to college was with the Florida State Highway Department. Russ Davis, a local pharmacist and a friend of our family, used his influence to assist me in getting this job. I worked as a rodman on Billy Hale's survey crew. I learned a lot about road building, surveying, drafting, and people. I formed friendships with Billy Hale and Walter Skinner that lasted throughout their lifetimes. They were good to me.

My Jacksonville cousins, Monteen and Phil Tomberlin, owned a farm east of Lake City. Phil was employed by the Florida Alcohol, Tobacco and Firearms Department. He traveled all over north Florida, and I frequently saw him in Lake City, Gainesville, or some other place where we both traveled. Phil was just a few months younger than my father. Since he and Monteen had no children at the time, he took me under his wing. Every time he saw me, he will fill my car with gas or leave me with several dollars in hand after a parting handshake. He would check my car to make sure I was taking care of it as I should. If he found anything that needed repair, he would often take me to his favorite mechanic and have repairs done. Often, his help came at just the right moment!

My third year in college was without major incident except for the breakup with Carolyn which I mentioned in a previous chapter. I stated that it took me two years to get over the emotional blow of that failed romance. I stayed in school, but my heart was not in it. I maintained a 2.0 grade average, but I needed to be making a 3.0 average to raise my previous poor grades to the required level. I also began dating other girls, but I was very unsure of myself in terms of how to relate to them. It was like starting all over, but with time I became more at ease and was enjoying the company of several young ladies.

One of the discoveries I made while recovering from a failed romance was country music. Hank Williams Sr. was writing and recording one song after another. When I first heard his songs, I could hardly believe the lyrics because they told the story of my recent broken romance. He described my emotional state of mind. The songs about unrequited love, broken trust, and deep heartache seemed to resonate with all that was happening in my life.

One of the girls that I dated was Joanna Vaughn, a high school junior at the time and a member of New Oak Grove Baptist Church. I dated her against the advice of other ministers and people who were friends. Joanna was the younger daughter of Myrtle Vaughn, a widow in the church. We were often together in the company of other young people in the church and our behavior was always exemplary. I always treated her like a lady. I dated her, though not exclusively, until near the end of my college career. We cared for each other, but I told her that I could not consider marriage until I finished seminary. I never proposed marriage because I did not feel that I loved her the way a man should love the woman he chose to marry. When she finished high school, she was ready to marry, and I was not. We came to a parting of ways. It was explosive, but we remained friends. She married, had a family, and died from cancer in 1992.

My service in the New Oak Grove Baptist Church was going well. The attendance was good, and new people continued to join our church. The church expanded to include four Sunday School rooms making it possible to minister to youth and adults more effectively. I continued to study and prepare for my preaching ministry and believed myself to be improving at that task. I had taken several speech courses in college which helped me improve my delivery, sermon preparation, and general speaking skills. I was spending more time working as a pastor and was beginning to gain a strong following in the church.

The deacons in the church had always controlled and given direction to the church. As I became a stronger leader, they appeared to feel threatened. I do not think they realized what was happening, but usually when criticism begins to mount you are either doing something that is wrong, or you are doing some things that are right. Looking at the success we were having in terms of growing attendance, new members, and a good spirit in the church, I felt we were doing something right. However, the deacons came to me late in the summer and suggested that I look for another place to serve. They said they needed someone who would be more effective with the young people, but that was the group with whom I was being the most effective. I decided that I did not want a church fight on my hands, so I quietly resigned, folded my tent and departed. I had been there nearly three years. The church had grown and prospered under my ministry.

At this point in time, I had completed three years of college. Having transferred from Stetson University to the University of Florida, I was in the process of changing my college major. Which meant that I would probably be in college at least two more years. After that I had at least another three years of academic study at a seminary. The education highway did not seem to be getting any shorter.

Having resigned as pastor of New Oak Grove Baptist Church, I met with our Director of Missions and made him aware of my availability which he shared with two half-time churches. They were Athens Baptist Church and Mt. Zion Baptist Church, both rural churches in Columbia County near Lake City. My pay was $25.00 per week, the same pay that I received at New Oak Grove, but now I had more miles to drive. However, these were half-time churches having church only two Sundays a month, and I did not have to lead a midweek prayer service. I had every fifth Sunday free to speak elsewhere and often found a place to preach.

The Athens Church was made up predominately of the Kirby family with a mixture of a few smaller families. The church had potential, but the congregation had little vision. We had an effective Vacation Bible School and revival during the year I was there. I baptized several people in Ichtucknee Springs at the close of the summer. They invited me back in July 2005 as the homecoming speaker. It had been more than fifty years since I had served as their pastor.

The Mt. Zion Church was basically a maintenance ministry. The church membership was small. They had money but were not inclined to invest it in ministry. They were good to me but had no vision for a greater or future ministry. Later, I learned that they had closed the doors of the church because of dwindling membership and lack of interest.

My summer job after completing my third year in college was in a small wood fence factory housed in a hangar at the old Naval Air Base in Lake City. The Dubois Fence Company fabricated snow fence from small pine saplings that had been removed from pine forests destined to be cut later for pulp wood. The finished product was shipped by rail back north for distribution. The entire labor force in the factory was black. We employed both men and women. The manager of the operation was a retired tennis professional from New Jersey. He hired me as a foreman to oversee and give direction to the day to day work of the black employees. The pay I received was reasonable, but the working relation with the manager was unpleasant. He was not mean or vicious, but he had a negative opinion of Southern people. He seemed to be constantly watching for someone to do something wrong thus giving him an opportunity to be critical. It was not a pleasant work atmosphere, but it was the only summer job available to me.

During my third year at the University of Florida, I decided to try living at home and commuting the three days, Monday, Wednesday, and Friday, that I had classes. I traveled to and from Gainesville with Herb Wright, pastor of Southside Baptist Church in Lake City. Herb had talked with my mother, telling her that I could ride with him at no cost since he was going anyway. I contributed to my keep at home, but my stepfather insisted all year that I should be giving him the money instead of my mother. I told him that I would give what I had to contribute to my mother. The tension between us continued to mount. He tried several times to bait me into physical conflict, but I refused knowing that one of us would do serious harm to the other if that happened. He usually did this when he was drinking.

I improved my academic performance during that third year, but I still had a way to go before I made up the grade point deficit that I had incurred my first year at Florida. I was still in the University College since the College of Education would not accept me until I had the 2.0 average. Had they accepted my grades from Stetson, I would have been fine, but the rule was that all transferred credit was accepted as a 2.0 grade. Most of the courses that I was then taking were either senior level courses or graduate level courses. I petitioned the College of Education to allow me in on probation at the beginning of my fourth year. They declined telling me that I had to get the grade point average to the 2.0 level before I would be admitted.

In the summer of 1953, I obtained a job with the U.S. Department of Agriculture measuring tobacco, peanut, and cotton crops in Columbia County. It was an interesting job. I tried to choose farms located in the same section of the county and close together each day as I went out to work. There was a small mileage allowance for the use of my car, but it was not wise to abuse it. Since I used a chain in measuring the crops, I needed a helper. I chose my brother who was fifteen years old. We worked together all summer which was enjoyable. When we arrived at a farm, we introduced ourselves and asked for permission to measure the crop being grown. Once we were finished, we usually shared with the farmer the results of our work reminding him that our figures were unofficial. The official results would be mailed to him from the local Department of Agriculture office.

Previously, my brother had worked jobs where he made five or ten dollars a week. He always gave a tenth of what he made to the church. His first pay check for working for me was over forty dollars. When he started figuring his tithe, it surprised him. He protested that it was too much to give. I asked him how much he gave when he made less money. His answer was ten percent. I reminded him that the ten percent rule still applied even though it meant more money. He grumbled, put the money in his church envelope, and gave it the next Sunday. It was a valuable lesson.

As I was preparing to go back to college, the Ft. White Baptist Church contacted me asking me to consider becoming their pastor. This church was in a village of about four hundred residents, half way between my home of Lake City and Gainesville. I do not remember the size of the church membership, but it was larger than that of Athens and Mt. Zion combined. Traditionally, they had preaching twice a month and were paying fifty dollars for each Sunday. After we had talked, I told them that I was not interested in serving another half-time church. I proposed that they call me and begin having services every Sunday. They said that they were not sure they could do that and keep the minister's salary at fifty dollars a week. I proposed that I would preach twice on Sunday and lead a midweek prayer service for thirty-five dollars a week. I assured them that if we tried that and had financial problems, we would find a way to work it out. They took that proposal back to the church and issued a call to me to be their pastor with that agreement. I served Ft. White a full year, resigning in late 1954 to attend seminary. It was a happy experience.

Beginning my fourth year at the University of Florida, I moved out of my mother's home for the last time. I would be back for brief visits, but I would never live under her roof again. I found a small apartment which contained a bedroom, a bathroom, and a separate entrance. The home was an excellent place to live in old downtown Gainesville.

When school began, I knew that this was probably my last chance to make the grades necessary to raise my grade point average to the level needed for being admitted to the College of Education. I signed up for a full load of classes with every course being either senior or graduate level. I scheduled a conference with every professor. I explained to them my academic problems and told them that I intended to do whatever was necessary to make the necessary grades. I asked for their guidance should they notice that I was not doing what was necessary to reach my intended goal. They were all sympathetic and helpful. When the semester was over, I had made all A's and one B, which gave me a better than the needed 2.0 average. I was admitted to the College of Education.

My last semester in college involved completing a fifteen-hour block course called Practice Teaching. We had two weeks at the beginning of the semester in preparation before being sent to our assigned schools to work in a classroom setting with a certified teacher. My assigned school was Callahan High School in Callahan, Florida. My supervising teacher was a Miss Hardee who was a first cousin to my stepfather. It was a delight to work with her. We never had a cross word or any discipline problems the whole ten weeks that we worked together. She gave me a grade of A for my work under her direction.

When I returned for the last two weeks of class at the University of Florida, I submitted all my written work. As grades were being given, I went by my field supervisor's office for a conference with him and was surprised to find that he was not available. One of the other professors, an unattractive, tall, leggy blonde, in her mid-forties, explained that she had been assigned to me for my last conference. She came over where I sat on the couch in her office and sat very close to me. Her skirt was above her knees and her face was very close to mine. In a soft, husky voice she explained that they had already given out all the A's that the school would allow. She said that my supervising teacher had recommended that I be given an A for my work at her school, but it was necessary that my grade be reduced to a B. She sat even closer to me as she explained this. As I left her office, I had the distinct feeling that I had been toyed with shamefully. As I later reflected on that meeting, I realized that had I responded positively to what had been an obvious invitation for more than a professor/student relationship, I would have received my A. Conversations that I had later with other male students confirmed my suspicions. But the sad fact is that I got fifteen hours with a B grade when it should have been an A.

Later, the academic standing for the students in the College of Education were sent to me and to my Military Draft Board. I learned that I ranked twelfth in my class of thirty-eight full-time male students. That put me in the top one-third of my class which was not bad for a country boy who began this endeavor being totally unaware of what the college experience would bring his way.

Chapter 7

Early Seminary Years

The summer of 1954 was one of the most eventful and interesting summers of my entire life. It is hard to believe that so much activity could be packed into such a short amount of time. I enjoyed a delightful summer romance; I had a good summer job; I also continued to faithfully serve the Ft. White Baptist Church as pastor. Further, I was able to get most of the things done that I felt were necessary before leaving Florida for my years at Southern Baptist Theological Seminary in Louisville, Kentucky.

My graduation from the University of Florida took place on Monday evening, June 7, 1954. There were about six other students from Columbia High School in Lake City that received degrees that evening, including Morris Williams and Richard Addicks. My mother and brother were both present for that event. Later, in the August 1954 graduation, several of my former teachers and close friends received master's degrees.

My summer job was with the Engineering Department of the City of Gainesville. The father of one of my Lake City classmates worked for the City of Gainesville. Knowing that I wanted to stay in Gainesville for the summer, my friend's father arranged for me to be interviewed for a job as an inspector on a construction job. The pay was good, and the work was not hard. When the summer was over, I was offered a permanent job with the city. I thanked them for the offer but declined saying that I was going to continue my education.

As the summer began, I became acquainted with Jo Anne Browne from Bradenton, Florida. She was in the College of Education and had previously dated a friend of mine. When they stopped dating, I asked him if the romance was over and he said it was. I asked her for a date and we began an enjoyable summer together. She was a Baptist and visited my church at Ft. White several times during the summer. I knew that she had been involved with a young man who was overseas in the military, but it did not appear that she was overly committed to him.

As the summer progressed, a strong romantic relationship began to develop, and we began to talk about the possibility of marriage. She invited me to Bradenton to meet her family. Her parents were Kentuckians who had moved to Florida years earlier. She had two sisters, but she was the best of the bunch. I thought the visit to meet her parents went well. However, I was unaware that some of her family preferred that she marry the young man who was in the military. He came home just as I was getting ready to leave for Kentucky.

My thoughts are that word got to him that he would be wise to arrange to come home and protect his interests. During that visit, he gave her an engagement ring which she accepted. She did not tell me about this until much later, but when we talked on the phone, I could tell that something was wrong. When she finally told me what had happened, I was quite shocked. But I began to see that forces other than the fact that she might simply be in love with this man were at work. I did not realize until much later that her family may have been pressuring her to marry the other man. We kept writing each other through most of my first semester at seminary. When I came home for spring break in April 1955, I was scheduled to preach at Parkview Baptist Church. When the worship service began on Sunday morning, I saw Jo Anne in the congregation.

After the worship service, we met at her car and had a long, tearful conversation. She was confused but declared that she loved me. I asked if she loved me enough to give the ring back, break off with the other fellow, and go against her family. She said that she did not know. I told her that though I cared for her, until she could make that decision, there was not much reason for us to keep hanging on to a broken relationship. We hugged and kissed goodbye. We exchanged letters briefly, and then I quit writing. It was a bitter sweet ending, but it was over. She married the other guy.

In late July 1954, my Aunt Hallie in Panama City sent word that she and Uncle Hiram wanted me to visit them before I went to seminary. She indicated that Uncle Hiram wanted to do something for me in a financial way. I made the visit. Uncle Hiram had been a captain in the Florida National Guard when World War II began. His company was activated, and he spent several months at Camp Blanding near Starke, Florida. Later, he was assigned to duty in Alaska where he remained until the War was over. He had returned home after the War, remained in the Florida National Guard and achieved the rank of brigadier general. After his military service, he became a highly successful building contractor.

During my visit, Uncle Hiram told me that he wanted to make some funds available to me as I went to school. He wrote a check to the Ft. White Baptist Church for six hundred dollars. With the check was a letter instructing the church to keep one hundred dollars for the church and write me a check for the balance to be used in my educational efforts. That five hundred dollars turned out to be just enough to see me through the lean, hard times that I experienced during my first year in seminary. I will always be grateful to Uncle Hiram for his generosity.

During the early months of 1954, I made the congregation of Ft. White Baptist Church aware that I would be enrolling in seminary in September. They were gracious telling me that they understood my desire to further my education but would be happy for me to remain as their pastor. I have in my files a copy of the church resolution recommending me to the seminary for enrollment in the School of Theology. It was signed by Robert F. Persons, Deacon Chairman, and J. C. Christopher, Church Clerk. I ended my service as pastor of the church on Sunday, August 29, 1954.

On the first Sunday in September 1954, I preached at Parkview Baptist Church, which had just been formed by about 180 members from First Baptist Church, Lake City, Florida. There had been tension in First Baptist Church for a long time. The Parkview Church was formed by persons signing a petition asking for their membership to be transferred for the purpose of forming a new congregation. For better than forty years, members of my family were members of the Parkview Church. My mother was still a member there when she died in April 1994. Her funeral was held at the church.

Early in September 1954 I left Lake City for Kentucky to begin the new adventure of my seminary education. The first two years were not happy years. I went through a time of spiritual trial and struggle. I re-examined my call to the ministry and recommitted myself to it with even greater intensity. The struggle was be harsh and bitter, but I emerged from it a better and more mature person.

My first trip to Kentucky is still a vivid memory after more than fifty years. I made a stop in Dublin, Georgia, and visited briefly with the Tomlinson family. I had dated their daughter, Vivian, when they lived in Lake City. Mr. Tomlinson and his son, Charles, both worked at the Mercury dealership in Lake City and had been helpful as I tried to keep my 1950 Mercury in good repair. My next stop was in Atlanta where I visited with my cousin, Pat Tygart. Pat, an electrical engineer, was working for Lockheed. From there I drove to Irvington, Kentucky and spent the night with the grandparents of Bill Cowley, whom I had befriended at the University of Florida. They were gracious hosts.

Kentucky roads proved to be a nightmare for me. Florida highways were usually straight and wide with a nice sloping shoulder to the drainage ditch. Kentucky highways were crooked and narrow with small shoulders that dropped off quickly to the drainage ditch. Driving on Kentucky highways was not an enjoyable experience for a boy who had traveled all his life on Florida highways. Most Kentucky highways have improved dramatically since 1954, but we still have some of those narrow, crooked roads with a sharp drop off from a narrow shoulder.

I arrived on the campus of Southern Baptist Theological Seminary near the noon hour on September 15, 1954. Since I was much farther north, the noonday sun appeared to be about as bright as it would be in Florida at mid-afternoon. There were many differences between Florida and Kentucky, which I was about to learn. I checked at the information desk and was sent to get my room assignment. I was assigned to a room in Mullins Hall on the third floor. My roommate was to be James Corbett from Tennessee. At the Registrar's Office, I met Dr. Hugh Peterson, who called me by name. Dr. Peterson was known for learning the names and faces of new students from studying their admission photographs.

Having obtained my room key, I went to Mullins Hall and began moving into my room. My roommate had not arrived. Mullins Hall was one of the most depressing places that I had ever seen. It was a large brick building that had the same brown brick walls on the inside as on the exterior. The halls were dark and dreary. The floors were a dark brown tile. Each room had a sink for shaving and other personal hygiene, but the toilet and bath facilities were of the communal variety down the hall. The only phones were pay phones on the first floor. I did not like the place, but I was determined to make the best of it. However, I was so depressed by the surroundings that I could barely keep from crying.

During my last year in college, I met and became close friends with William A. Cowley, a Kentuckian who was working on his masters in speech. Bill and I went places together, ate meals together, and enjoyed the company of many of the students who frequented the Baptist Student Union next door to the university campus. He assisted me in some of the writing I had to do, and I helped him with the research for his master's thesis. One of the persons with whom we kept company was the Baptist Student Union Director, Audrey Evans. Bill was about three years my senior, and Audrey was about eight years older than Bill.

When Bill learned that I was planning on going to Southern Seminary in Louisville, he began promoting the idea that we might room together. He was a mission volunteer and seminary was a requirement for appointment by the Baptist Foreign Mission Board. Further, since Bill was from Kentucky, he assured me that with his connections, it would be no problem for me to find a student pastorate. It all sounded too good to be true, but I was convinced that it would somehow work out.

During the early part of the summer, Bill and Audrey announced that they were in love and would be getting married in late summer. They had a nice wedding. I was best man and helped return all the things that Bill had borrowed to decorate the BSU Chapel for the wedding. It was a gala affair. Bill shared with me soon afterward that he had been offered a teaching position at Georgetown College, and that Audrey would be working with the students as she had done at the University of Florida. I was told that they would be in touch with me as soon as things settled down for them at Georgetown.

However, several weeks went by after I arrived in Kentucky and I heard nothing from them. I made several attempts to get in touch with them and finally made contact. They invited me over for the weekend and I stayed with them in their small apartment. The weekend was full of their social activities. I returned to Louisville and that was the last I heard from them. They never called, never wrote, and if they made any attempt to help me get before a Kentucky church, I never heard about it. They were at Georgetown for a year and received a special appointment to serve as missionaries in Nigeria. Later, Bill joined the faculty of Samford University in Birmingham, Alabama. I saw them several times while I was serving a church in Birmingham, but the college friendship simply vanished. It was a bitter disappointment. I could have lived with a statement from Bill that he may have promised more than he could deliver, but I found it hard to understand that after allegedly being close friends, our relationship was suddenly terminated without explanation or ceremony.

What I learned from this experience is that marriage often changes many things. I have seen it happen often. However, long standing and close friendships ought to survive the tests and changes that life brings. Many of my friendships have survived, and for that I am thankful.

As the week of orientation began at Southern Seminary, I discovered that many of the students whom I had known at Stetson University were there. Even some of the professors from Stetson were now members of the seminary faculty. Henlee Barnette, who had been my Old Testament professor at Stetson, was now teaching Ethics at Southern. His first wife had recently died in childbirth, and he soon began courting Helen Porch, one of my very attractive classmates. They later married and had a long, happy marriage.

I found the seminary classes to be challenging and threatening. It was a challenge to learn and complete the work assigned; it was threatening when you were called upon in class to stand and answer the questions asked by your professor. That method of teaching seemed to fall out of favor as my seminary experience continued. I tried to carry a full load of classes each semester, but soon learned that working forty hours a week and serving a student church made an academic load of twelve semester hours to be about all I could handle. Most of my classes were four-hour classes meeting Tuesday through Friday. There were some two-hour classes, but most were four-hour classes. No classes were held on Monday, thus giving students who served churches some distance away time to return to campus.

If a student carried a full academic load, it was possible to earn the Bachelor of Divinity degree in three years. By carrying twelve hours per semester, I completed the degree in four years. I regret that by working as much as I did, I did not perform well academically. I may have used work as an excuse for not being a better student, but the academic demands were strenuous.

Early in my first semester, economic matters began to be of great concern to me. Since I had very little savings, I needed to be employed to provide the necessary funds to survive while in school. Few preaching opportunities were available to first year students without some Kentucky connections. I took a job as a psychiatric aide in the psychiatric ward at Norton's Hospital. It paid minimum wage which was eighty-five cents an hour. It was just barely enough to get by. The job was approved through the Pastoral Care Department at Southern Seminary. I enjoyed the work and learned a great deal about emotional and mental illness. Also, I found myself to be very interested in what I was learning in the field of medicine.

This began a career struggle that lasted almost a year. I found that I had an amazing ability to absorb and remember medical information. Further, I had a hunger for such knowledge. My experience at the seminary both spiritually and academically was proving to be disillusioning and frustrating. I did not like the seminary class work. The personal flaws of both the faculty and students were obvious and disturbing. Also, theological education seemed to be content to remain far behind the cutting edge of needs that existed in our world. Medicine seemed to be where the action was and where I felt that I wanted to be.

I went to the School of Medicine at the University of Louisville and obtained an interview with Dr. Arch Cole, the faculty member who had the final decision concerning who would get into medical school. After a brief discussion, he outlined a thirty-hour course of study at the University of Louisville, instructed me to enroll, take the classes, and make at least a B average. He assured me that I would be admitted to medical school if I would do as he said. I took the information he gave me, applied for admission at the University of Louisville, was accepted, but never enrolled.

During the summer of 1955, I worked as a laborer on bridge construction on the Kentucky Turnpike which began at Watterson Expressway in Louisville and ended just south of Elizabethtown, Kentucky. I worked on the bridges beginning at the Ford Plant in Louisville all the way to the Salt River Bridge at Shepherdsville. Throughout the summer, I kept praying about what the Lord wanted me to do. Finally, near the end of August as I walked across campus one evening on my way to my room, I told the Lord that if He would make it possible for me to come back to seminary without financial anxiety and stress, I would come back, and He would hear no more complaints from me.

Within two weeks, I was called by General Electric at Appliance Park for an interview. I had been trying for months to get such an interview. I was hired for a second shift job beginning early in September. With that job secured, I quit my construction job and went to pack for a trip to Florida. As I was taking my clothes to my car for the trip home, Dr. Hugh Peterson came into the foyer of Mullins Hall and called me by name saying, "Brother McDonald, I have been trying to find you. A church has requested that I arrange for you to preach for them. They are without a pastor and would like for you to come preach in view of a call to be their pastor." I replied, "Thank you, sir. Would you please tell them that I will be with them on the second Sunday of September? I am leaving for a brief trip home and I can be with them then." Dr. Peterson assured me that he would relay the message. He gave me information about the church and I left for Florida. I was aware of the church because a friend had told me he was giving them my name. My friend had kept his word, and I was ready to visit the church. God had heard my prayer and had given me an answer assuring me that my call had not been rescinded. I was at peace for the first time in a long time.

My trip home in late August 1955 was pleasant. My mother noticed that I was more at peace than when I had been home the previous April. I preached at the Parkview Baptist Church while I was home, which became a sort of ritual each time I came home. The congregation continued to be interested in my progress in the ministry. Their various pastors were always gracious in opening the pulpit to me so that the people who had supported me could hear me preach. Other young ministers from the church were given the same treatment.

Upon my return to Kentucky, I began my job at General Electric. I also went to Franklin, Kentucky, and preached for the congregation at Shady Grove Baptist Church. It was a rural church composed mostly of farmers and small business people in the area. Economically, they were from the middle class. Perhaps a few were from the upper middle class. They were staunch Baptists and were very gracious people. The church had only a morning worship service. After I had preached for them most of September, the church called me to serve as pastor. It was to be a happy arrangement that lasted slightly more than four years.

Perhaps one of the biggest adjustments that I had to make when I came to Kentucky had to do with the difference between Florida weather and the bleak Kentucky winters. Having always lived in Florida, I had never seen snow, or all the leaves fall off the trees during the winter months. I had never experienced prolonged periods in which one did not see the sun. I am certain that this was the reason I became so depressed during my first year in Kentucky. In fact, in late December 1954 into mid-January 1955, the temperature dropped to about ten degrees below zero and remained there for several days with little or no sunshine. I promised myself that if I ever finished school, I would go back south and never return to Kentucky.

I did become extremely depressed during that first winter I spent in Kentucky. I cannot say that I became suicidal, but I had some serious thoughts about driving my car into a tree or one of the stone formations that are often found next to Kentucky highways. I was miserable. Had I not found some friends to whom I could talk, I am not certain how things would have turned out. Looking back, I can see that my mood improved as the weather began to improve in the spring. Once I got through that first year, I was better able to handle the changes that came with the winter months.

It is appropriate that I should say something about the theological beliefs I brought with me to the seminary and the changes that took place during my seminary years. The fact is that most of us change with the passing of time. The Bible is a living document that shapes and changes us with time and the insights that God gives us. I have found that if we continue to read the Bible and other literature related to it, we will continue to grow and our outlook toward life and how God deals with man will continue to be filled with fresh new insights. God's revelation continues if we are open to it and are willing to listen to His voice. I am grateful for that.

I grew up in the culture of religious fundamentalism in north Florida. The fundamentalists will take a literal stance toward the interpretation of the Bible. They are dogmatic in their views, narrow in their focus, and judgmental to the point of being harsh in dealing with those who do not agree with their views. Fundamentalists are combative by their very nature. They constantly look for those with whom they disagree in order to point out their flaws regarding scriptural interpretation or doctrinal beliefs. Fundamentalism appears to need an ongoing controversy in order to survive or to prove its worth.

When I decided to attend Southern Baptist Theological Seminary, several people warned me that there were liberals on the faculty. I was cautioned not to allow any of these people to undermine my faith. I was even told that I would be more acceptable in terms of returning to Florida to serve if I went to any of the other Baptist seminaries. However, I felt Southern offered the best course of study among our Baptist seminaries. I did not feel that my faith would be harmed by studying there. This proved to be true. However, I believe that leaving my home in Florida, coming to Southern Seminary, and remaining until I finished was the most difficult thing that I have ever had to do in my entire life. Looking back over a span of time that is beyond a half century. I have faced other difficult circumstances, and saw them through to the finish, but this was the most difficult one for me.

One of the first things that Henlee Barnette told us during orientation in September 1954 was that the seminary is a place of study, spiritual growth, and learning. He said, "If you think this is going to be a three-year camp meeting, you are in for a great surprise." The seminary was a place of academic endeavor. Often, it was too much that, but it was certainly a place of spiritual growth. I grew as a Christian while I was there. My faith grew, and I acquired the mind-sharpening tools that prepared me for ministering in a lost world.

I came to the seminary believing that the Bible was the inspired word of God. I believed in the miracles recorded in the Bible. I believed in the Virgin Birth, the Divinity of Jesus, His miracles, His Resurrection, His Ascension to sit at the right hand of the Father, and His imminent return. I believed in salvation by grace through faith alone. I also believed in the autonomy of the local church, the priesthood of the believer, and the perseverance of the saints.

None of these beliefs changed as I studied at the seminary. However, my reasons for believing changed. I discovered better, more mature reasons for believing the great truths set forth in the Bible. Not all of my beliefs are founded on reason. Faith comes into play as we accept the teachings of the Bible. Faith is tempered by both reason and experience. I have found that as a person walks with God, depends on God, and seeks to do His will, God reveals Himself to us in ways that are almost impossible to describe. We do walk by faith, but our faith is assured by our past and our continuing experience with God in which He reveals Himself giving us a confidence in Him and His Word that we could not have known otherwise. There are spiritual truths and insights that come to us by revelation through faith. Without faith, we could neither discover nor understand them. They come to us from God. They make sense to the person of faith. The unbeliever may not be able to grasp or understand them.

I wish I could say that my seminary experience was one continuing mountaintop experience. But the truth is that it was not, and that is the way it should be. There were struggles and low moments. There were times that I was disappointed in myself, my fellow students, and my professors. We all have feet of clay. Our flaws and failing become even more obvious and visible in the climate of studies that touch on the spiritual nature of our lives. But the truth of the matter may be that in these struggles in which one makes his way through the highs and lows of life, we discover so much about ourselves, about our fellow man, and about God. We learn how to deal in a redeeming way with our fellow man, because that is the way God chooses to deal with us and how He would have us deal with others.

Much about my second year in seminary seems to be a blur in terms of clear memories. I was working at General Electric and preaching each weekend at Shady Grove Baptist Church. My life seemed to be on hold in many ways. Earlier, P. C. Brown Jr. and I became close friends. He was from South Carolina and a graduate of The Citadel. I had the privilege of introducing P. C. to Doris Jean Bowman, who later became his wife.

Early in January 1956, my social life experienced some changes. I simply stopped seeing any of the ladies who had been a part of my life. In late February. I complained to P. C. and Doris Brown that I was quite lonely. They began to tell me about a young lady who had recently become church secretary at Broadway Baptist Church. Doris and P. C. were members at Broadway and Doris served as the church organist. They suggested that I return early from preaching on Sunday evening and meet them and this young lady at church. The plans were for us to go out to eat when the church service was ended.

On Sunday evening, March 4, 1956, I drove back to Louisville early enough for the evening service at Broadway. Doris and P. C. met me at church and we took seats about six rows from the back on the right. They told me that the young lady, JoAnn Ensslin, would join us shortly. I was watching the door near the front of the chapel when she entered. She was an attractive redhead. We went out for a meal and I took her home. We talked briefly before I walked her to the door. I asked her if I could call her again and she said yes. We said goodnight and I went to my room.

Later in the week, I called JoAnn and asked if she could meet me for lunch. She said she could, and we met, ate lunch, talked about several things and became better acquainted. Neither of us suspected then that our relationship would become seriously romantic. It was a quiet, easy relationship. Neither of us seemed to be overly impressed with the other, but we enjoyed being together. At that point, I had no idea that what was developing would lead to marriage. But after we had gone together for about a month, I began to realize that I was forming a strong emotional attachment to this young lady. About a week later, I told her that I felt that I might be falling in love with her. Her reply was that I should not say that unless I meant it. She did not reveal any of her feelings to me.

On the Mother's Day weekend, JoAnn went home and spent the weekend with her family. Later, she told me that she was almost certain that I was going to propose marriage. She said that she needed some time to pray and sort things out. She shared none of this with her family, but by the time she returned to Louisville, she had decided that if I did ask her to marry me, she would say yes. She said that she felt that we had been brought together by the Lord. I felt much the same way.

We continued to date. It was a comfortable relationship. I began to ask the Lord for some guidance about what I should do. I did not receive any negative leadership from the Lord. One evening near the middle of May, I met JoAnn after my work and we drove to a public park down on the Ohio River. We parked, talked for a while, and watched the boats on the river. Then, I told her that I had brought her out there to ask her to marry me. After a brief conversation about the fact that being a preacher's wife was not an easy role, she said, "Yes." I was almost in a state of disbelief. We had met and courted for about three months. Our relationship seemed to be so easy and natural and I was in love in a way that I never had been before. Now, we had to tell her parents and get their permission to marry.

JoAnn had grown up in London, Kentucky, a three-hour drive south of Louisville. She was the daughter of Paul and Hazel Ensslin. Her mother's family had been for several generations part of the coal mining culture of eastern Kentucky. Her father's parents had emigrated from Germany in the late 1880s. Hazel was Baptist, and Paul was Lutheran, but he attended the Baptist church faithfully with his family. Paul was in the business of drilling oil and gas wells. He worked all over eastern Kentucky and was a successful businessman. JoAnn had one younger sister, Bobbie Jean. Her mother and sister were both redheads and very attractive.

One of the goals that Hazel Ensslin had for her daughters was that they obtain a college education. Hazel had wanted to go to college, but her family did not believe in girls getting an education, so she had been denied the opportunity. JoAnn had finished the requirements for a high school diploma when she was fifteen years old. Her mother enrolled her in Sue Bennett Junior College which was located in London, Kentucky. When she completed her studies at Sue Bennett, she enrolled at the University of Kentucky where she graduated in 1955 with a degree in Commerce Education. Her pastor had recommended her to Edwin F. Perry, pastor at Broadway Baptist Church in Louisville, for the position of church secretary, and that is how she came to be in Louisville.

In late May, near the Memorial Day weekend, JoAnn and I went to London so that I could meet her parents and ask permission to marry their daughter. Arriving on a nice, warm, sunny day, and we gathered outside in a patio area that the family used during the summer months. JoAnn's mother had gone into the house while I visited with her father, Paul, and her sister, Bobbie Jean. What seemed to me to be the right moment presented itself, and I told Paul that I had asked Jo Ann to marry me and that we had come to request family permission to proceed with wedding plans. He did not even respond to what I said. Instead, he turned to Bobbie Jean with a pleased look on his face and said, "See, I told you that JoAnn was bringing a young man in here to tell us that she was going to get married." Apparently, he and Bobbie Jean had a bet on what would happen once JoAnn and I arrived.

JoAnn and I sat there for what seemed like forever while her father and sister had a discussion over who had won to the bet. Hearing the conversation, Jo Ann's mother came out and Paul told her that JoAnn and I were wanting to get married. Hazel seemed to be completely surprised. She appeared to be almost in shock, but soon regained her composure. However, she kept saying, "I never dreamed that this was about to happen." At this point, Paul had yet to respond to my request for permission to marry JoAnn. Finally, as we continued talking, I pointed out that her father had not answered my request. He laughed and said that if JoAnn wanted to marry me, he and Hazel would give us their blessing. I was relieved, but I do not know what I would have done, or what JoAnn and I would have done, had he not given us his approval.

With family permission to proceed with wedding plans, the summer was going to be a busy one. JoAnn and I had discussed a possible wedding date. I had time off from General Electric with a summer shutdown in late August. We decided to set the date for August 19. Having done that, we began making and carrying out all the plans for a wedding that would help us begin a life together. It was a step of faith for both of us, but we felt that we loved one another enough to begin such a journey. Further, we felt God had brought us together and He would bless us as a family.

Chapter 8

Late Seminary Years

Once we gained permission for the wedding to take place, we set the date, and JoAnn began to do all the things that prospective brides do in preparation for the wedding. My next move was to purchase an engagement ring. Since my friend P. C. Brown had recently become engaged and then married, I called on him for advice thinking he might know a good source for purchasing a nice ring.

P. C. put me in touch with a gentleman at Citizens Jewelry Company in Atlanta, Georgia. I called there and placed an order for a half carat diamond in a solitaire setting. He told me that he would be back in touch with me in a day or so. In less than a week, he wrote saying he had the diamond and needed a ring size along with a bank officer and address where he could send it for approval. I sent the information to him, and in about ten days my banker called telling me the ring had arrived. I had previously made the banker aware that the ring was being sent.

I went to the bank immediately, and the bank officer brought the unopened package to his office. With another bank employee present, he opened the package and looked carefully at the ring. Then he passed it to the other bank employee for a close look. All the time I was sitting there anxiously waiting to see the ring myself. When they finally passed it to me, I was pleased with what I saw. To me, the diamond appeared to be as big as a grapefruit, but I know it was nowhere that large. I wrote a check for $250.00 to the Citizens Jewelry Company and gave it to the banker who placed it in a return envelope for mailing. I took the ring and went straight to Broadway Baptist Church where JoAnn was working. I was excited.

I arrived at the church just before the lunch hour and I went to JoAnn's office asking if she would like to go to lunch. She said yes, and we went to the car. Unknown to her, I had placed the ring in the glove box of the car. As we were about to pull out of the parking lot, I asked her to hand me my sun glasses which were in the glove box. It was a ruse; only the ring was there. I could not resist the element of surprise. When she opened the glove box, she saw the ring. I do not know which one of us was the most excited. I took the ring out of the box and put it on her finger. It was now official, we were engaged.

The members of Shady Grove Church in Franklin were unaware of my romance with JoAnn. It was time to introduce her to them, to share the news of our engagement and our approaching marriage. I shared with Paul and Martha Allen what was happening. The plan was for me to bring JoAnn by their home the following Sunday morning. She would accompany them to church. I would introduce her and announce our engagement and wedding plans. It all went as planned. The Shady Grove folk approved of her and she heard me preach for the first time. It was a momentous and exciting day.

When I told John Oakley, a friend and student at University of Louisville School of Dentistry, that I was getting married and did not want to live in seminary housing, he suggested that I look at the apartment that he and his wife had been renting. He said that he was graduating soon and that it would be available. JoAnn and I looked at it and agreed that it would be acceptable. It was located near the seminary at 2321 Glenmary Avenue and would be convenient for both school and work. John's mother offered to sell us the gas stove in the kitchen, a dinette set, and a wooden hutch plus the curtains that were in the apartment. We took the offer and rented the apartment. I moved in and lived there all summer before our wedding.

As soon as we rented the apartment, JoAnn's parents came to Louisville and took us to Belknap Furniture Warehouse. They told us to select a bedroom suit and living room furniture. Both of us were careful not to choose anything too expensive. We chose a nice three-piece bedroom suit plus a good mattress and box springs. Then we selected a couch and chair set, a coffee table, and two end tables. I personally chose and paid for a sling-type leather chair. All of this purchase, except the chair, was a gift from Paul and Hazel. They were generous and good to us. JoAnn moved her furniture from her apartment the week before we married.

Before we knew it, August was upon us. I had two weeks off from my job at General Electric. The first week I spent at the Shady Grove Church conducting Vacation Bible School in the morning and preaching a revival at night. A seminary classmate, Bill Billingsley, led the singing for the revival and assisted with Vacation Bible School. By the time the week was over, I was exhausted.

When the revival services ended on Friday night, I drove to London. My mother and brother were already there. JoAnn was there and our friends who were going to be in the wedding would be arriving the next day. JoAnn and I had reserved a number of motel rooms for family and the wedding party members from out of town. Many of JoAnn's relatives from both sides of her family would be arriving for the wedding festivities. Paul and Hazel had met my mother and brother at the bus and had looked after them until I arrived. My mother and brother had not met JoAnn until they arrived for the wedding, but when they did, they fell for her immediately. I did not expect otherwise.

JoAnn's father loved to tease and as soon as I arrived, he began to tell me all the pranks that they were planning to pull on me as soon as the wedding was over. I had a relatively new car and was convinced that they would probably turn it into a pile of junk before I could get out of town. Paul kept telling me stories from time past of what they had done to other grooms. As my anxiety level kept rising, I asked my friend P. C. Brown, go with me to nearby Corbin where I arranged for my car to be hidden at a service station right across from Colonel Sanders' Motel and Restaurant. Also, I reserved a room at Colonel Sanders' Motel for the wedding night. Then, we returned to London with P. C. assuring me that he would tell no one about my wedding night plans.

The wedding rehearsal took place without a problem. I had purchased a copy of The Book of Common Prayer which I gave to Rev. George Phillips, JoAnn's home pastor. We asked that he use the wedding ceremony in that book. At first, he seemed uncomfortable, but once he read the ceremony, he remarked that it was similar to the one he often used. As we were leaving the rehearsal, I realized that I had not arranged for an after-rehearsal dinner. I turned to JoAnn's father and began to apologize for the oversight. He told me not to worry; he had arranged for the dinner. I was relieved.

On our wedding day, JoAnn's father kept up the good-natured kidding about the pranks that were going to be my fate. Even though I felt that it was simply fun on his part, I was nearly a nervous wreck when it came time for the wedding. While Paul appeared to be having the time of his life, I have since wondered if he was not covering up some anxiety about his daughter getting married. Hindsight causes to us see much that we miss in the heat of the moment. I kept trying to figure out how I could escape his alleged plans. Little did I realize that the best plan for me was to have no plan at all.

The wedding took place at First Baptist Church, London, Kentucky, on Sunday, August 19, 1956 at 4:00 p.m. It was the typical church wedding of that day and time. The bride wore a flowing white wedding dress; the bridesmaids wore ballerina-length crystal blue dresses; and the men wore formal tuxedos. There was organ music and three solos, "O Promise Me," "Because," and "The Lord's Prayer." My brother, Ralph Hardee, Jr., was my best man and JoAnn's sister, Bobbie Jean, was the maiden of honor. I arrived at the church about an hour before the wedding. The wait seemed to me to be the longest hour that I have ever experienced but being married to JoAnn was and is more than worth the wait.

As soon as the wedding was over, and the photographs were taken, we went downstairs to the reception which was held in Fellowship Hall. There was a three-tiered wedding cake, an abundant supply of punch, and a variety of finger-food items. More than three hundred guests were present. I remember how happy and excited everyone seemed to be. I kept watching my father-in-law fearing that he really had planned some mischief, but nothing ever materialized. As soon as we could get away from the reception, we headed for P. C.'s car. He was supposed to take us to the motel in Corbin. JoAnn was still in her wedding dress and she insisted on returning to the church to change into street clothes. Once that was done, we were off to Corbin.

When we arrived at Colonel Sanders' Motel, I asked P. C. and Doris to wait while I changed out of my tuxedo and packed it for him to return to the rental store. He was kind enough to gather all the rented tuxedos and return them for me. Just as I finished getting dressed there was a knock on the door. JoAnn opened it to find her sister, who was saying that she had left a pair of leather gloves in the room where JoAnn had dressed at the church and could not find them. Had JoAnn picked them up when she changed clothes? Suddenly, I was hit in the face with a handful of rice. Rice began to fly around the room. P. C. and Doris joined Bobbie and Ralph in filling our bed, our luggage, the room, and the bathroom with rice. They even filled my car with rice. I was still getting rice out of the luggage and car months later. Later, I learned that P. C. had whispered our plans to Doris who told Bobbie and my brother. So much for concealing our whereabouts.

We all had a good laugh about the rice and other surprises. Also, I learned that my car had been properly decorated. Since I had paid the service station owner to wash it and get it ready for our trip, I requested that he wash it again before we left. He laughed and did as I asked. After friends and family left, JoAnn and I went into Colonel Sanders' Restaurant and ordered our evening meal but could hardly eat. I think both fatigue and excitement had taken our appetite. This was before Colonel Sanders became famous for his Kentucky Fried Chicken. He was in the kitchen cooking when we entered. Knowing that we were newlyweds, he came out and greeted us in his friendly, outgoing way.
We had barely gone to sleep that first night when a rather strong thunderstorm hit the area awakening us. There was a lot of lightening, thunder, wind, and rain. The lightening knocked out the power to the motel leaving us without air conditioning. After that, it was difficult going back to sleep. Both of us were still tired from the previous week and all the wedding festivities. Further, neither of us was used to sleeping with another person. The thunderstorm lasted for most of the night and neither of us slept well.

The next morning, we headed south for the Smokey Mountains and the Gatlinburg area. On the edge of Knoxville, we found a nice motel, one of the first Holiday Inns, and stayed there. We drove into Gatlinburg and browsed around the town several times. Most of our time was spent getting used to each other in this new relationship. We were both amazed at how comfortable we were with each other. We did not seem to have any problems as we began to adjust to sharing our lives together. Late in the week we went back to London and began to prepare to go to Franklin, Kentucky, for my regular preaching appointment. JoAnn was about to begin her career as a pastor's wife.

The people of Shady Grove Baptist Church had not said much to me about my marriage. I do not recall any special gifts. I was not expecting them to do anything unusual. However, on that first Sunday after the wedding, they took a few minutes early in the service and gave us a card along with a rather thick envelope. We opened the card and read it. Then we opened the envelope and found it to be full of cash in ten-and twenty-dollar bills. They had taken up over four hundred dollars and presented it to us as a gift. We were completely surprised by their generosity. It came at a good time because with the wedding, honeymoon, and other expenses, both our bank accounts were nearly empty. As we accepted this generous gift, they knew we were both surprised and genuinely grateful for this expression of love. A member of the church, Mrs. Reed McCreary, was the person responsible for promoting this gift and taking the contributions from the members of the church. She remained a close and loving friend.

As the waning days of August slipped away, September brought the beginning of seminary classes and a nagging awareness that I still had two years to go before completing the requirements for my degree. I had thought about completing my degree at Southern Seminary and then going to Edinburgh, Scotland, for studies toward a doctorate. I knew that my academic performance at Southern would not allow doctoral studies there. Further, I was disenchanted with the academic program at Southern. I felt that there was too much emphasis on the academic and not enough on the practical things that would help one become a better pastor, missionary, or church staff member. Southern trained great professors, but prospective pastors did not receive the practical direction they needed. Though I earned three degrees at Southern, Bachelor of Divinity, Master of Divinity, and Doctor of Ministry, I still have that opinion. Also, I learned that the same problem existed at our other Southern Baptist seminaries. There was something about my entire seminary experience that did not challenge me to be the student that I was capable of being. However, that does not excuse me from not doing better academically. I was responsible for my performance and I did less than I should have. This is something that I truly regret. However, during my later doctoral studies at Southern, I was a much better student than I had been previously. And in fairness to Southern Seminary, it was there that I learned the necessity of being a continuing student. I have never given up on the quest for more study.

Shortly after JoAnn and I returned to Louisville, Kentucky from our honeymoon, JoAnn told her pastor that she would not be present on Sundays because she wanted to go with me to my church. Nothing had been said about the necessity of her being at Broadway on Sunday when she was employed. Dr. Perry told her that he would prefer that she seek employment elsewhere because he wanted the church secretary to be at Broadway on Sunday. JoAnn was surprised by this, but word quickly spread. One of the deacons at Broadway, Bill Moore, worked at Reynolds Metals in the business office. He offered her a job and she took it. She worked there until her surprise pregnancy caused her to resign.

Life seemed to move at a happy pace for us as newlyweds. My seminary classes were scheduled for the mornings. JoAnn was working at Reynolds Metals. I was working second shift at General Electric. I preached at the Shady Grove Church each Sunday. Occasionally we went to London on Friday night and then drove to Franklin early Sunday morning. This made for a long weekend, but we did enjoy seeing the family. JoAnn's mother quietly but firmly told me to call them by their first names, Paul and Hazel. She wanted none of that Mom and Dad stuff. She said they were not my parents. There was no tension, but this was the way she wanted it. Since London, Kentucky, was close and Florida was too far away for holiday trips, we spent both Thanksgiving and Christmas holidays with JoAnn's family.

It was during the Christmas holidays that JoAnn became pregnant with our first child. She did not understand what was happening at first because the sickness that usually accompanies early pregnancy came at night instead of each morning. When I arrived home from my second shift job, I found that I had a sick wife. A brief trip to our doctor a few weeks later confirmed our suspicions. We were going to be parents and if our calculations were correct, the baby would be born shortly after we had celebrated our first anniversary. We had not planned to start a family this early, but the child was on the way. JoAnn became quite upset at first thinking that she would be the cause of my not going to Scotland to do further studies. I did my best to assure her that I was not disappointed. Rather, I was elated; my doctorate, if I ever got one, could wait.

As the spring months passed, JoAnn made the decision to resign her job at Reynolds Metals. This happened before companies began providing maternity leave to expectant mothers. When a lady's pregnancy became physically obvious, she was expected to leave the work force. The loss of income from JoAnn's job caused us to decide to move into seminary housing in Fuller Hall. The apartment was small. It had a living room, Murphy kitchen, one bedroom, and a bathroom. There was a community phone in the hall near the elevator. There was no air conditioning. I purchased a window fan which helped make conditions a little more bearable. We enjoyed the friends we made on campus and adjusted to the new living conditions.

JoAnn had no sooner left her job than we began to hear some ominous stories at General Electric. The national economy was slowing down and so was the demand for household appliances. Company layoffs were becoming a distinct possibility. This economic downturn came to be known as "the Eisenhower Recession." The rumors continued to circulate at General Electric about layoffs. A new building was about to be completed at Appliance Park that was to house the manufacturing of window air conditioners. I was given an opportunity to transfer to that building into a day shift job, but I was assured that by the time school was to begin they would have a second shift. I took the job and worked all summer helping get everything set up for production to begin. By late August it was obvious that no second shift would be operating because there was no production on the first shift. I needed to get back into a second shift job, so I could stay in school. It was a problem that would soon become much more serious.

The birth of our first child was about to take place. Our doctor had told us that the baby would arrive sometime during the first two weeks of September. On Labor Day weekend, JoAnn began to have contractions that would come and go, never getting regular enough for her to go into full labor. I called Paul Jackson, one of my deacons, on Sunday morning and explained what was happening. He advised me to stay with JoAnn saying they would take care of church. I kept thinking that JoAnn might begin having regular labor pains by the next day, but that did not happen. We called our doctor who said that if she had not gone into labor by Tuesday he would induce labor.

When I came home from work on Tuesday, JoAnn had her bag packed and was waiting on me. I took a shower and we headed for Baptist Hospital. To this day, she reminds me that she had to wait to go the hospital while I took a shower. The doctor was waiting when we arrived. They took her right in and broke her membranes and labor followed. JoAnn had been admitted to the hospital at about 6:30 p.m. and by 9:30 p.m. our first son had arrived. We named him Paul Ensslin McDonald after JoAnn's father. It is interesting to note that he was born on September 3, which was my father's birthday. After I visited briefly with JoAnn to make sure she was all right, I went to the phone and called her parents and my mother. Everyone was relieved and proud.

Both of us had assumed that the doctor would not send her home with the baby for four or five days. She spent two nights in the hospital, and when I called her before leaving work on the afternoon of the third day, she told me to bring the things she had packed for bringing the baby home. She was coming home as soon as I could pick her up. When I arrived at home, I was so panic stricken that I could not find anything that JoAnn had packed. I frantically went through several "baby things" packed away in a drawer and found some diapers and a snow suit, items that one would hardly use in early September to bring a baby home from the hospital. When I arrived at the hospital, I found JoAnn to be nearly as nervous as I was. What were we going to do with this baby? The doctor happened to come by and saw how anxious we were. He assured us that we would be fine. I remember him saying, "Take the baby home. Keep him dry and feed him when he is hungry. Everything will be all right." We were not convinced.

When we arrived at our Fuller Hall apartment, one of the first things we had to do was prepare formula for feeding. Neither of us could remember how to do this. Fortunately, a couple from across the hall came by just as we were trying to figure out what to do. They came in and helped us prepare the formula. It was simple once we did it.

We had all the baby books and had read everything we could find about being parents, but it is one thing to read a book and another thing to deal with a real live baby. Our Paul only slept about two hours at a time and he never took more than two ounces of his formula, which meant that JoAnn got very little rest since she was constantly taking care of his needs. He seemed to cry a lot, which made her anxious and fearful that she was not being a good mother. Often, I would come home from work and find her crying. She was not one to cry. The headaches began soon after she came home from the hospital. We felt that the saddle block spinal that she received as she went into labor may have caused the headaches since she had not had headaches prior to this. Whatever the cause, the headaches seemed to stay with her for much of her adult life.

With school about to start, I arranged for my transfer back to a second shift job at General Electric. There were still rumors about impending layoffs, but I had no choice in terms of accepting a transfer. The problem was that my transfer took me into a building where everyone had more seniority than I did. Should layoffs come, I would be one of the first to go. I needed to work even more since I now had a family and JoAnn was not working.

I registered for classes for what was to begin my last year in the seminary. From this vantage point I could see the finish line, and I was willing to make some genuine sacrifices to complete what I had begun three years earlier. I was determined to improve my grades. I did better work in school, but my grades remained about the same. Later, I learned that the graduate students who served as assistants to the professors did the grading. They had access to the student's previous grades. If you did well during your first year, you would continue to do well. The grades you received during the first year usually set the pattern for you for the rest of your seminary career. Grading was done on a curve basis. If you had been making C's in most of your classes and managed to do A work in a class you were now taking, the chances of your getting an A for that present class work was very slim. Your grade would likely be scaled back to a C because that was what you had been earning. It was almost impossible to improve your grades at the seminary after that first year, which was another of my frustrations with my seminary experience. Only when I began work on my doctorate did I break out of this grading pattern.

As seminary classes began in mid-September, JoAnn and I were adjusting to the task of being new parents. Paul was a pretty child, and we were beginning to enjoy the role that parenthood had given us. I cannot remember when Paul and Hazel saw their grandson the first time, nor do I remember when we took him with us to Shady Grove Baptist Church for the first time, but those times did come, and we enjoyed showing him off to everyone.

Near the end of the second week of October, I got my pink slip, my layoff notice, from General Electric. I had worked there twenty-seven months, but it appeared that the relationship was about to end. I was aware of layoffs in other companies all over Louisville. I began looking for other work, but the job market was very limited; there were simply very few jobs available.

JoAnn decided to check the job opportunity board in the lobby of Norton Hall which was the seminary administration building. While she was there, Badgett Dillard, the Administrative Assistant to the President, walked by and told her that there was an opening for a secretary in the President's office. She went in, was interviewed, and was offered the job as secretary to Dr. McCall but learned that the job only paid minimum wage. When she told Badgett that she would have to earn more than that, he told her about a teaching position in nearby Shelby County that had just been listed. He gave her a phone number and the name of the school superintendent. She called him, and he insisted that she come for an interview immediately. We went for the interview, she was hired, and would begin teaching at Simpsonville High School immediately.

We were faced with some changes in our lifestyle with JoAnn going back to work. My classes were in the morning, so we would need a babysitter for Paul until noon. Also, since there was the possibility that some emergency could arise, we decided that the car would remain with me and JoAnn would ride the bus to and from Simpsonville. I took her to the bus stop at Bacon's in St. Matthews each morning and met her there each afternoon. The bus schedule would put her at school in Simpsonville before the janitor arrived. Often, she waited on the steps of the building until he came to open the doors. On class days, I took Paul to the wife of one of the students in Fuller Hall who cared for him until my classes were over at noon. I was responsible for taking care of him, doing some housekeeping and some of our laundry. I realized then how fortunate I was for a mother that insisted early in my life that I learn how to do some things around the house.

School was different now that I did not have a second shift job. I was more relaxed and was enjoying my classes more, but there were still some negative undercurrents at the seminary that bothered me. I did not know exactly what was taking place, but it was apparent that some kind of conflict was developing within the seminary family. It was early in the second semester when that conflict between the faculty and administration broke out into the open.

We spent Thanksgiving with JoAnn's parents. It was the first time that they had been around their grandson for more than a day. The weather was cold and wet when we left Louisville going to London, Kentucky. We traveled on two-lane highways since this was before we had interstates highways. We drove through rain, sleet, ice, and snow, but JoAnn was determined to spend Thanksgiving with family. She drove part of the way, with Ohio traffic passing us as though it was a dry, sunny day. The Ohio travelers paid no attention to weather conditions.

When Christmas came we made a brief visit with JoAnn's family in London and then drove to Florida. My family had not seen Paul, and JoAnn had never been to Florida. We did some of our traveling at night so that Paul would sleep. Further, there was less traffic at night. Our visit with my family was pleasant. Also, we visited in Jacksonville with some of my father's family, who were meeting both JoAnn and Paul for the first time. JoAnn said that it did not seem like Christmas to her since there was no cold weather or snow in Florida.

Once we returned from our Christmas visits with family, I was immediately involved in my last semester at Southern Seminary. Calm seemed to prevail at the seminary until sometime in March when conflict between seminary President Duke McCall and a group of professors broke out into the open. Dr. McCall had been instructed by the Board of Trustees to implement some changes in the seminary administration, but some faculty members opposed his actions. Charges and counter charges were being exchanged daily. Open discussions about differences between the administration and faculty were taking place in the classrooms and every other gathering place on campus. Chapel speakers even felt called upon the address the problems. The students had closer contact with the professors and were inclined to be more sympathetic with them. Dr. McCall was more removed from the student body and remained somewhat aloof in terms of sharing his point of view with them. It was not a happy scene.

The atmosphere on campus affected everything that went on in the classroom. If a chapel speaker said something with which a professor disagreed, that disagreement was aired in the classes that followed. The discussions of the differences continued to spill over into the halls after class. Students would often wait outside the President's office and ask questions of Dr. McCall as he entered the hallway from his office suite. The topics of faculty meetings which had been previously kept among the faculty were now discussed openly with the students. Everyone was taking sides, and the sides taken were often influenced by a student's relationship either to the faculty or the seminary administration. Everyone's emotions seemed to be almost out of control.

I was in a Greek exegesis class studying I Corinthians, taught by Henry Turlington, one of the best professors that I had while in seminary. One day he took more than half of our class time telling us some of what was happening and his view of the possibility of ending the conflict. He was not mean-spirited, but it was apparent that the disagreement had become a win-lose proposition between faculty and administration. What we did not grasp at the time was that there would be no real winners in this battle. The seminary was about to suffer a grievous blow.

With graduation time being near, it appeared that I was going to earn my degree. In those days, a student had no assurance of graduation until Dr. McCall called their name for them to walk across the stage to receive their diploma. I had previously seen individuals in the graduation line, wearing cap and gown, being removed from the line as the graduates were making their way to the chapel for graduation ceremonies. It always seemed to me that there had to be a better way of dealing with these circumstances. Unless a student had done nothing in class, some grace ought to be exercised to avoid such harsh treatment.

My graduation from seminary took place on May 16, 1958. Along with JoAnn, the only people attending in my behalf were Reed McCreary and Mabel Jackson, members of my church in Franklin, Kentucky. I was bitter about my seminary experience. Walking across campus with JoAnn on the way to join the graduation line, I told her, "If I graduate today, I will never set foot on this campus again as long and I live." This was an extreme statement and one that I would not keep, but it would be a long time before my bitterness would diminish.

About two weeks after my graduation, the trustees met and took action that resulted in the firing of thirteen professors. These thirteen professors had stated collectively that they would resign rather than continue teaching under the administration of Dr. McCall should he carry out the changes which the trustees had instituted. The trustees, most of whom were pastors, saw their action as insubordination as though it were a pastor/staff conflict. They instructed Dr. McCall to terminate the professors, which he did. Of those who were fired, one, J. J. Owens, asked to be reinstated, saying that he felt called to teach at Southern and that he would accept the changes. That being done, the others soon found teaching or pastoral places of service elsewhere. Dr. McCall remained as seminary president until retirement. It was a sad ending to an unnecessary conflict that spiraled out of control. A lesson to be learned from this event is that when strong people disagree, it is often difficult to find middle ground on which to work out a compromise. This event weakened the seminary and still casts a shadow over its history in Baptist life.

Chapter 9
Full-Time Ministry-Early Years

With my graduation from seminary, JoAnn and I were also facing the end of the school year for JoAnn's teaching position. This meant that we would soon be moving out of Fuller Hall, away from the seminary campus, and away from the city of Louisville. Though I had spent four eventful years in Louisville, I confess that I did not mind moving to another area of Kentucky. The move involved renting a truck and carefully loading our belonging for the trip. Earlier, when we moved into Fuller Hall, we had stored some of our belongings in London with JoAnn's parents. This meant that we must go by London to pick up our stored goods as we made our way to our new home in Franklin, Kentucky. On JoAnn's last day at Simpsonville High School, I loaded the truck and departed for London with our son traveling with me. JoAnn drove to London when she finished her last day at school. Both of us were looking forward to having our own home instead of an apartment, even if it was a rented home.

Our move to Franklin marked the beginning of my full-time ministry as a pastor. The move took place during the last week of May 1958. I remember that I had to return the rental truck to Louisville and catch a Greyhound Bus back to Franklin. A seminary friend, Bill Green, met me at the truck rental place and drove me downtown to the bus station. The return was completed in one day.

The first day of June 1958 fell on a Sunday. We arrived in Franklin early enough in the week before that first Sunday to allow us to get halfway settled in our new home and for me to be prepared to lead the worship service that Sunday. We had rented a house from Elmore Gregory. It was near the Franklin city limits on state highway 100. The house had three bedrooms, one bath, a kitchen, a combination living and dining room, and a full unfinished basement. It was small but much larger than our apartment at the seminary. Several of our church members came by for a brief visit while we were in the process of unloading the truck and putting our furniture in place. They seemed to be excited to have a full-time pastor, and we were excited about the opportunity for ministering to the community.

As we moved to Franklin, we were aware of the economic changes that we faced. JoAnn had left her teaching job in Simpsonville and the church was providing us with about two thousand dollars less annually than the combined income we were receiving during my last year in school. However, we felt we could live on that salary. We were frugal with what the church provided and took care not to go in debt, but we were disappointed with the response of the church members to the demands of a more active church life. They had been used to having only a morning worship service plus special services such as a revival or Vacation Bible School. I felt that they should have an evening service and a Wednesday night prayer service. The response of the church members was disappointing. They were willing to pay for my being there, but they were unwilling to support the expanded church activities with their presence. I was frustrated, but I kept working trying to make things turn positive.

What I failed to see at the time was that I was coming face to face with the idealism that many ministers face early in their careers. Webster's Dictionary defines ideal as "existing as a mere mental image or in imagination only; lacking practicality." Webster goes on to define an idealist as "one that places ideals before practical considerations." Without realizing it, I had inherited from my mother much of the idealism that had influenced her life. She was one who would take a less that promising situation and try to turn it into a success. Further, many on the seminary faculty were guilty of encouraging this frame of mind. They should have been sharing ways to evaluate opportunities for ministry that had a reasonable chance to meet with some measure of success. In my opinion, failure to succeed does not glorify the Lord, even if the cause may have been worthy.

I was aware that the Shady Grove Church had two factions within the congregation. One faction was matriarchal in that the women in the family made the decision as to how they wanted things to be and the men followed their lead. This group was often able to gain the ear of the pastor, influencing him and thus exercising some measure of control over the church. The second group was more traditional in their roles. Both the men and women expressed their opinions, arrived at some form of consensus, and tried to carry on the work of the church without deception or the use of undue influence. Previously, there had been strong conflict between these groups, which the matriarchal group believed was the cause of a pastor, whom they valued highly, to abruptly resign and leave the church. My idealism came into play when I decided to lead the church in trying what the previous pastor had failed to accomplish. I believed that since I was sincere in trying to lead them forward, that they would unite behind the effort and help it succeed. Sincerity is a good thing but does not heal old wounds or secure the cooperation of adversaries in worthy endeavors.

While conflict between these two groups did not frustrate the effort for a greater ministry, it certainly did not help it succeed. The matriarchal group attended church but gradually withdrew most of their support. If what we were trying to do succeeded, it would do so without their help. The traditional group cooperated to a point, but the demands of getting the church on a more solid footing were greater than most of them wanted to meet. We enlarged our Sunday School. JoAnn and I both worked with the youth and managed to attract several young people in the community but were unable to reach their families on a continuing basis. Our Vacation Bible Schools were always successful, but again, we were not able to reach many of the families from which the children came. Revivals were well attended and former members in

Franklin would attend special services, but we did not experience much growth in the church.

I believe changes in the community itself greatly influenced the effort we were making. Many of the farms in the area were being sold or leased to families that were moving from north central Tennessee. These people were not from Southern Baptist backgrounds. Some of them were Baptists but of the anti-missionary or anti-education Baptist movements that were common to rural Tennessee. When they moved to Kentucky, they either did not attend church, or they started a church locally like the one they attended back in Tennessee. When people from other church backgrounds moved into the area, they often continued in their same church tradition. With old established families moving out of the community and being replaced by people with other denominational loyalties, our prospects for growth were greatly diminished. Hence, the success that we had hoped for did not materialize.

We had not been in Franklin long when we discovered that JoAnn was pregnant with our second child. This was our second unplanned pregnancy. In fact, when JoAnn had a physical examination before we married, the doctor had told her that she would likely be unable to get pregnant. It is slightly unnerving to be on the receiving end of erroneous medical information. Her pregnancy with this child seemed to be normal and without complications.

JoAnn's labor pains for the birth of our second child began shortly after we went to bed on Saturday night, February 28, 1959. Shortly after midnight, she told me that the pains had become regular and we needed to go to the hospital. However, making that short trip proved to be a difficult task. The weather was cold with the temperature hovering in the mid-twenties. A neighbor came over to stay with Paul. Wanting to be helpful, he offered to start the car and let it warm up. But he flooded the car and failed to start it. I failed to get it started and then called the only service station in town that was open. The attendant explained that he could not make a service call because he was the only person working. I explained my situation, persuaded him to close the business an come start my car. I promised to intervene with his boss should he get in trouble. It was a promise I did not have to keep. Our second son, Joseph Bryant, was born on Sunday, March 1, 1959, at about 8:45 a.m. in the Carter Moore Hospital in Franklin, Kentucky. The hospital had no labor room, so I stayed with JoAnn, caring for her until she went to the delivery room. Bryant really made a fuss at the moment of birth; I heard his very first cries. Further, he was ravenously hungry, resulting in his being fed long before the usual twenty-four-hour waiting period for newborn babies had taken place.

Dr. Lee Venzil cared for JoAnn during her pregnancy and delivered Bryant when he was born. He was good to us. The medical care that we received from him was excellent, and Bryant was a healthy child. Our only problem with Bryant was keeping him fed. He was born with a good appetite and has never lost it.

JoAnn lost a more weight after Bryant's birth than I felt was good for her. She dropped down to about 105 pounds. Her sister threw a fit when the family came to see Bryant. She kept complaining about how skinny JoAnn was and giving me a critical look as though it was all my fault.

At this point in time the Annuity Board of the Southern Baptist Convention had not begun to make health insurance available for ministers and their families. All they had for ministers was a retirement program. I had begun to participate in the retirement program, but we had health insurance through Blue Cross and Blue Shield. What we had did not cost much, but it did not pay much. Local physicians had the practice of providing care for ministers and their families without cost. This was a courtesy that my family and I greatly appreciated though it would have been nice to have been able to pay for what we received.

In early July 1959, my maternal grandmother passed away. When I shared this news with the Shady Grove people, they told me to take whatever time I needed to go to Florida to be with my family. Several of the men came to me with money in hand asking if I had the funds that I needed to make this unexpected trip. When I said that I had what I needed, two or three of them pressed large bills in my hand anyway and told me to take it and not worry about paying it back. They knew how to be kind and generous.

My grandmother was a more powerful influence on my life than I was aware until I was well into my adult years. I have shared several things about her in other chapters of this work. She became a widow in her late fifties and lived with her children, most of the time with my mother, until her death at age seventy-three. She was a devout Christian and faithfully served where she could in the various churches where she was a member. When she and my grandfather were members of Mt. Carmel Baptist Church near Lake City, Florida, she always prepared the unleavened bread that was used when the church observed the Lord's Supper. She was strong-willed and very opinionated which served to alienate her from almost every close family member except my mother. Her pastor, E.L. Mixon, conducted her funeral, and she was buried next to her husband in the Mt. Carmel Church Cemetery, in Lake City.

It is my observation that every pastor needs to have one or more laymen in the congregation with whom he can have honest, open, and confidential conversations in regard to the church and the pastor's ongoing ministry. One of our deacons, Paul Jackson, was that man for me at Shady Grove Church. Paul was a local farmer and business man. He owned a tobacco warehouse in Franklin where he also had other business interests. Paul and I always seemed to be able to talk and understand each other. He had a committed interest in the church and gave me his strong support. His wife, Mabel, was the same kind of person. Paul was a sportsman who loved to hunt and fish. While I was his pastor, he loaned me a twenty-gauge double barrel shotgun and furnished me all the shells that I could use during hunting season. We hunted dove, quail, and squirrel and fished together. He would coach me about how to shoot and rejoice when I hit my intended target. He was a good man, deacon, and friend! As every pastor needs good laymen to help him lead the church, he also needs a mature, experienced pastor who is willing to serve as a role model and confidant. That person for me was J.V. Case, the pastor of First Baptist Church in Franklin. Through his influence, I became active in the work of Simpson Baptist Association. I served as the Associational Sunday School Superintendent and I was elected to serve a term on the State Executive Board. Both of these offices gave me a chance to develop leadership skills and to meet Baptist leaders on a local and statewide basis. He also encouraged me to attend the State Evangelism Conference for the first time. J.V. proved to be a great friend and an excellent mentor. His guidance and friendship were a blessing to me.

By early summer of 1959, I began to realize that no matter how hard I worked, the Shady Grove Church was at a standstill. I had obtained all of the effort that these people were willing to give. This is not to say that they were not good people. It is to say that what I wanted for them and what they wanted were two different things. There was no hostility. There was a good spirit among the people, but the fact was that with the community changes that were taking place and with the level of commitment that the church was willing to give, further growth was highly unlikely. I felt that I had given my best effort, but perhaps I had expected too much. So I began to let my connections know that I was interested in moving.

Near the end of the summer, E.N. Perry, pastor of First Baptist Church in Richmond, Kentucky, visited some of his relatives in our community. He came to hear me preach. We spoke later, and he told me that the Calhoun Baptist Church was without a pastor. He had relatives in the church and would like to suggest that they come hear me. I was delighted with the prospect of having a pulpit committee visit my church. I gave him permission to place my name before the church as a possible pastoral candidate.

In late September the pulpit committee from Calhoun Baptist Church came for a visit. I did not know that they were coming, but I had prepared a good message on Romans 12:1-2. The arrival of six well-dressed strangers at a church that usually ran between 45 to 65 regular worshippers was not something that could be concealed. Everyone knew what they were and why they were there. I was leading the singing and almost lost my voice when they entered during the singing of one of our first hymns, but I regained my composure and did a good job preaching. The committee did talk with me after church, though I do not recall any of the details of that meeting. Our sons were too young to know what was happening, but JoAnn and I were both excited.

Later, I had both phone and mail communication with the Calhoun chairman, Wendell Davis. We agreed on a date for me to visit the church and preach for them. The pulpit committee had all of their information about the church in order. They shared with me the proposed salary and other benefits. I was going to receive about a six hundred dollar increase in salary and benefits, and I was going to have a much greater opportunity for growth and ministry. Also, I was pleased to learn that the church had a history of being good to their pastor. I preached for them in early October. The church gave me a unanimous call which I accepted. By late November we were living in Calhoun and I was hard at work.

Calhoun, Kentucky, was the county seat of McLean County. The church belonged to the Davies-McLean Baptist Association. Calhoun was a rural, farming community of about eight hundred residents that was located on the Green River. There were four high schools in the county, located in the small towns of Calhoun, Livermore, Island, and Sacramento. Most of the residents of the county were related either by blood or marriage or both. One learned quickly never to make negative statements about anyone because by sundown everyone would know what you had said.

The Calhoun Baptist Church had not enjoyed a great history. The Methodist Church and other churches in the county had enjoyed much more success in terms of growth and ministry. In fact, the church suffered from an inferiority complex, having never developed a vision for a future, dynamic ministry. However, the previous pastor, James Baggett, had led them to demolish an educational building that was deteriorating and build a newer, more adequate building. When I arrived, the outside brick veneer was unfinished. The top floor had been roughed in but was also unfinished. The local bank had loaned the church only enough money for that much construction. The fact that the building was left half-finished helped explain the depressed state of mind of the congregation.

When I arrived, I concentrated my efforts on getting to know the people and the community. I was gifted at learning and remembering names. Further, I was willing to visit, try to win people to the Lord, and encourage them to come to church. This was a time in which revivals were often greeted with much enthusiasm. We usually had two revivals a year. I always tried to invite a preacher who was gifted in the pulpit. Our Sunday School grew, and we began baptizing more and more people each year.

One of the strengths of the Calhoun Baptist Church was its laymen. There were several men with whom I could talk and who would be honest with me when I shared with them various programs that might be used to strengthen and build the congregation. Among those men were Dr. Gerald Edds, Wendell Davis, Walter Fee, and Bill Quisenberry. Dr. Edds was the most respected man in the community and if he gave his support to something, it would most likely be met with success. He had helped push the church building program toward a successful completion.

One of the needs of Calhoun Baptist Church was more land. The church was boxed in on every side; the Christian Church owned land to the north, the Catholic Church owned the land behind, and a widow owned a home and a nice sized lot to the south. All the land that the church owned was the land on which the church buildings were located. In time past, the church had become involved in a property line dispute with the husband of the widow. The dispute wound up in court, and the church had lost the case. The husband had instructed his wife before his death to never let the church purchase the property. So we were locked in from every direction.

However, I began a public relations campaign with the widow who owned the property next door. She lived with her daughter in Florida most of the year but came to Kentucky every summer. I visited her in Florida one year when she had not been able to come to Kentucky. During that visit, I told her that should she ever decide to sell the property, the church would like to have first refusal. She told me that she would take that into consideration.

In the meantime, a member of the church came to me with her checkbook in hand. She said, "I want to give the church the money to put the brick on the educational building, but I want to challenge the church to do more than that. The money I am going to give is seed money. I will give the money for the brick plus having it laid if the church will raise the money to complete the top floor. Will you take this proposition to the church and lead them to complete the building?" My answer was, "Yes, I will take it to the church and do all in my power to get our people to finish the building." The church accepted the gift and the challenge, and we began finishing the building.

While that was taking place, the Catholic diocese decided to sell its old church site which backed up to both the Baptist Church and the Christian Church. I began talking to the church leaders and insisted that we make every effort to buy the property. However, the Christian Church also wanted the property. The moderator of our church, Leroy Northington, was asked to represent our church in the negotiations and he worked out a very equitable deal for us. The agreement was that the Christian Church would purchase half of the Catholic property, and the Baptist Church would purchase the other half. However, to make the deal equal and to square off the property the Christian Church agreed to trade us a portion of the lot they owned on our north side so that there was a straight property line from the Main Street to the back property line. Both congregations found the deal equitable and gave their approval.

Next came the problem of working out the financing. The local bank had a policy that limited the amount of a loan to one individual or institution. Since we already had a loan with that bank and had been faithfully making our payments, we asked them to loan us what we needed purchase the property and complete our building. This would involve making the loan and converting the entire loan to one promissory note. Our loan request would put the entire loan above the usual loan limit for the bank which was twenty thousand dollars.

Much to my surprise, the bank refused our request. It appeared that all our efforts were for naught. I was almost overcome with frustration and anger, but I went to see Charles Blancett, who was the Chairman of the Bank Board, the local Ford dealer, and owner of about half the rental property in town. I explained that I was disappointed in the decision of the bank. He said the church really did not need the property and indicated that he thought we were being greedy and land hungry. His arrogance was almost more than I could bear. I looked him squarely in the eye and said, "Mr. Blancett, you have the right to refuse to give us the loan, but your opinion about our church is small and childish. The future of our church and its ministry is hanging on whether or not we are able to get this loan. I am already in touch with another financial institution that will loan us what we need. In fact, they will loan us enough money to make this land purchase plus enough to pay off our loan at your bank. If we are forced to go outside of town for this money, we will do it. Further, we will pay off our note at your bank and we will tell everybody in this county and every county that joins us how shabbily you have treated us. Please take that back to your board meeting and share it with the members. Good day, sir." Of course, Mr. Blancett did not appreciate my words, but the next week the president of the bank called to tell me that the bank had reconsidered, and our loan was approved. Charles Blancett always appeared to be less than friendly after this encounter.

Dr. Gerald Edds was generous and kind to our family while I served the Calhoun Baptist Church. The medical treatment we received at his hands was always excellent and without cost to us. I came down with the flu at least once every year. Also, I suffered a great deal with allergies. Our young children experienced ear infections, strep throats, respiratory infections, and many of the early childhood diseases during the three and one-half years we lived there. Also, JoAnn had appendicitis which necessitated surgery at the McLean County Hospital. This hospital was a thirty-four bed facility built with Hill-Burton funds.

Our house in Calhoun was the church parsonage. It was a two-story white frame house that had little or no insulation; the upstairs floors were not level and the windows leaked cold air during the winter. The house was difficult to heat. JoAnn and I believed that living there was a major contributing cause to our many respiratory infections which we experienced during the winter months. I discussed this with some of the church leadership, but none of them were willing for the church to pay us a housing allowance and thus allow us to live in better conditions. This was a contributing factor a few years later when I made the decision to begin looking for another place of service. It may have cost the church more for us to have our own home, but they would have had a pastor and his family that experienced much less sickness.

We had been in Calhoun only a few months when leaders from the county school system approached JoAnn about teaching at Calhoun High School. She accepted a teaching position in the business department of the school and taught there until we moved away. Her principal was L. D. Knight, who was a member of our church along with his wife, Edna, our church organist. Corine Woodfork, a member of our church, cared for our two sons while JoAnn was at work.

The last year of my service at Calhoun saw the completion of our educational building. With more educational space available, we expanded and reorganized our Sunday School. I continued to study, preach new material and visit as much as possible. This kept our Sunday School in a good growth pattern and opened doors for me to do some counseling with people in the church who had problems. We continued to win people to the Lord and baptize the new converts.

During the last months that I was in Calhoun, I tried to lead the church to install air conditioning in our church sanctuary. My goal was to get it done without having a large payment for the equipment and installation. Cost ruled out conventional equipment and installation, but there were natural gas compressors that were available through the Texas Gas Corporation which provided natural gas service to our community. They proposed a deal that would cost about $6,000.00 which could be added to our monthly service bill for a period of five years with no interest. I was so excited about the proposal that I could not see any reason for not doing it. Of course, the electricians and the heating and air conditioning people in our church would not even listen to my arguments for this kind of project. I took the proposal before the Property and Grounds Committee, the Finance Committee, and the Deacons only to have it rejected. I was disappointed.

My "I told you so day" came in early June just before departing to serve as pastor of Lone Oak Baptist Church, in Paducah, Kentucky. We had a formal wedding in the church on a Sunday afternoon with an outside temperature of 105 degrees and high humidity. We all sweltered in the sanctuary. Just as the groom leaned forward to place the ring on the bride's finger, all of the perspiration on his face seemed to run to the end of his nose. It hung there until a drop that appeared to be nearly the size of a golf ball accumulated before falling to the floor. In all my life, I have never seen a drop of liquid that big collect in one place before falling. At least a dozen people mentioned this sight to me after we went downstairs for the wedding reception. I just smiled and said, "Well, if we had air conditioned the sanctuary, all of us would have been more comfortable today!" Some nodded affirmatively and said, "We will have to get it done soon."

In defense of the church leaders, I must say that my suggested plan for getting the air conditioning done was a poor choice. Today, I would say that it bordered on being harebrained. I chose it because I felt it would work and we could handle it financially. To their credit, they did air condition the building in about two years and they did it the conventional way. I think that was a better choice though I was bitterly disappointed at the time.

In late spring of 1963, I learned that several churches in western Kentucky were without a pastor and were conducting active searches to fill their pulpits. First Baptist Church Earlington and Lone Oak Baptist Church Paducah were both looking for a pastor. Friends submitted my resume to both churches. Word came to me later that the committee from Lone Oak Baptist was to visit on the following Sunday. Just as that word arrived, I learned that the Earlington committee was planning on visiting the same day. Guy Gordon was the former pastor at Earlington. Since he was a friend, I called him and explained my desire not to have two committees present at the same time. He understood and said he would get word to the Earlington committee and suggest that they visit at a later date. He did alert the committee from Earlington and they chose to visit later. The Lone Oak committee came as scheduled and we entered into serious talks that ended with my becoming their pastor.

The congregation at Calhoun Baptist Church had been gracious to me and my family throughout my ministry to them. They had provided me with my first challenging opportunity to continue developing and using the skills that I had been learning while gaining my education. They were aware that eventually, I would have an opportunity to move to a larger challenge. They accepted my resignation with regret. As a parting gesture, they gave JoAnn and me a nice farewell reception and a large crystal punch bowl set which we still possess and have used many times. I look back on my service there with great joy and with a sense of genuine, lasting accomplishment.

While I was pastor at Calhoun Baptist, I had suggested that the church take each fifth Sunday offering and place it in a building fund. This was in anticipation of a later date when they would have the opportunity to enlarge their church buildings. I had forgotten about leading the church to do that until late in the summer of 1990. I had a call from the present Calhoun pastor telling me that the church had eventually been able to purchase the land next to the church which had been owned by the widow. They had built a new sanctuary on that site and were inviting me to come preach the dedication sermon. It was a wonderful day with many old friends, and it was a blessing to have had a part in what was accomplished there.

Chapter 10

Paducah: The Early Years

When the pulpit committee from Lone Oak Baptist Church came to visit Calhoun Baptist Church in search for a pastor, JoAnn and I sensed a positive chemistry with them from the beginning. The committee members were warm and friendly. They were enthusiastic about their task and knew how to conduct themselves. We were at ease with them and they seemed to be at ease with us.

On the Sunday that they visited our worship service, everything appeared to go well. When the service concluded, they waited until most of the Calhoun members had left and asked if we could talk. We talked briefly and then drove to Madisonville to a restaurant where we could eat and continue our conversation. It was a relaxed visit. I do not remember a great deal about the visit except that it was a positive experience. One of the men kidded me saying that if I came to Paducah, I would have to learn to drive a little slower. He assured me that the Kentucky State Police would not allow me to get away with breaking the speed limit. I did not think I exceeded the speed limit, but since I was leading the way, he may have had to drive a little faster in order to keep up with me. Further, since ministers are known for exceeding the speed limit, he may have been pulling my chain. That is my story, and I am sticking to it.

The Lone Oak committee invited us to visit the church for the purpose of meeting some of the church leaders and seeing the community, the church facilities, and parsonage. Arriving in Lone Oak, which was a suburb of Paducah, we found the church and community to be vibrant and expanding, thus providing a great opportunity for growth and ministry. The previous pastor, B. R. Winchester, had served the church for eighteen years. His early ministry had been effective; both the church and community had grown and changed during his tenure. He was a college graduate but had not been to seminary. However, there were lay leaders in the church who for unknown reasons had successfully frustrated and limited his leadership during the last years of his ministry. I could see the results of a dispirited and frustrated leader everywhere I turned. I determined that I would not allow that to happen to me. A majority in the church wanted strong pastoral leadership and was willing to follow a visionary, able leader. It is unfortunate that this group had not asserted itself and provided the pastor with stronger support.

A group of four or five older men who were deacons and trustees in the church had controlled much of the church ministry in recent years. They were good men, but they were misguided and lacking in vision in terms of the future of the church. Their goal was control, and they guided the church budget and finances as though it was their private domain. If they could avoid spending money, they would do so at almost all costs. My first experience with them came in this visit when we went to look at the parsonage. The home was a nice sized brick house located across the parking lot from the church building. It had two bedrooms downstairs and two bedrooms upstairs. One of the upstairs bedrooms became my home office. There was a living room, a dining room, and a large kitchen with a dining area included. The home had one and a half bathrooms. There was also a large unfinished basement. An enclosed back porch was off the kitchen that opened into a double carport. The house had hot water heat, and window air conditioning units. The Winchester family had lived in this house the entire eighteen years that Rev. Winchester had served the church.

Once we entered the house, it was obvious that it had not be kept up in terms of painting, floor coverings, and general repairs. The kitchen cabinets were shabby and in poor repair. The floor covering on the back porch was worn bare. I began to make a list of the things that would have to be done before we moved in should the church call me to serve as pastor. The trustees who served as the property and grounds committee immediately balked. They insisted that everything was in good condition. I told them that my requests were not unreasonable and that it represented poor maintenance to let such things go undone. They continued to resist. I told them that none of their wives would move into that home in the condition that currently existed. They continued to resist my requests. I finally told them that if they refused to meet our requests, we would either not move into the house or I would not accept the call of the church if it was extended to me. They grumbled but finally agreed to do what we asked. I was, at the time, unaware that this was a prelude to all that would follow. Once I became their pastor, everything that was to be accomplished for several months came about as the result of confrontation and the use of ultimatums. I felt then, and still do, that this was an unnecessary atmosphere in which to serve and work.

My official visit with the church on the weekend of my trial sermon was positive. We stayed at the local Holiday Inn and took our meals there. Our boys loved it because they had use of the swimming pool. Both Sunday worship services were well planned, and I felt that I was at my best in my preaching. I do not recall the title or text of either of my sermons. The vote was to be taken by secret ballot the following week. I received a call from Ed Wilkins, the committee chairman, on the day of the vote, telling me that it was affirmative. I told him that I would give my answer by the following Sunday. Later in the week, I received a letter from W. D. Kelley telling me the results of the vote and opening the door for further communication in regard to the possibility of my coming to serve the church. Both Ed and W. D. told me privately that the improvements at the parsonage were being made.

I wish I could say that the experience of negotiating with the pulpit committee was pleasant, but that is not true. The conversations were highly stressful for me. In fact, all such dealings with pulpit committees have been stressful. In retrospect, should I be able to relive this part of my life, I would never again become personally involved in such negotiations. I would request that the committee give me their proposal in writing. I would then go over it with my attorney and have him present in writing my requests for salary, benefits, time off, housing, and professional study time away from the church. If there were matters that needed discussion and negotiation, he could do it. Such a procedure would relieve me from being exposed to dealing on this basis with individuals with whom I would later have to work or to whom I would have to minister. My experience in these negotiations is that someone in the group invariably demonstrates a less than charitable attitude which provides one with a lingering negative memory.

If a person or a committee does not exhibit a generous and willing attitude, it is best that prospective minister does not have to carry that memory with him throughout his entire relationship with those involved. Human nature being what it is, I believe it is extremely difficult to put negative experiences in the back of one's mind and not allow them to influence later relationships. People that have a positive and respectful attitude toward their pastor will always find a way to express that in their dealings with him. One can get an accurate perception as to what a person's attitude is by the way people speak to you and in how they deal with you personally. It is not a simple matter for a person to conceal their real feelings. If they have respect for the office of the pastor, it will show. If respect is lacking, that will be revealed also.

My resignation at Calhoun took effect almost a month before our move to Lone Oak. I remained at Calhoun for two weeks and took two more weeks off before arriving in Paducah to begin work on the first of July. The following Sunday, July 7, 1963, was my first Sunday in the pulpit as pastor of Lone Oak Baptist Church. We planned a special installation service which was perhaps the most formal type service that had been conducted in the church in its history. W. R. Osborne, chairman of deacons, presided over the opening part of the service. When I shared with him the plans and program for the service, he objected to our having it, his reason being that the church had never done anything like that in the past. While that may have been true, it was not a good reason for not doing it now. It took about an hour of strong persuading on my part, but Brother Osborne finally agreed to having the service and participating in it. I still have in my files the copy of the program which I used along with my notes and instructions for the various persons who took part. It turned out to be a good service and a very nice day. I believe that such a service serves to impress upon both the congregation and pastor the sacredness of the relationship that is being formed and that it must be done with a deep sense of commitment and reverence.

During my first weeks as pastor at Lone Oak, I busied myself with getting acquainted with the church leadership and meeting as many of the people as possible. The minister of music, Jimmy Driver, was from a long-established family in the Paducah area. However, he had resigned just as I was in the process of dealing with the church. He was an able church musician but had just bought a Kentucky Fried Chicken franchise, the first such franchise in the Paducah area. Most of his attention and energy was being directed toward his new business. We talked but it was obvious that he had no interest in continuing his ministry at Lone Oak, meaning that we had an immediate need for an interim minister of music and later a permanent replacement. A church member, Billy P. Spears, agreed to serve as the interim and did an excellent job.

The church secretary was Louise Osborne, wife of W. R. Osborne Jr. She stated that her job consisted of answering the phone and taking messages for the pastor. She performed other tasks but did not appear to be interested in seeing any changes or in raising the level of ministry in the church. Within a month of my arrival she resigned, meaning that we also had to search for a church secretary. I do not remember how many applicants I interviewed, but one of the applicants was Betty Hunt, a member of the church. She was one of the best church secretaries that I ever hired. She remained in that position during my eight years as pastor and for several years into the next pastor's tenure. She and her husband, Roger, along with their family have remained close friends over the years. JoAnn and I still get together each summer with the Hunt family and one other couple from the church for a brief reunion and a renewal of our friendship.

These first months at Lone Oak provided us with a growing number of visitors each Sunday. These visitors seemed to respond positively to my pulpit ministry. The church began experiencing growth both in attendance and membership. It was my practice to visit recent visitors and new prospects each week. A result of this was new members being added and the church was growing. Lay leaders joined with me on improving our Sunday School. We began by reorganizing and relocating many of the departments and classes. Since reorganization would provide us with a clearer picture of our future needs and was easier to accomplish, we chose to do it first. Then we faced the issue of making better use of our space. Whenever changes of this nature are attempted, one is likely to encounter resistance. Some classes of older members did not want to be reorganized or change their meeting places. When we began to move classes and departments in order to better utilize our space, we almost provoked a rebellion. But with each move, we experienced a surge in enrollment and attendance. I was careful to go to those who had made changes pointing out to them that their cooperation had made it possible to reach more people. Some who had cooperated grudgingly were unconvinced, but many rejoiced.

Our next task was that of improving the entire church record system. We began with the Sunday School record system completing it department by department. We also began using the church envelope system for Sunday School attendance and church offering. That practice began a growing increase in our offering which continued during my entire tenure as pastor. Finally, we began working on the master list of our church members. Our church family may not have noticed the results but doing this made it easier to keep up with our members and minister to them in good times as well as in sickness, death, and personal crisis.

Reading about the various changes that were in progress at Lone Oak Baptist Church, one might assume that nothing else was happening, but that was not the case. Ministry to our people continued without fail. Most of the changes being described took place over a period of about three years. However, we were constant in continuing the effort until we had improved and restructured our organization making it as effective and inclusive as possible. Also, we began expanding and rotating the church committees. Each committee appointment was for a three-year term with two people being appointed each year. This rotation kept the committee structure from becoming stale and kept people from assuming that the committee on which they were serving was their private domain. My philosophy was that every person who wanted to serve ought to be given an opportunity. With numerous committees, each person who wanted a job could be given one. I felt that one major job plus one minor job should be near the limit for each person who had the ability to serve. Of course, there were some who only wanted to attend. We did our best to eliminate the practice of one person having too many jobs, believing that if a person had too much responsibility, burn out could occur, and the person may quit doing anything. That was to be avoided.

"The Baptist Faith and Message Statement" adopted by the Southern Baptist Convention on May 9, 1963, states that each "church is an autonomous body, operating through democratic processes under the Lordship of Jesus Christ." I quote this document because it best describes how local Baptist churches organize and govern themselves. Each local congregation governs itself by decisions made at regular business meetings. This was the practice that was carefully followed under my leadership as pastor of the church. When a decision was to be made by the church, it was presented at the monthly business meeting and church action was taken. This meant that no person, committee or unofficial group of persons could impose their will on either the pastor or the church congregation.

The process described in the above paragraph precipitated several heated confrontations in my office, but the process continued. Several times, those who had controlled things in the past came to me and said, "Preacher, you must stop this, and you can do it if you want to!" My reply was that the church was in the process of moving forward and that I would not to stand in the way of progress. Once they came to me bitterly opposing some church action and demanded that I not allow it to happen. My reply was, "Gentlemen, the train of progress is on the tracks and moving forward. My advice to you is to get on the train and go with it. If you persist in laying down on the tracks, I don't think I can stop the train. If you remain on the tracks, you will get run over. If you get on the train, you can have a part in something that is bigger than anything you have imagined up to this point. Don't miss your opportunity." They were not convinced but grudgingly went along.

A few weeks after our move to Lone Oak, it became apparent to JoAnn and I that the salary and expense arrangement we had received from the church was not going to meet our needs. True, the church had paid for the movers to bring our household goods to Lone Oak. But there were additional expenses that we had not anticipated. In fact, being inexperienced in the moving process, we did not know how to anticipate it. Also, it is highly possible that few in the church had ever made any kind of professional move. Hence, our committee seemed to be unaware of any other kind of relocation expenses or the need for an adjustment in their salary provisions. The truth is that the raise in salary over my previous salary at Calhoun did not match the increase in my responsibility or the increase in ministry expenses that I faced daily as pastor at Lone Oak. We were in a financial bind for several months. Early in our stay, we did not have money for food. On one occasion, two weeks went by without a drop of milk or loaf of bread coming into our house. I resorted to picking up apples that had fallen off trees in church members' yards in order for my family to have food to eat. I am aware that I could have gone to some of the church leaders and explained our needs, but I was too proud and embarrassed to do so. Further, I was disappointed that none of them appeared to be sensitive to our needs.

I share the above story to point out the need for younger, less experienced ministers to seek the advice and counsel of older, more experienced ministers in matters such as I have described. It may appear that I am portraying myself and my family as victims in the above story, but that is not my intention. I have often sought the guidance of older ministers and have never failed to be helped by it. Less experienced ministers would do themselves a favor by seeking the wise counsel of more experienced ministers as they face the many issues of serving a congregation.

The church asked me to preach the fall revival that first year I was there. I was more than happy to do it, but I learned a hard lesson. If the pastor becomes the evangelist for a revival in his own church, it doubles his work load. I had to do my regular work plus all the work involved in being the evangelist. Further, there must be a clear understanding about receiving an honorarium for this extra service. When the revival concluded, I discovered that checks had been written to the music leader, organist, and the pianist, but not to me. When I asked why I had received no honorarium, they said, "You received your regular pay." My reply was, "If you had asked an outsider to preach for you, you would have paid him. Why would you treat an outsider better than you treat your pastor, who has given you an extra measure of service?" They then asked for the amount of a proper honorarium. My reply was, "Treat me like you would treat a stranger." It seemed that every measure of progress came at the cost of this kind of leadership. It took a lot of the joy out of making progress.

Telling this story, I am aware that sounds like I was having to insist on things being done right on every occasion, but that was not entirely the case. Looking back, I realize that previous leaders had simply failed to teach the people how to respond to leadership and how to relate to those who were leading them. We always pay for the failures of others. I resolved to teach the people how things should be done without fail. Even though I did not enjoy doing what others had failed to do, the task needed to be done. The people may have enjoyed my ministry more had I not felt it necessary lead them in a more proper way, but, in the years since I was there, I have never heard a single complaint about my leadership in this area. If anything, they have been grateful and so have those who succeeded me.

Our first year in the Paducah area was one of changes. Many of the younger couples in their twenties and thirties often included us in their social activities which we enjoyed immensely. Our oldest son, Paul, started attending Lone Oak Elementary School. Our second son, Bryant, entered kindergarten, which was sponsored by our church. Also, we experienced a growth spurt in the size of several of our younger families. It was a baby boom that began in late winter and ended in the spring. There were nineteen babies born to families in our church by late spring 1964. JoAnn and I were included in this growth spurt as our youngest son, Philip, was born on Sunday, April 12, 1964. Later, our church kindergarten program was filled with most of these children from various young couples in the congregation. Also, both Paul and Bryant learned to ride their bicycles using the church parking lot that was next to our house. It was a safe place to ride.

The local television station was WPSD-TV, an NBC affiliate owned by the Paxton family in Paducah which also owned the local newspaper, known then as the Paducah Sun-Democrat. The television station made time available to the area churches and ministers for a brief daily telecast during the week and a slightly longer worship telecast on Sunday morning. Since the station was only equipped to telecast programs from their studio, we went there for our presentations. The weekday Daily Devotion program was telecast at noon Monday through Friday, featuring a pastor and lasting about thirteen minutes. The Sunday morning telecast included music by the church choir and a message by the pastor. It was a live telecast at 8:30 a.m. and lasted twenty-seven minutes. Both telecasts required a great deal of planning.

We presented our first Sunday morning telecast on April 12, 1964. I have mentioned before that all of our children were either born on Sunday or labor pains prior to their birth began on Sunday. In the early morning hours of Sunday, April 12, JoAnn woke me telling me that her labor pains had started. I called the doctor and then called a neighbor to come stay with our boys while I took JoAnn to the hospital. I admitted her at the hospital with just enough time for me to go back home, change clothes, and arrive on time for the television program. The doctor assured me that she would not deliver before I returned. However, just as I walked into the television station, my minister of music, Bill Fowler, came over and told me that the hospital had called and that my wife had delivered our third son. I thanked him and told him not to mention it until the program was over and we were off the air. It was our first telecast, but it was a flawless presentation.

I went to the hospital as soon as we finished the telecast and found JoAnn doing well. She did not tell me until much later, but she had a hard time with this birth. Her doctor and the anesthetist got into a heated argument and she did not receive any anesthesia until after Philip had been delivered. I complained later to all the doctors involved, but it was after the fact and did little good. Philip was our largest baby weighing eight pounds and six ounces. Labor and birth took about four hours, which was the same for all our children.

The day of Philip's birth is a vivid memory in some ways, but some things are difficult to recall. I do not remember preaching except at the television station. I do remember people congratulating me after our morning worship service at the church. Some wondered how I had the composure to speak at the television station after learning about Philip's birth. One lady in the church was praying that we would have a little girl. This lady later came to me in all seriousness and asked, "Preacher, I want to know what you have done that the Lord would not give you a little girl instead of another son?" Some questions have no answer, and that was one of them. Further, I was and still am proud of my boys.

Shortly after Philip's birth, I met Ben Brewer, Administrator of Western Baptist Hospital, in the hospital hall while doing my regular visitation duties. He asked me to come by his office when I finished my visitation. When I arrived, he told me that the hospital had a new chaplain who had not completed his clinical pastoral education, CPE, as it was known. They had arranged for John Boyle from Southern Seminary to spend part of the summer in Paducah and lead a seminar for the new chaplain. It had been decided to ask three local pastors to share in the seminar for which they would receive academic credit. Would I be interested in being a part of that study group? My reply was yes, if my church would grant me permission to participate. The seminar would meet for two hours each weekday morning for six weeks. I would be able to do my regular hospital visitation while I was there. When I asked the church for permission to participate in this seminar, they graciously granted it.

Other participants in this CPE seminar were Harley Dixion, Jim Gerren, and Bob Dunn. Harley Dixon was the hospital chaplain and became a lifelong friend. Jim Gerren was pastor of First Baptist Church, Wickliffe. Jim and I have remained close friends and still keep in touch. Bob Dunn was pastor of Olivet Baptist Church, Paducah. He became a dear friend also, but over the years our relationship became more distant. He later retired as a pastor, went to China to do some teaching, and died while there. This group formed a close bond as we studied and worked together.

In fact, each member of the group still comments about how he has been blessed by the relationship that developed between us.

Three other events stand out in my memory of my first three years at Lone Oak. The first was the discussion of a recommendation for the church to adopt the rotation system for a deacon's term of service. One of our deacons, Wallace Adams, brought the recommendation to the church. It was explained that this would make deacon service less stressful. Men who had served as a deacon would be allowed at least one year off before being called upon to serve again. Bill Spears, also a deacon, stood in the business meeting and asked if this was scriptural. His question became the source of much good-natured kidding from his friends. We have never let him forget that event. Brother Adams replied that there was no scripture indicating that this should or should not be done. He did point out that many other congregations were using the rotation system quite effectively. The church approved the rotation system, and it proved to be good for our church.

The second event was the writing and adoption of a church constitution and bylaws. One of our deacons, Ed Luttrell, was the driving force behind this effort. Ed was a University of Kentucky graduate, a farmer, and a successful business man. He had been quite active in the Kentucky Farm Bureau along with several other organizations that used parliamentary procedure in conducting the organization's affairs. Ed's view of both the constitution and bylaws was that each should be as simple as possible. He felt that they should give direction to the church without binding it with a set of hard and fast rules. I am grateful that his views prevailed because we developed both a constitution and bylaws that told who we were, affirmed what we believed, and gave practical direction for carrying out our beliefs and business.

The third event had to do with a personnel matter. The church custodian had been hired by the men who had served as trustees and who had taken on the responsibility of running the church. When I first arrived at Lone Oak, nothing was said about my being his supervisor. I gave him the freedom to do his work, but occasionally I did ask him to perform certain tasks. Sometimes he did what I asked, but there were times that he did not. I finally asked him why he had not performed a task that I had repeatedly asked him to do. He informed me that I was not his boss, and he had been told that he did not have to do it. I asked him who told him that he did not have to follow my requests. He named the previous trustees, many of whom were no longer serving as trustees. I informed him that some changes had taken place and that he would have to adjust to those changes. He informed me that he would never do that.

I discussed this with the chairman of the church personnel committee telling him what had happened. He informed the custodian that I was his supervisor. Thinking that the custodian understood this new relationship, the chairman told me that all appeared to be well, but it was not to be. The custodian went to the old trustees who encouraged him to stand his ground. He did, and we had another conversation about requests that I had made which had not been carried out. I told him that he two choices: he could do as he was instructed or else he could resign. He laughed and said that he was not going to do either. I informed him that should he persist in that frame of mind, he would be terminated. He said we would see.

Several members of the church personnel committee met with the custodian. The outcome was that he resigned, and the church accepted his resignation. However, the custodian was not without supporters in the church, one of whom was the Bob Summers family. They had been constant critics of the Winchester family and now they focused on me. Bob and his wife Loraine made a point of not speaking to me or JoAnn. Bob was well known for his temper tantrums. He appeared to stay just a small step away from exploding in a fit of temper most of the time. I did my best to ignore his antics. On this occasion, he followed me out of the building, across the parking lot, and into the driveway of my home. He asked several questions and was not satisfied with my answers. Joe Morris happened to be standing next to me. When Bob persisted with his questions and allegations that I was not telling the truth, Joe spoke up and said, "Bob, you have called the preacher a liar several times in this conversation. It is time that you apologized, shut up, or both." Bob put his head down and left. He was never friendly to me after that, but he never confronted me that way again.

At this point in my ministry at Lone Oak, I had led the church through many significant changes. The Sunday School had been graded by age groups that matched the church literature we were using. The Sunday School enrollment records were brought up to date and we had begun to use the church envelope system for recording attendance and promoting church offerings. Further, we were using the space in our facilities more effectively and wisely. Three pieces of adjoining property had been purchased with the intention of future expansion of our facilities. The church committees were expanded and reorganized with rotating membership. The church had reorganized the deacon body and had begun the rotation system for their service. Church bylaws and a church constitution had been written and adopted by the church. The church was adopting a yearly church budget and was actively using it. Church business was conducted at the monthly business meeting with the congregation making decisions concerning the work and ministry of the church. During this time, the church had called Bill Fowler as minister of music and education. The music ministry and choir program of the church were flourishing.

The church had wanted these changes when they called me to be their pastor. However, these changes came quickly. It may be that getting the changes implemented quickly was the best decision. If we had gone slower, I believe we would have encountered much more resistance making it more difficult to bring about the changes. However, with this much change taking place so quickly, one could expect some backlash. It came in the form of some grumbling and visible discontent among those who had been the champions of change. To say that this surprised me is an understatement. I was surprised and hurt by some of the negative reactions that took place. But I hunkered down and kept on preaching, visiting, and ministering as best I could hoping that time would resolve the issue.

I spent some time praying about this problem, but I had absolutely no idea how to solve it. I felt that it might be wise to move and serve another church. Little did I realize what God had in store for me. In my wildest dreams, I could have never imagined what the future was about to bestow upon me and this growing congregation. It turned out to be the opportunity of a lifetime, but it did not appear that way when it arrived. Blessings often come disguised as disasters.

Isaac Burkhalter McDonald, Jr.
3 Months March 26, 1932

Isaac at 8 weeks with cousins Billy
Harrell and Mary Hollie Sperry

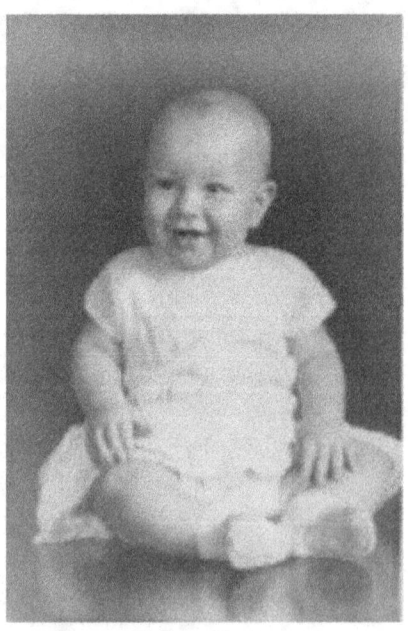

Isaac B. McDonald, Jr.
8 Months

Ike, Jr. (hands on knees) with
cousin Billy Harrell
August 25, 1934

Isaac B. McDonald, Jr.'s
Mother Meldred Young
Hardee 1960

Ike, Jr. and brother Ralph, Jr.
Ages 7 and 9 Months
September 1938

Maternal Grandparents
"Nettie" and William Young
Summer, 1943

W.P. Young, Sr., Meldred
McDonald, Ike, Billy in
background, Summer, 1934

Ike and Mother
Meldred Young
McDonald

Ike McDonald, Sr.
Winter, 1944

Isaac Sr. and Tallmadge
McDonald
Winter-Spring 1943-44

Isaac McDonald, Sr.
Biak Island, New Guinea
Late 1944

Paternal Grandfather,
Robert Lee McDonald,
Sr.

Paternal Grandmother Lilla Woodson McDonald (standing) with twin daughters Lillian and Vivian, grandchildren and son-in-law. Richard Clements

A Journey Remembered

Pastor of Ft. White Baptist Church 1954

Isaac McDonald having baptismal fo Athens Baptist Church at Ichetuckne Springs August 29, 1953

Ordination Photo of Isaac McDonald, age 19

Seminary graduation photograph Isaac B. McDonald 1958

A Journey Remembered

Jo Ann Ensslin
Engagement picture 1956

Jo Ann Ensslin McDonald
1957

Jo Ann McDonald
1976

Jo Ann McDonald
2002

A Journey Remembered

Jo Ann Ensslin McDonald

August 19, 1956

**Burma Sue and Ralph Hardee
(Ike's Brother and Sister-in-law) with Ike.
Summer 1998**

**Isaac McDonald family 1966
(seated) Jo Ann, Philip, Ike; (standing) Bryant, Paul**

Isaac McDonald Family 1971
(L to R) Bryant, Paul, Jo Ann, Philip and Ike

Isaac McDonald Family 2005
Front row: Susan, Emma, Adam, JoAnn
Second row: Philip, Paul, Benjamin, John Tanner, Rachel
Third row: Bryant, Leslie, Isaac

Chapter 11
Paducah: The Later Years

On Sunday, January 30, 1966, I awoke to a ten-below-zero winter morning. The wind was blowing about ten to fifteen miles per hour out of the northwest. At eight a.m. my phone rang. It was Dwayne Boyd, a church member who lived across the street. He asked if I had looked at the church building that morning. I replied that I had glanced over there but had not looked carefully at the building. He said, "There appears to be either some steam or wisps of smoke coming from around the windows on the top floor. The wind quickly takes it away, but it needs to be checked out." I told him that I would step across the parking lot and check the building. I dressed as fast as possible and went to the side door. When I opened it, the heat and smoke nearly knocked me down. The building was on fire, but the fire was contained within the building. I closed the door and quickly ran home to call the fire department.

When I finished calling the fire department, I put on some insulated underwear under my other clothing, got my camera, and went back outside. In a matter of minutes, the firemen were there. Crowds of people began to gather in the parking lot and across the street. Window panes began to break, and the fire began to get fresh air. In a matter of minutes, the fire had broken through the roof of the educational building. The entire building had been framed out of heart pine shipped in from Mississippi, Alabama, and Georgia. The fire apparently had been smoldering most of the night and had used up most of the oxygen in the building. When the windows began to break, it did not take long for the fire to consume the educational building and then the sanctuary. It was a total loss.

With my camera in hand, I began taking photos of everything that was happening. A few days later I realized that my slide photos had documented most of the fire and the efforts of the firemen. I also moved among the people who were standing out in the cold watching the fire. Everyone was in a state of shock. I kept assuring them that though it was bad, it was not the end of the world; God was not going to desert us even if our building burned to the ground. By noon that day, nothing was left of what had been our church buildings but crumbling walls and smoking ruins. Some of the walls had collapsed and others were about to follow them. Safety demanded that we call in a crane to push the remaining walls down so that they would not fall into the street or on those passing by. We saved the corner stones from previous building projects and a time capsule that had been placed behind them.

Having lost our buildings, we needed a place to meet at least on a temporary basis. W. D. Kelley was the assistant superintendent of McCracken County schools and a member of our church. I called him and asked if we could arrange to meet in the gymnasium of the Lone Oak Elementary school that evening. He made the arrangements and we had it announced on both the radio stations and the TV station. Further, we asked the chairmen of our various church committees to have their committee members call as many of our church members as possible. We had a big crowd that night and I assured them that we would be able to rebuild if we stayed close together and close to God. It was the beginning of a great adventure.

In the months before the fire, the church had purchased three houses and lots that joined the church property. After the fire, the church office was set up in one of these houses and the other houses were used for part of our Wednesday children and youth activities. We arranged to rent Lone Oak Elementary School for Wednesday Prayer Service, Sunday School, Church Training, and Sunday worship services. All church literature and office supplies were lost in the fire. We immediately placed orders to replace them. We bought a small travel trailer and installed shelves in it for church literature and supplies that would be needed at the school facilities on Wednesday and Sunday. Sitting on bleachers and in folding chairs for worship in the gymnasium was not comfortable, but our people did it with a minimum of complaining. We used these school facilities for a total of twenty-two months.

When the fire took place, I was entering my fourth year as pastor of Lone Oak Baptist Church. I had become weary of the confrontations and struggles for leadership within the church. I had begun to share with friends and those in a position to assist me that I was ready to move. Bill Fowler, who was serving as our minister of music and education, had shared with me that he was also ready to seek another place of service. Neither of us had received any contact from churches that might be seeking our service. However, after the fire, we both decided that the church had suffered enough loss without losing the established leaders that were there. We made a covenant that neither of us would consider leaving until the building program had been completed. Bill did leave during the first year that we were in the new building. My tenure went four years beyond that time.

The bad news in this story is that the church facilities burned, and it was a total loss. The good news is that we had good insurance coverage. I do not recall the insurance agent's name or the name of the insurance company, but I do remember that our claim was paid and paid quickly. We were insured for replacement value which was about three hundred sixty thousand dollars. Having received that amount from the insurance company, we went to the First National Bank in Paducah, Kentucky. James C. Rickey, the bank president, advised and guided us as we invested the funds we received in U.S. Treasury Bills. This assured us of a good investment return on our funds while we were preparing to build. Later, when we decided to sell church bonds for the remainder of our financing, Mr. Rickey guided us through that process. Finally, when some of the bonds failed to sell near the end of our building program, Mr. Richey provided us with a loan from the bank. We repaid that last loan a short time later when we sold the old church site. It always helps to have a good financial person close by, and James Rickey was that person for the leaders of Lone Oak Baptist Church.

I was disappointed that some of our church family chose not to invest in the church bonds. They were a good investment and they paid a good dividend. I learned during this process that once a church decides to enter into a building program, some of its members will start "an open mouth and a closed pocket book campaign." The bonds were later paid off about four years ahead of time.

Within days after the fire, some of the older members of the church began to talk about the fact that the old church site was an inadequate place for the kind of growth that our church had been enjoying. We simply did not have enough property on which to rebuild and continue to grow. Their suggestion was that we consider looking for another site on which to rebuild. It is interesting that the people taking the lead in this effort were those "owners of the church" who had been in control before I arrived on the scene. The present leaders advised me to stay quiet and see what happened. I followed their advice and the older folk found a site less than a mile from the old location facing US 45 and bordered on the back side by a main county highway. They negotiated for thirteen acres for the price of thirty thousand dollars. When this deal was brought to the church for approval, the decision was unanimous in favor of purchasing the property and relocating the church facilities. It was a great move for the future of our church.

With the vote to purchase a new church site and to rebuild on that new location, a new enthusiasm seemed to fill the hearts of our people. A church building committee was appointed with the understanding that their recommendations would require church approval before we could move on to the next step of the building process. Led by Allen Ross as Chairman, the Building Committee consisted of Ernest Owen, Roy Reynolds, W. D. Kelley, Robert Summers, Bill Fowler, and me. Bill Fowler and I were on the committee because we were church staff, but we had full voting status. The first step for the building committee was to select an architectural firm. We chose Peck Associates of Paducah and received excellent service and cooperation from them.

The next step was developing a written description of what we wanted in the new building. Then straight-line drawings could be produced, and a model of the new building could be made so that the congregation would have a visual idea of how the new building would appear. We did quite a bit of traveling to see new church buildings and to confer with the people involved in building them. I felt that we got the most help from pastor Sidney Maddox, who had recently led First Baptist Church in Hopkinsville during the construction of a new sanctuary and additional educational space.

Later, I arranged for the entire building committee and one of the architects to visit the Church Architecture Department of the Baptist Sunday School Board in Nashville. The Church Architecture Department was on the cutting edge of church building construction for the entire Southern Baptist Convention. I believed they could provide us with valuable guidance as we entered into the rebuilding process. The disappointment we experienced from that visit was overwhelming. Learning that we had chosen not to use traditional Georgian Colonial Architecture in our new building, the leaders in the Church Architecture Department refused to meet with us. When I protested to the leaders that I had brought the entire committee along with our architect to confer with them and stated that using traditional architecture would increase our building costs by at least ten percent, they condescended and sent one of their draftsmen to talk to our committee. After that experience, we decided to develop our plans to meet the needs of our congregation and to forget about getting any help from the Church Architecture Department. Further, we realized that we were on the cutting edge of a new trend in the use of modern architecture for church buildings. What we were in the process of doing was setting a new standard rather that following established tradition. It was exciting.

We met with the leaders of the various organizations of our church to determine what they felt our needs would be for the future. Armed with this information, we asked the architects to begin preparing working plans from which we would be able to obtain bids for the various parts of the building project. We decided to act as our own contractor and to employ an experienced and reliable builder to supervise and direct to the building project. Doing this would provide us with an immediate two percent savings on all purchases of building materials, plus we would not have to pay the five percent sales tax. With the hiring of Bill Harper, a highly reputable building contractor, as the superintendent for the building project, the architects informed us that it would not be necessary for them to inspect the work, thus providing us with additional two percent savings. We estimated later that we had saved between ten and fifteen percent of the building costs simply by acting as our own contractor.

When the building committee began to meet, we decided that once work began on the building only one person would be authorized to give direction to Bill Harper, who was supervising the project. We agreed that when decisions had to be made, we would discuss the issue before us, make the decision, and the chairman, Allen Ross, would share that decision with Bill Harper. We felt this procedure would avoid confusion and conflict. It is interesting that the entire building project was completed without a cross word being spoken or a serious conflict arising. Bill Harper stated that it was the best experience that he ever had in any building project.

When the building was completed, our sanctuary had the largest seating capacity of any church in the area. The seating capacity was fifteen hundred people. We had educational space for nine hundred people, which was about three hundred and fifty more people than we had been averaging in attendance when the fire occurred. We began using the building in December 1967 even though the carpet and pews were not installed in the sanctuary until late spring 1968. Lone Oak High School accepted our invitation to hold the school baccalaureate service in our sanctuary in May 1968. We filled the entire building, which gave me the pleasure of reminding our prominent critics that we were not guilty of overbuilding. They had stated that we would never fill the building, but we did it soon after the building was completed.

Once the carpet and pews had been installed in the sanctuary, we began planning the dedication of the building. The decision was made to have an extended series of dedication services rather than one big day. Our plans were to have one special dedication service each month beginning in June and ending in December. There were at least two reasons for scheduling the dedication services over an extended period of time. First, this would make it possible to have more denominational leaders visit our church and see what we had done, and it would allow our people to see and hear these leaders. Second, there was an economic factor. Extending the dedication festivities over a few months would allow us not to incur one large financial expenditure but to spread the cost over a period of several months. In June, our dedication speaker was Dr. James L. Sullivan of the Baptist Sunday School Board. In July, US Congressman John Buchanan of Alabama, an ordained minister and a seminary classmate, was our speaker. In August, we invited Dr. Baker J. Cauthen of the Baptist Foreign Mission Board to be with us. In September, our guest speaker was Dr. Duke K. McCall, President of The Southern Baptist Theological Seminary. In October, Dr. Arthur Rutledge of the Home Mission Board came to speak. In November, we had Miss Alma Hunt of the Woman's Missionary Union as our guest speaker. This was the first time that a woman had been the guest speaker for a worship service in our church. In December, I brought the Pastor's Dedication Message.

Some have asked why Duke McCall was included as a speaker. It was personal because the two of us became acquainted when I first entered Southern Seminary. He was a leader that I admired, respected, and found approachable. All three of my seminary diplomas were signed by him. He always called me by my first name, even when presenting me my doctoral diploma at graduation. I simply wanted him to see that the seminary had helped me develop leadership skills that made that dedication event possible. Also, I wanted our people to hear this able leader preach. Finally, I wanted Dr. McCall to see and preach in our beautiful new sanctuary.

You may notice that no one from the Kentucky Baptist Convention was invited to our dedication activities. The reason being that we had been ignored as a congregation by the convention leadership when fire destroyed our building. Neither the State Executive-Secretary nor anyone else from our state Baptist organization made any contact with us or made any mention of our loss. Further, no interest was shown from our state Baptist leaders in our efforts to rebuild. That being the case, the choice was made not to involve them in any of our celebration or dedication activities.

However, time has caused me to realize that returning in kind the perceived snubs and indifference of others is not the best or wisest course of action. Success is the best revenge and success needs to be shared even with those who have been less than friendly or supportive. For some reason, Kentucky Baptist leaders had chosen to ignore us at a time when we could have used their good will, support, and encouragement. The better part of wisdom would have been to have invited the State Executive Secretary or the Editor of Western Recorder to be one of the speakers.

Shortly after the completion of the dedication services, we were faced with the need to fill the vacant staff position of minister of music. Allen and Linda Henson were music educators and members of First Baptist Church Paducah. Allen was on the faculty of Paducah Community College and Linda was a faculty member at Reidland High School. Both were able musicians who were familiar with church music ministry. We called them as a team, and they provided excellent leadership for our music ministry. However, they were plagued with family discord and problems in their marriage. They concluded their ministry with the church shortly before I left Lone Oak to serve a church out of state.

The first degree that I earned at Southern Seminary was a Bachelor of Divinity. This was a graduate degree requiring the completion of ninety-seven semester hours of academic studies. I had always felt that the first degree earned at the seminary should be at least a master's degree. The American Association of Theological Schools finally made the decision for its institutions to do exactly that. They suggested a simple degree exchange for those who had earned the Bachelor of Divinity degree. However, Southern Seminary faculty decided to require those holding the Bachelor of Divinity degree to return to the seminary for two months of study which would be offered in July in 1968 and 1969. Once that was completed, the new degree would be conferred.

In a casual conversation with one of my deacons, I shared with him the letter from the seminary announcing the offer for the degree upgrade. To my surprise, he took the letter to the next deacons meeting and shared it with the deacons. The deacons immediately voted to recommend to the church that I be granted the time for the proposed studies and for the church to pay the expense involved. I was totally surprised and gratified by this generous gesture. The church passed this recommendation and I immediately began making plans for this welcome time of study. These July studies, which took place in 1968 and 1969, took me away from the church during the week, but I returned home each weekend for my preaching duties. It was a time of renewal for me which proved to be a blessing both to me and the church.

As the church experienced continued growth in membership during the post-fire years, leaders within the congregation began to see the need for a minister of education. Up to this point of my tenure, I had given direction to the education ministry, but the demands within the church were now suggesting a growing need for this staff position. A search committee was appointed, and I began to work closely with that committee.

The committee focused on Carlos Anderson, who had been a Student Minister at Southwest Baptist College in Bolivar, Missouri. He had reasonably good credentials, but there were several red flags that most of the committee failed to see during the interview process. Carlos managed to obtain good letters of recommendation which we accepted at face value. I learned during this search that one must never to fail to dig deeper when trying to fill a staff position. If there is even a small hint of a problem, always investigate it.

The church called Carlos and he accepted, but it turned out to be a bitter, exasperating experience for me and a source of division within the church. He would not work, and he could not tell the truth. He was passive-aggressive in his relationship with me and any person who had authority. He was highly skilled in knowing how to twist the truth or misrepresent facts to make his case for those who were foolish enough to listen to him. Also, he had no sense of loyalty to those with whom he was supposed to work. He began a campaign of seeking out those who were unhappy with me or other church leadership and currying their favor to his advantage. Never to my knowledge did he develop any sort of educational ministry that would help the church grow. Early in my ministry an older minister had said to me, "It takes a damn good staff member to be better than none." To my sorrow, I was learning this first hand.

When I began sharing these staff problems with church leaders and the Personnel Committee, everyone saw the problem, but no one was willing to take any positive corrective action. My opinion was that there was only one solution to this problem: Carlos must be terminated from his staff position. It was going to be messy, but it had to be done. He was doing much more harm than good. The sad thing about this event was that there were people who believed his stories and were defending him. In their eyes, I was the problem, not Carlos.

This situation was finally resolved in a church business meeting in which I was called upon to explain to those present the full story of the problem from my perspective. Carlos presented his case which was followed by a church vote. The vote to terminate Carlos passed, but all of his supporters turned their hate and invective in my direction. They continued in that frame of mind until the day I left to assume another pastorate.

A sad footnote to this event was that we learned that Carlos had followed a similar pattern of behavior in his previous employment and continued it after he left our church. It is my observation that he was and continues to be an emotionally unstable person who never seemed to get his act together. He did great harm to our church and to my ministry there. We had given him the opportunity to serve as a member of our ministry team; he returned that favor by sowing discord within the congregation, using deception, dishonesty, and disloyalty.

This kind of stress and turmoil takes a toll on a person in many ways. For me it came in the form of physical problems. Most of my frustration and tension found its way to my digestive tract. With the onset of the staff problems, my stomach stayed in a knot until the day that the church dismissed Carlos. But more stress was on the way. Being in the hospital visiting church members, I was always in contact with the medical staff. When I shared some of my physical problems with one of the doctors, he insisted that I make an appointment and see him as soon as possible. When I became his patient, he admitted me to the hospital for a series of medical tests which revealed that I had a hiatal hernia, a spastic colon, and mild depression. He recommended that I resign as pastor of the church and temporarily find another line of work. When I told him that his suggestions were out of the question, he put me on a series of drugs which seemed to help my physical problems and depression. We concluded that my depression was from overwork, sleeping too little, and not getting away from the stress of the pastorate on a regular basis. According to my doctor, my problems were common to ministers. With time and some changes, I did improve.

Since Paducah is located on the Ohio River and both Kentucky Lake and Barkley Lake are nearby, JoAnn and I found that we had ample opportunity to participate in and enjoy summer water sports. I learned to water ski and we often went boating and with members of the church. These outings usually involved the entire day in which we would picnic and cook hamburgers on a selected site along the river or at someone's second home on the lake.

Several people let our family use their homes on the lake. Bob and Dorothy Mae Rogers had a boat and often invited us to spend the day with them and others on the river. Both Otis and Sybil Brittain and Roy and Florence Reynolds did the same. Jack Pressly loaned me a ski boat which I ferried up the Ohio River, through the Kentucky Dam locks, and to a lot on the lake that we later bought. This trip was done by the seat of my pants and without a map. I made the trip and went straight to my destination without missing a turn. It was an adventure.

As our boys enjoyed the water and were learning to be good fishermen, JoAnn and I begin thinking about finding some lake property. We began looking and found a nice site on Malcolm Bay. The owner was said to have built a house that had later burned, but I could never find any evidence of a building or a fire. The property also had a small, flimsy boat dock which was still in good condition. The lot was narrow at the entrance but fanned out into a pie shape toward the water. We had over two acres and three hundred feet of waterfront.

Prior to this, JoAnn's parents had sent us, without explanation, about six thousand dollars in U.S. government bonds. We learned later that they had given her sister and husband a similar amount for down payment on a house where they were living and teaching school in the Cincinnati area. Believing that they should treat each daughter the same, they had sent us the bonds. With the funds we had, we felt we could make payments on the balance of three thousand dollars and the property would soon be ours. At first, several people told us that we were paying too much for the property, but six months later, they were saying that it was a good investment. Along with the purchase of this lake property, we soon found an Apache fold-out travel trailer which slept four. Since Paul was a light sleeper and my snoring allegedly kept him awake, he usually slept in the car. When I later purchased from Otis Brittain a twelve-foot aluminum boat with a small outboard motor and a trailer for transporting it, we were completely in the camping business. We spent many a happy night on the lake, away from the phone and pressures of church work. It was one of the wisest decisions we ever made.

After looking for a better place to tell this story, it seems to fit better here than anywhere else. After moving to Alabama and living there for several months, JoAnn and I discussed the fact that we might never return to Kentucky to live. So, we decided to sell our lake property. I had a friend paint a "for sale" sign with my address and phone number on it. I drove to the property and nailed the sign to a tree. Within a few months, we sold the property for twice the amount that we had paid for it. Then we reinvested the money in a mortgage with a dentist in Birmingham. The dentist was to make monthly payments into an account which belonged to us. We used the proceeds of that money to pay for college expenses for both Paul and Bryant. I believe we even used it for Philip's first year expenses as well. It did not pay for everything, but it did pay for the big items at the first of each semester. It proved to be an excellent investment. This was to be our first investment in real estate. but it would not be our last. We learned from this and other experiences that wise real estate investments would be most helpful to us as we made our way through life. As it has turned out, we have never lost money on real estate. We always turned a profit.

I was now into my eighth year as pastor of Lone Oak Baptist Church. The church was experiencing some inertia resulting from the effort made to relocate and rebuild its facilities. However, we were still experiencing excellent growth. I began to concentrate on preaching, evangelistic and pastoral visitation, and leading the church in trying to improve its ministry in any way possible.

Further, we were actively trying to find a buyer for our old church site. The real estate community in Paducah had told us that there was no market for our property. They insisted that everything was moving to the Reidland area. However, I had seen the official proposed corridor for Interstate 24 which was to pass through the area. The proposed interstate highway was an east/west corridor located about halfway between Paducah and the Lone Oak community. Further, U.S. 45, the main route south from Paducah to Mayfield, was in the process of being expanded to a four-lane highway. The new site location of Lone Oak Baptist Church faced U.S. 45 on the south side of the present Lone Oak community. This clearly meant that Lone Oak would experience growth beyond normal expectations. With this knowledge in mind, I kept promoting the property as an excellent opportunity for a wise investor. I began negotiating for and nearly completed the sale of the property before I left to serve another church. On leaving, I turned the negotiations over to Ned Buchanan, a deacon who was also a banker. He completed the sale in about six weeks. The property sold for two and one-half times more than what the real estate people said it would bring. This sale put the payoff on the church debt about four years ahead of schedule and was a huge positive lift financially and emotionally for the church.

During my entire ministry, I have been involved in only three or four revivals that I felt were truly led and blessed by the Holy Spirit. One of those revivals took place during my last months at Lone Oak. Our church was blessed with a group of young people, all in their early teens, who were as bright and energetic as I have ever seen. They were involved in all the church activities but had been slow to make any commitment to Christ or the church. During this revival, we conducted a special evangelistic service during Sunday School hour. Over thirty of those young people made a profession of faith in Christ during that service.

Once we moved into our new church buildings, I began to study the records of our church growth during the time I served as pastor. We averaged losing about fifty members each year either by death or transfer of membership. This meant that we had to enlist fifty new members each year or we would face a negative growth factor. During the two years that we met in the school, we averaged sixty-two additions to our church each year. After we entered our new buildings, our church membership began to experience rapid growth. If my records are correct, we led the West Union Baptist Association in baptisms the last two years I served as pastor. Further, we were in the top five churches in baptisms for several years. This was no small achievement in the face of some of the criticism I was receiving.

In spite of positive events taking place in our church and the growth we were experiencing, we did face some discontent. Some kept insisting that the church increase its contributions to missions. Our church suffered from the influence of the past that had emphasized missions as being something away from one's local church ministry. Since we had been forced to build by the circumstance of the fire and since our contributions had not grown significantly, we were sending less to Baptist mission programs than we had previously. Those who were unhappy with this had significantly reduced their giving and had encouraged others to do the same, which put the church in a financial bind.

Despite our growth, I was facing increasing opposition to my leadership as pastor of the church. People found fault with my every move and decision. I continued working hard while keeping a low profile. I did my best to let the church committees do their work with as little input from me as possible. I realized then and more so now that the life and ministry of the church was moving forward so fast that many were reacting to the fast pace in which change was taking place. But being a strong leader made me an easy target for those who found fault with my leadership style, even though it had brought the church to where it was at that time. I deeply felt that the church needed to see a new face in the pulpit and to hear a new voice challenging them to serve their Lord.

I faced these circumstances with mixed feelings. I loved the church and would have been content to remain as their pastor for the rest of my life, but I had collected a large amount of baggage while leading them the last eight years. Churches often need and want change, but they do not always appreciate those who help those changes take place. My critics were highly vocal while those who supported me seemed to have lost their voice. Financially, the church had never provided me with the support that I needed to care for my family. My wife was making more money teaching at Draughns Business College than I was making as pastor of the church. Since the church was still trying to get its finances on a more solid footing, I had little hope of getting any increase in salary. Some of my supporters within the church kept telling me to create a lower profile and hope that the opposition would wear itself out, but I did not think that was going to happen. Finding another church that I could serve as pastor seemed to be the only solution to the problems that I faced at Lone Oak Baptist Church.

Contacts from other churches began to come my way. The one that materialized into a call came from Ruhama Baptist Church in Birmingham, Alabama. It was a much larger church located in the suburbs of this large, Southern city. It was going to be an entirely different experience for me and my family. We looked forward to that experience with eager anticipation, but the pain of parting from our friends in Paducah was greater than we anticipated. They gave us a nice reception and presented us with a set of Gorham sterling silver candlesticks. It had been an eventful eight years and the most productive years of my ministry in terms of a variety of accomplishments. Some of the best and lasting friendships of my life were made while we served in Paducah. Adjusting to a new place of service would not be easy, but that was the step that we had now chosen to take. It was going to be another adventure.

Chapter 12

The Early Alabama Years

In early summer of 1971, I learned that the Ruhama Baptist Church in Birmingham, Alabama, was without a pastor. During the two previous summers while updating my degree at Southern Seminary, I had become acquainted with Norman "John" McCrummen, Pastor of Woodlawn Baptist Church in Birmingham. He was a personable individual with whom I had played tennis when our seminary classes were over each day. We had formed a good friendship which lasted until his death.

I called John and asked him to share with me what he knew about Ruhama Baptist Church. He asked for some of my biographical information during that phone conversation and told me that he would get back to me. In a few days he called back and told me that he had been in touch with Reeves Sims, Chairman of the Pulpit Committee from Ruhama, and that he believed that I would be hearing from Mr. Sims shortly. He went to great length to assure me that these were good people and that I would be impressed with them. He was right. Reeves Sims called me, and we had a most pleasant phone conversation. He asked if it would be acceptable for two members of the committee to visit with me in the near future. I replied that it would, and he assured me that they would call before they came so that time could be arranged for a brief visit with them.

In about two weeks, Bob McClain and Malcolm Pledger visited Lone Oak on a Sunday morning. Bob had called during the week to be sure that their visit would not conflict with any other plans that I might have for that weekend. They visited on a Sunday morning and we went out to eat after the service. I do not recall any of the details of that visit except that it seemed to go quite well. I was impressed with the professional way in which the members of this committee were conducting themselves. We agreed that we would talk further to work out a visit of the remaining members of the committee and for us to visit Birmingham.

In the meantime, JoAnn and I attended the Southern Baptist Convention where I saw one of my seminary classmates, Hilton Olive, talking with George Bagley, the Executive-Secretary of the Alabama Baptist Convention. I knew Hilton was from Alabama, that he wanted to move, and that Ruhama had his resume. Knowing how church politics work, I assumed that with his

Alabama connections, he would probably get the nod from the Ruhama committee. But that was not to be. When I returned to Paducah, Reeves Sims called me telling me that I was their top candidate and that as soon as conflicts resulting from summer vacations could be worked out, the rest of the committee would be paying us a visit. I assured him that we were looking forward to meeting them.

Both Bob McClain and Malcolm Pledger stayed in contact with me during this time. Bob was in sales as a stock broker with a large investment firm in Birmingham and Malcolm was an engineer who was in sales with a large firm that built steel tanks mainly for fuel trucks. They kept assuring me that I was their top candidate and encouraged me not to get impatient with the rest of the committee. The remaining members of the committee would visit with us as soon as summer vacations were over. I told them to take their time because we did not want to get in such a hurry that we failed to be responsive to God's leadership.

In late June or early July, the remaining members of the committee visited our church. We met with them briefly on Saturday evening and they attended our worship service the next morning. Following that our family visited Birmingham and I preached the traditional trial sermon. It seems that two visits were made, a preliminary visit to look things over and then the more formal visit with the congregation. The outcome of these visits was that the church issued a nearly unanimous call and we accepted, agreeing to begin my ministry as pastor of the church on September 1, 1971.

Ruhama Baptist Church was the oldest Baptist church in Birmingham, founded early in 1819, shortly before Alabama became a state. The membership was keenly aware of this fact and quite proud of the history of the church. A history of the church had been written and published in 1969 as part of the sesquicentennial celebration of the church. Two members of the church, Fanna K. Bee and Lee N. Allen, shared in the authorship of the history.

I was just a few months short of my fortieth birthday when I accepted the call from Ruhama. I had been in the ministry over twenty years and had learned that pulpit committees always present their church in the best light possible. They seek to conceal anything that is negative. I tried to ask all the right questions, interviewing a number of people, mostly ministers, who were not associated with the church in any way. I regret that I did not talk with any of the previous pastors, though I am not certain they would have been honest with me. The pastor immediately before me was Roland L. Jarrard. He had been arrested for shoplifting on New Year's Eve, 1970, and consequently resigned and left the church. I have never met him, but because I followed him as pastor of Ruhama, I feel that I know him quite well. He was a gifted and able man but a person with numerous conflicts and problems. His ministry was brought to a virtual end as a result of his being unable to resolve these issues in a positive way. Following his departure from Ruhama, he and his wife divorced.

However, it was obvious to me that I was going to have to clean up a mess and reestablish some respect for the office of pastor. In trying to get a clear picture of the church and its needs before I accepted its call, I talked with Arthur Walker, vice president of Samford University, who had served as interim pastor of the church; Dotson Nelson, Pastor at Mountain Brook; and Oley Kidd, Director of Missions for the Birmingham Baptist Association. While these men were as truthful as they knew how to be, none of them had the inside information that I sought and needed. I do not think anyone could have told me the true story except some of the men who had served the church. I still wonder if any of them would have told me the truth since it would have involved making extremely negative statements. Pastors have a way of trying to be positive once they are no longer serving a church. Further, it involves some risk if a person chooses to tell the unvarnished truth to a person that he does not know well. Telling the truth often makes one vulnerable to those that have little appreciation for the truth.

There is another factor that comes into play when a prospective pastor is evaluating a church where he has an opportunity to serve. It is the ego factor that says, "These other men failed to succeed or enjoyed limited success because they were not as able as I am. I would not have made the mistakes that they made. I am a more capable leader than they were in this situation. I can do what they failed to do because I have leadership gifts that they did not possess. I can get this job done." While there may be more than a small amount of truth in these assumptions, they can give a prospective pastor false hope and assurance that success will not elude him as he seeks to lead a congregation. A church that is not moved to follow pastoral leadership will find a way to avoid doing so. It is just that simple. And the power brokers in Ruhama Baptist Church had no intention of following the leadership of any pastor. Those who were in positions of power and leadership had little or no trust in or respect for pastors.

Several people did finally tell me some of the truth about the church, but it came only after I had accepted the church and was in the midst of the struggle to establish myself as pastor and leader. Bill Longshore was an attorney and Dr. Joe Bancroft was my personal physician. They were deacons who had joined the church while Roland Jarrard was pastor. And both shared with me their insights into some of the leadership problems telling me that Ruhama was going to be a most difficult church to serve. They spoke the truth.

I had just accepted the church and was still in my last days at Lone Oak when the first indication of problems at Ruhama took place. Joe Blass was the incoming chairman of deacons at Ruhama. He called one morning wanting to discuss the deacons retreat that would take place the first week I was in Alabama. He had the entire program worked out and shared with me in detail exactly what he expected me to do at the retreat. I got the impression that he saw himself as being my supervisor. I was not long in discovering that my first impression was right. He was mean-spirited and overbearing. Before his term as deacon chairman was over, I was refusing to take phone calls from him because he was so abusive in those conversations. An adversarial relationship developed between the two of us that was never bridged. He later suffered a serious heart attack that left him with a large amount of heart damage. His wife came to me during the last year I was there and asked me to try to work out some sort of reconciliation with him. She stated that she could not bear the thought of him dying without our working out our differences. I did set up a lunch meeting with him. He was obviously extremely uncomfortable during this this meeting. In fact, in that meeting, he never once looked me in the eye. I approached the matter of reconciliation directly, but never could get any kind of commitment from him. I told him that I did not want to leave it that way, but it would take both of us working at it if we were to have an agreeable relationship. He said I was right, but he was not sure we could do it. We shook hands and parted, but we parted more as adversaries than as Christian brothers.

I began receiving anonymous, poison-pin hate mail from Birmingham before I left Paducah. It was obvious by their wording and form that the letters came from an educated person. All the letters were type written, with fictitious return addresses, but there was never a signature. There were weeks in which I received as many as three or four such letters. They were all filled with hateful, venomous personal attacks that were designed to hit one below the belt emotionally. I finally concluded that they were coming from Cass Johnson, a prominent leader and deacon in the church. Many in the church leadership knew about these letters and personal attacks, but because this man was a lifelong member of the church, was involved in many ways, and contributed to various causes, no one would confront him about this abhorrent behavior. He never ceased these activities and even wrote me after I left the church. I tried to get church leaders to confront him about this sick, unchristian activity, but no one would. One person told me that they would not believe he was the guilty party even if he confessed being guilty. I was later told by a deacon that he and another deacon had confronted the writer after my departure and told him that if he persisted in that kind of activity in the future they would expose him. I never learned if any changes were made. More will be said later about this man's unchristian activities. I remain keenly disappointed in those two deacons and other church leaders that they did not take a strong a stand while I was still pastor of the church.

I received so much hate mail that I became able to detect a poison pen letter and identify it as such before it was ever opened. In dealing with this issue, I would ask my secretary to open a suspected letter to see if it had a signature. If it did not, we destroyed the letter without reading it. I did take some of the letters to postal authorities to see if any legal action was possible but was told that unless the letters contained threats or suggestions of violence there was little that could be done.

When we arrived in Alabama, I was aware that the culture of the deep South was quite different from what we had known in Kentucky. There were many more black people and the old prejudices were still alive. My wife and children were not used to hearing the "N" word used in reference to black people. We had taught our children not to use that word in reference to blacks under any circumstances. For the first time, our children were to have black teachers in the schools that they attended. Philip's second grade teacher was a black lady from south Alabama. Her accent was such that it took him most of the first semester to understand what she was saying. Bryant had a black teacher also. During the first week of school in 1971, there was a race riot at Banks High School because the black students resented a rendition of "Dixie" which was used as the school fight song along with the waving of a Confederate battle flag in a school pep rally. Paul managed to get to a phone and call his mother to come get him. There were racial tensions at Banks High School the entire time we were in Alabama.

We encountered the realities of reverse discrimination early in our Alabama experience. When JoAnn applied for a job in the public school system, she was told that they would be happy to employ her but could not because she was not black. This incident was repeated each year we were in Birmingham.

Earlier, in order to avoid busing, the Birmingham public school system had agreed to integrate its faculties on a 52:48 percent ratio. Each teacher's credentials were accepted without regard to the quality of their training. There were some very able and well-trained black teachers, but there were others with inadequate training who were not classroom ready. JoAnn's credentials from the University of Kentucky were not the issue. His skin color was the issue. She could have taught in one of the private Christian academies, but we believed in the public school system. Further, the private schools paid about one third less than the public schools with no retirement of medical benefits. JoAnn chose to work on her master's degree at Samford University, which she completed shortly after we returned to Kentucky.

As soon as I began work as pastor of Ruhama on September 1, 1971, I encountered resistance to my efforts toward pastoral leadership. It was my policy to meet with the various committees, not to tell them what to do, but to be acquainted with what was happening and to give any counsel that might be needed. When I inquired about the Nominating Committee and the Budget Committee, the Deacon Chairman told me that they had completed their work. Later, I learned that the committees were still meeting and working. It soon became obvious to me that pastoral leadership was the last thing some of the church leaders wanted or intended to accept.

There was hardly a week that went by that I did not learn something that revealed deception on the part of church leaders and their efforts to keep me out of the loop in terms of knowing what was happening in the life of the church. Several people commented to me during this time that I did not appear to be at ease or to feel comfortable with my role in the church. They were right, I was totally uncomfortable with the way things were. Every day I was learning that I had been deceived, lied to, or totally misinformed. It was an unnerving experience in which I was blindsided several times with facts and information which was in total conflict with what I had been led to believe. I became so unsure of who might be trustworthy that I soon trusted no one.

I decided that I would try to do what I could and stay out of conflict with the control group as much as possible. I tried to excel in the pulpit, but my critics constantly found fault with my preaching. Joe Blass even called demanding that I use a different version of the Bible when I preached. I was very careful to do all the pastoral and evangelistic visitation that I could do. I worked as closely with the church staff as possible. We had a minister of music, a children's minister, a youth minister, a church hostess, a building maintenance supervisor who directed the work of several black maids and janitors, an educational secretary, a financial secretary, a personal secretary for the minister of music and Pastor and a church receptionist. In all, we had a total of twenty-one full and part time employees. I found it was a monumental task just to keep the employees happy and pointed in the same direction. The saying of my older preacher friend proved to be true once again: "It takes a damn good staff member to be better than none."

Since all of the church organizations were in need of attention and direction, I began trying to do what I could to improve them and increase the outreach of our church. Sunday School was our largest organization, so I gave it the lion's share of attention. No matter what we did, our attendance and enrollment continued to decline. Church Training was always in need of help, but the Woman's Missionary Union and other mission organizations seemed to fare best. It was about this time that the church called Earl "Bo" Wascom to serve as Minister of Education. He served in that position for about three years and had a good ministry. However, the opposition group continually worked on him in their efforts to discredit me. Later, he left to work in the Sunday School Department of the Alabama Baptist Convention.

Our Minister of Music was John Atherton. John had served with Roland Jarrard when he was pastor at First Baptist Church, Selma, Alabama. An able church musician, John was from the Chicago area and strongly influenced by the pietistic Wheaton College philosophy. He had acted as senior minister of the church during the interim and was emotionally drained from the experience. He was also working on his master's degree in music at Samford University. The church had given him permission to pursue those studies. John had been trained in the classical tradition and instilled that in both the choir and the congregation. He was familiar with most of the problems at Ruhama, but he was unable to find a positive resolution to these problems. He had gathered his own group of supporters in the church and thus insulated himself from much of the power struggle. He was unhappy to the point that he would welcome any chance to move. Reeves Sims spoke to me about John, saying, "John is a 'do gooder' and a 'soul searcher," he is never sure of himself and he has doubts about everyone else. Sometimes folks like John can do you more harm than good without intentionally meaning to." I always thought that was a good description of John. I liked him, recognized his creativity, and appreciated his musical ability, but I never knew for certain where he stood.

After I had been at Ruhama for a year, a new church budget was passed. Elaine Manning, the church Financial Secretary, came to me and asked what she was to do about a small increase in the pastor's Automobile Allowance. Was she to increase the amount I was receiving? I told her that in all the churches that I had served, when the church passed the budget, that authorized the expenditure of the funds, and unless Ruhama followed a different procedure, my automobile allowance had been increased. Without further discussion, she increased the amount allocated each month for that purpose.

Four months into the new budget, the Church Personnel Committee scheduled a meeting with me but would not tell me their agenda. Arriving at that meeting, I was informed that the increase in my automobile allowance was the subject of the meeting. Joe Blass spoke for the committee which included Cass Johnson, Marvin Jones, and one other person whose identity I cannot recall. Joe informed me that I had absolutely no right to authorize Mrs. Manning to increase what I received for that purpose. I was accused of "giving myself a raise" and of misappropriating church funds. My position was that the church had given me the increase. They contended that only the Personnel Committee could do that. The meeting became contentious. I have never before or after been subjected to such harsh and hostile treatment. The harshest words ever directed at me came in that meeting. Since my previous secretary had resigned, JoAnn had been serving temporarily as my secretary. The group began to find fault with her service. I told them that I had listened to all that I intended to hear, that I would not tolerate another word about my wife's service as my secretary, and that I would refund the three hundred dollars to which they said I was not entitled. They replied that they did not want me to repay what I had received, but under no conditions was I to continue to receive the increased amount. Something was said about my tenure as their pastor. I told them that I really was not enjoying serving them and that if I had another place in which to serve, I would be on my way to that place without delay. But I told them that I would be there until I had opportunity to serve elsewhere. It was a tense and unnecessary confrontation.

I left the meeting abruptly and went home. When I shared with JoAnn what had happened, we decided that I would write a check to the church for three hundred dollars and mark it as a refund for overpayment on my automobile allowance. The next morning, I waited until the banks were open, went to Elaine Manning's office, and told her to get a deposit slip and accompany me to the bank. She began to apologize for what had happened and for not making me aware of the problem. She told me that the Personnel Committee had told her she would be fired if she warned me of their impending action. I said little to her, but we went to the bank, I gave her the check and she made the deposit. She kept apologizing, but I told her that the trouble was not of her making. She had the misfortune of being caught in the middle of a situation that should have never happened. She explained that what had happened was not right, but that she was powerless to do anything about it, which was true.

On the following Wednesday evening, Joe Blass met me in the hall as I was making my way to the Fellowship Supper and Prayer Meeting that followed the meal. He appeared to be nervous and ill at ease. He was unable to look me in the eye. He told me that the Personnel Committee had not intended for me to refund the so-called "excess" automobile allowance which I had received. I told him if I was not entitled to it, I did not want a penny of it. I also told him that there was no reason for the Personnel Committee to treat me as they did in regard to this matter. He asked me if I would reconsider my refund and withdraw it. I said that under the conditions they had laid out I would not. That ended the matter.

As I write this account of events at Ruhama, I do not wish to give the impression that all was conflict, pain, and unhappiness. There were many good people in the church. Most of them were totally unaware of the power struggle that was happening between lay leaders and the pastor. The church did have a history of not being kind to its pastors, but most of the people were kind and respectful. They were an older congregation. Their community had changed, and they were bewildered by the changes that were going on all around them.

Howard College had been the co-educational Baptist college in Alabama. For years, the church and college had adjoining campuses. However, Howard College had moved across town to a new campus and had changed its name to Samford University. With this move, both the faculty and students were no longer a major presence in the congregation. Corridors for two interstate highways that were to pass through the middle of the community had been purchased. The people whose homes had been located in those corridors had sold their homes, moved out of the community, and joined other churches. The church was visibly in decline. Few new people were moving into the community. New congregations had been started near the borders of the old Ruhama community and there was strong competition for new people as they moved into the area. Additionally, conflict in a church is hard to conceal. People sense it, feel it, smell it, or see it, and few want to join a church where they sense ongoing conflict or the possibility of conflict developing. Then, there was the race issue. The black community was slowly but surely moving out of the inner city to the suburbs toward Ruhama's community. All of these facts served to fill many in the congregation with anxiety, fear, and uncertainty.

I have already mentioned that Ruhama was an older congregation. That being true, dealing with death and grief became a constant part of my ministry. Some pastors boast about baptizing one hundred people each year. Previously, in my last Kentucky pastorate, I averaged more than fifty baptisms a year. But at Ruhama, I was conducting nearly one hundred funerals every year. During the first twelve days of 1972, I conducted fourteen funerals. Hardly a week went by that I was free from ministering to a family as the result of a death.

One constant source and encouragement for me was Reeves Sims. He was always a person that I could speak to freely without fear of the confidence being broken. He never misinformed me or led me in the wrong direction. I have always thought he understood what was going on but really did not want to get involved in a leadership fight. He took the Deacon Chairmanship following Joe Blass's term just to give me some time for less conflict as I was trying to establish myself as the leader of the church. I believe he felt that my tenure would be brief and so he tried to suppress as much strife as possible. Malcolm Pledger, another deacon and a former member of the pulpit committee, was a reliable confidant. He had influence with a group within the deacons who wanted the church to move forward without conflict. However, the group who wanted to remain in power had no intention of allowing anything to happen that they did not control. Had they not been so mean spirited and calloused in dealing with me, we might have been able to work together. Their methods involved intimidation and threats, which I resisted. They were wrong in what they were doing, and I had no intention of letting them dominate me. It was a no-win situation for everyone involved.

In the midst of all this turmoil and conflict, Danny Newman, also a deacon, came to my house and asked me to tell him what was happening. Danny lived about one block from me. He was a no-nonsense, plain-speaking person and I was reluctant to talk to him, but he insisted that we talk. I had been working in the yard when he arrived. I stopped work, took him in the house, and told him the story. I also told him that if he betrayed my confidence, I would never talk to him again. To this day, he remained a true friend and stood with me through all the difficult days that followed.

I had been involved in the leadership of the Kentucky Baptist Convention before moving to Alabama, but I never broke into the leadership circle in Alabama. I was not from Alabama. The native Alabamians were friendly but entrenched. Very few people are willing to move over or invite an outsider into the circle of leadership. I became acquainted with most of the leading pastors in Alabama because of Ruhama's history and received some acceptance, but I never had an opportunity to serve in the state convention in any way.

However, I did become involved the in the community life of Birmingham. Since there was no elementary school basketball program through the city school system, the YMCA had developed an excellent basketball league for the elementary schools. Our middle son, Bryant, lived from one ball season to the next, and I faithfully attended his games. His coach was out of town part of each week, so I volunteered to meet with the boys and assist with practice when he was absent. Early in the season, the coach informed me that his job was changing, and he must give up coaching the team. He asked me to fill his place which I agreed to do. I had not played basketball, but having lived in Kentucky, I had become an ardent fan. There were some things that I could teach the boys, but the rest was up to them. I focused on fundamentals such as shooting, passing, dribbling, and handling the ball. We won about half of our games.

When Bryant left the eighth grade to enter high school, Philip was in the fourth grade. I was recruited to coach the fourth, fifth and sixth grade boys in basketball. Unless I had a funeral or some other ministry conflict, my time was such that I could meet the boys as soon as school was out and practice for an hour and a half each weekday except Wednesday. We played our games on Saturday. None of the boys on this team had ever played basketball. I had to teach them the fundamentals before we could even have an organized scrimmage. I conferred with my brother-in-law, Ralph Rush, a former high school basketball coach, and the coaches at the local high school. They guided me in developing a program in which the boys learned the fundamentals of passing, dribbling, and shooting and a few plays which we occasionally managed to use with some success. No one ever questioned or challenged me about the time I spent coaching the basketball team. I think this was because I never allowed coaching the team to conflict with my pastoral duties.

It is unlikely that any in the church even knew that I was working with this boys basketball team. The highlight of my coaching came when Philip was in the sixth grade. We were playing the team that was favored to go to the YMCA State Tournament. Their coach was their elementary school principal who was a former high school coach. His twin sons were the guards on their team. They were leading us 17 to 0 at halftime. During the break, I told the boys that we were better than we were playing. We had one tall boy and I instructed the guards to take the ball inside and pass off to our big man if they did not have a shot themselves. They did exactly that and we began to score. At the end of the third quarter we were still down 19 to 11. In the last quarter we scored 8 points and our opponents scored 2 allowing them to win 21 to 19. If we had played one more minute, we would have won the game. The opposing coach was white as a sheet when he came across the court to shake my hand. It had been a good season.

Having completed my first two years at Ruhama, we seemed to enter a period of peace and quiet. I attribute much of this calm to the service of Reeves Sims who had come in following the stormy first year and acted as a buffer while serving as Deacon Chairman. I continued working with the organizations within the church to strengthen and build up their ministries. We had two fairly good revivals and did not seem to have any problems developing and passing our budget. Though the cost of living continued to rise, nothing was said or done in regard to my receiving a raise in salary. Other staff received a raise, but nothing was done for me. I kept thinking someone would notice and question this, but no one did. After the Automobile Allowance incident, I was not inclined to inquire about a raise. This pattern continued my entire time at Ruhama. The peace and quiet that we were experiencing was not going to last, but I enjoyed it while it was happening. Later, I realized that it was the quiet before the storm.

Chapter 13

The Later Alabama Years

With two years of service behind me, I began to see more clearly how things were developing at Ruhama. The group that seemed to hold the power was not happy that I was there. They appeared to be determined to make life as miserable as possible so that I would leave. I began to talk with those in my circle of friends and with Willis Bennett at Southern Seminary who was in a position to help me get placed elsewhere. They all encouraged me to hold on until a new opportunity came along. I was determined to do that, but each day it became more of a struggle.

As I indicated earlier, I was diligent in hospital, pastoral, and evangelistic visitation. I tried to build a strong visitation program but had only meager cooperation and success. However, the visitation that was done bore fruit. Even though large numbers of people were not joining the church, there was some response at nearly every service. When new converts came into the church, they were baptized almost immediately. This practice put me in conflict with the House Committee which arranged the preparation for baptismal services. My policy was to baptize new converts on Sunday morning at the beginning of the worship service. Jamie Gates, Chairman of the House Committee, was constantly insisting that I wait to baptize until we had a large group of candidates. His alleged concern was the cost of the water used for filling the baptismal pool. He never could see the value of the Sunday morning crowd witnessing new people coming into the church or that the baptismal service itself was a powerful proclamation of the gospel message.

Five of my deacons did a great deal to befriend and faithfully support me in my effort to lead the church. These men were Danny Newman, Malcolm Pledger, L. T. "Pop" Reed, Carl Calvert, and Reeves Sims. Carl was my visitation partner. He saw the activity of the power group and advised me to ignore them as much as possible. Pop Reed and his wife, Lucy, were very close to our family. Pop worked for the large Buick dealer in Birmingham and arranged for me to get a good deal on the first Buick LeSabre I bought. He and Lucy were generous and gracious to me and my family. Reeves was a realist and understood the inner workings of the church. When I needed someone with whom I could talk, he was always available. In fact, I had that kind of relationship with all of these men. I was very close to Danny and Malcolm. Danny was a long-term member of the church, while Malcolm and his family had only been in the church for about ten years. Both men were spiritually mature and were not inclined to ignore the problems that existed in the church. They participated in visitation with me, prayed with me and for me, and were a source of strength when the stress became almost unbearable. I played golf with these men and went to high school and college ball games with them. To this day, I am in touch with both of them.

In the spring of 1972, I was approached by Ray Hurlbert, a well-known Alabama educator, about the possibility of being a member of a new Rotary Club that was being organized in East Lake area of Birmingham by the Downtown Rotary Club of Birmingham. I was interested because John McCrummen had encouraged me to consider becoming a Rotarian. He said it amazed him how many doors it opened to him for ministry. Further, it gave him an opportunity to serve his community apart from his ministry through the church. Rotary is a service group which has an international outreach. The outcome of my conversation with Ray Hurlbert was that Birmingham East Rotary Club was organized and I became the Charter President of the club. I was honored at being chosen to lead the club and delighted with the additional opportunities for service that came my way because of my Rotary affiliation. Becoming a Rotarian in 1972 began a relationship with this service organization that has continued to this day and I hope will continue as long as I live.

One of the benefits of being Charter President of Birmingham East Rotary Club came near the end of my service as President. In 1972-73, Roy Hickman, a businessman from Birmingham was serving as President of Rotary International. Leslie Wright, President of Samford University, was serving as District Governor of Rotary District 681. The annual meeting of Rotary International was scheduled to be in Lausanne, Switzerland, in the middle of May 1973. Leslie Wright decided that we should try to take as many members from our district as possible and be in attendance as Roy Hickman presided over the meetings. Our Rotary District chartered a DC-9 and took about 240 people from our various Rotary Clubs. One of my deacons, Tom McCain, was a member of the club where I was serving as president. He offered to pay the full expense for JoAnn and me to attend the convention if we wanted to make the trip. It was an incredibly generous gift which we accepted with enthusiasm.

On our way to Switzerland, we flew first from Birmingham to Philadelphia, and from there we had a direct flight to Geneva. Traveling at night, we were approaching the French coastline just as the sun was rising the next morning.

It was a clear day and we arrived in Geneva before noon. Tom McCain had arranged for us to stay in a luxury hotel in Montreux, which was about fifteen miles from Lausanne on Lake Leman as the Swiss know it and Lake Geneva as the French know it. We traveled daily to and from Lausanne by train and enjoyed seeing the Swiss scenery. We went back to Geneva for a day of touring in the old city. We visited John Calvin's church and toured the park that is a memorial to those who fought for Swiss independence and participated in the Protestant Reformation.

When the Rotary Convention concluded, we divided into three different groups for tours of Switzerland, France, West Germany, the Netherlands, and England. These groups later reunited in England where we boarded our charter flight to return home.

As our group continued the remainder of our tour, we met in Lausanne and traveled north by bus to Basel where we crossed the Rhine and entered West Germany. This was the Wurttemberg section of Germany which contains the Black Forest. Upon leaving Switzerland and entering Germany, JoAnn noticed that the rural people had arranged their homes, outbuildings and gardens much as her father had done in London, Kentucky. We learned later that her grandfather had grown up in a small town in Wurttemberg. When he came to the United States in the 1880s, he brought those customs with him. His son, Paul Ensslin, was JoAnn's father; Paul had arranged his home, outbuildings, and garden area just as he had seen his father do when he was a boy. We realized that we must be in the area where JoAnn's grandfather had lived earlier. Unfortunately, we were unable to stop and visit. Passing through was all that we could do at the time.

We traveled by highway to Mannheim and visited Heidelburg before going on to Mainz where we boarded a small ship for a cruise down the Rhine to Koblenz. The trip down the Rhine took place on a beautiful warm day. We could stand on the deck of the boat and see the castles and vineyards that were on both sides of the river. We learned later that when the Romans had controlled much of this part of Germany, they had brought many of the grape vines to the area and taught the Germans the fine art of growing the grapes and making the wine. It was a beautiful area to visit. It was my hope that we would be able to return some day, but that does not appear to be something that we will now be able to do.

We went from Koblenz by bus to Dusseldorf where we spent the night. The next day being Sunday, I conducted a small worship service in our room for those of the group who chose to attend. I spent part of the night writing the message which was based on Matthew 7:24-27. I still have the notes of this message, written in longhand, which I delivered to a group of about twenty who came for that time of worship. Then our bus took us to Cologne where we spent most of the morning at the site of the famous cathedral which had been slightly damaged during World War II and was still secure and in use.

Before leaving Germany and entering Belgium, we ate lunch in the ancient city of Aachen which had been Charlemagne's capital when he was King of the Franks and later Emperor of the Holy Roman Empire. There was an abundance of history to be absorbed from a visit in Aachen, but for some reason no stop for that purpose had been scheduled. I would love to return and tour the city.

Departing Aachen, we crossed the border into Belgium and came to the city of Liege which is where part of the World War II Battle of the Bulge took place. There is a large American military cemetery there. Our tour bus made a stop at the cemetery and several of the older men got out and began to walk among the graves of men with whom they had served during World War II. These men were survivors of the Battle of the Bulge. One of the men kept saying in my presence, "Look at all the graves of the young men who died in this battle." He repeated that several times. Soon I noticed that some of the men walking among the graves were being overcome with emotion and some began to weep openly. Several of us went to those who seemed to be weeping almost beyond control and began to assist them as gently as possible on their way back to the bus. When our tour bus departed that scene, hardly a word was spoken by anyone in our group for nearly an hour.

We did not enjoy Belgium. Brussels was a dirty city that was filled with immigrants from North Africa. The Watergate scandal had just been given full exposure in the U.S. and the immigrants took it upon themselves to remind us of that as they passed us on the street. They were aggressively hostile and rude as we worked our way through the crowds wherever we went. I did not enjoy the hotels, the food, the sights, or anything about Belgium. The best part of being in Belgium came when we crossed the border into the Netherlands.

We came to a nice rest stop shortly after entering the Netherlands. It was entirely different from anything we had experienced in Belgium. We entered a restaurant where I ordered a delicious cup of coffee and a serving of ice cream. It was the best food I had eaten since we left Germany. As we traveled, we stayed close to the coastline of the English Channel and the North Sea passing by Rotterdam, The Hague, Haarlem, and arriving at Amsterdam. The Dutch countryside was charming, just as we had seen in the many stories and travel brochures which told about the country.

Our visit in Amsterdam was brief. We visited the large art museum which contained many of the works of the famous Dutch artists. Rembrandt, one of their more prominent artists, had a large number of his paintings on display. Our tour guide seemed to be particularly fond of Rembrandt and provided us with a treasure trove of information about him as we toured the museum. Of course, there were works on display by van Gogh, Jan Steen, Jan Vermeer, and a host of others. We attended a Rotary Club in Amsterdam and were delighted to find that Roy Hickman and several other Rotarians from the U.S. were present.

From Amsterdam, we flew to London where we were reunited with the other two groups that had gone on different tours. London was a delightful city. A tour was arranged for us that took us to Buckingham Palace and Trafalgar Square. As we visited Westminster Abbey, I found the grave of the famous missionary David Livingstone along with other notables. Later, I learned about a small park that was near our hotel. I had been told that there was a great deal of history in the park. I walked to the park and discovered several statues of famous Americans as well as famous Englishmen. I discovered that the English people have little or no resentment toward the U.S. for breaking away from English rule. We also toured part of the Tower of London. Repairs were being made which kept us from a more extended tour. Our stay in London was brief but most pleasant because we were back where they spoke our language.

It was a long drive from our hotel in London to Gatwick International Airport. Driving through the English countryside, we could see the remains of military fortifications which had been a part of the preparation for the defense of England during World War II. Many of these fortifications appeared to still be in good condition. Our return flight home from England took us to Philadelphia and from there to Birmingham. This was a marvelous trip for JoAnn and me. The memories seem to be as fresh today as when the events took place.

Shortly before we left for Europe, our church had begun its first Family Life Conference. This event had been planned and scheduled for over a year. I had arranged for Dr. John Boyle, a friend and professor from Southern

Seminary, to lead the conference. I attended the first session, but the conference was to last through the weekend. Since our trip to Europe began before the conference ended, I had left my staff in charge of the continuing supervision of the event. I learned later that some of my adversaries had attended in force. Their intent appeared to be hostile, seeking to do what they could to disrupt or create enough distractions to keep the event from being much of a success or blessing to the church. The reports that I received from staff, John Boyle, and others who attended indicated that not much was achieved in a positive way. I saw this outcome as tragic because there were a number of dysfunctional families and troubled people in our congregation. Had they willingly sought for and accepted the help and good counsel offered by this Family Life Conference, they might have found some healing and direction for their troubled lives.

During my entire tenure at Ruhama, the church seemed to enjoy a highly effective youth ministry. This was due, in part, because of John Atherton's excellent ministry with the youth choir and its continuing presence in the church. Also, we had part time ministers of youth who were equally effective in their work with our young people. Add to that a highly supportive group of parents and the outcome for an active and successful youth ministry was almost guaranteed. Banks High School, where most of our youth attended, was located near Ruhama, providing an added binding force for our youth and their families.

One of the opportunities afforded me through Banks High School was the freedom to organize and lead a chapter of the Fellowship of Christian Athletes. Banks had an outstanding athletic program. The football team won three 4A state championships while I was there. With my interest in promoting the Fellowship of Christian Athletes came the opportunity to serve at Chaplain of the Banks High School football team. Jeff Rutledge, a young member of our church, was the quarterback of the team. He went on to play quarterback at the University of Alabama and had a career in professional football before retiring.

Besides meeting with the Fellowship of Christian Athletes each week during the season, I would often arrive at the football field just as practice was ending. Coach George O. White, also known as "Shorty," would see me on the sidelines and often concluded practice by asking me to gather with the team for a brief prayer. He was totally supportive of my work with the team and treated me as a member of his staff, providing me with the same clothes that the coaches wore on the sidelines at games. Before each game, I met with the team, led a brief devotional, boarded the bus with the team, and rode with them to the game. I was always on the sidelines with the team during the games. Once I was given the game ball after one of their playoff victories. If any of the boys or coaches seemed to be having a problem or needed someone with whom they could talk, Coach White would refer them to me.

These contacts provided numerous positive opportunities for ministry with the team members, their families, the coaches, the school faculty, and the administration. Further, it opened the door for an ongoing ministry for our church. However, some in the church failed to see the opportunities provided by this ministry. They began a concerted effort to criticize and block my involvement with the team and the school. The FCA group met at our church in the Youth Building for an hour on Wednesday evening, at a time when I had no other responsibilities and could meet with them. Some of my opposing deacons learned about the meeting and deliberately began scheduling conflicting church activities for that time, thus preventing me from meeting with the FCA group. I shared the problems with the team and we began scheduling our meetings to take place at the school in the morning before classes began. I raised enough private funds to make milk and doughnuts available to them at each meeting. We conquered adversity with a positive solution.

On one occasion, a Sunday School banquet was scheduled for a game night. I went to the banquet and stayed until my responsibilities were over. Then I slipped out near the end when a film was being shown. Only one person said anything about my leaving early. I can still see that person and hear her voice as she criticized me for what she perceived as being a divided loyalty. Finally, I stopped her ranting by telling her that she would have said nothing about my leaving to go to the hospital or to minister to a family during a crisis. I told her that my presence with the team and coaches on the sidelines was a ministry that was opening the doors for the sharing of the Gospel with young men, their coaches, their families, and others in our community. Only God knows how many other doors were opened by my work with the team.

It is true that the Gospel was shared with team members, their coaches, and their families. I do not have a count as to how many were saved during the three plus years that I served as Chaplain for the football team. I do know that Coach White came to know Christ as his Savior during one of our FCA meetings. I ministered intensely with several of the coaches during personal crises and illness. When I resigned the church to return to Kentucky, the

Banks High School Athletic Boosters voted to give me a lifetime Booster Club membership. This had been done only once prior to that time. Reviewing my service as Chaplain, I can say that it was one of the most rewarding and fulfilling experiences of my entire ministry.

During the last eighteen months of my tenure at Ruhama, I experienced increased pressure for me to resign and leave the church. I had previously begun enlisting the help of those who were friends and could be of help. I talked openly with Hudson Baggett, Editor of the Alabama Baptist; Dotson Nelson, Pastor at Mountain Brook Baptist; John McCrummen, President of Judson College; and numerous pastors who knew of my situation and were sympathetic with my problems. All of them counseled that a move was a necessity but such a move from Ruhama would be difficult. The church was large and had been a prestigious place to serve. Further, word had filtered out that there were problems, thus casting some question about whether I was the cause of the problems or the victim. It would be difficult to get search committees to look at me because of the questions about conflict where I was now serving. I was between a rock and a hard place.

Committees did visit the church, but I would hear nothing from them. I began asking my friends to help me determine why there was little or no response from these committee visits. We discovered that members of the Counting Committee that counted the offering while the worship service was in progress had been intercepting the visitor's cards. When it was obvious that a search committee had been in the service, my opposition had ways of providing them with negative information. I learned this from three different individuals in three different states. One Alabama pastor came to me saying, "Ike, I am going to tell you what is happening. When a committee visits your church, your opposition is using someone or maybe several people at Samford University to pass negative information about you to the committee. When that happens, they stop considering you. I have told you this in confidence. I am asking you not to use my name as you seek to put a stop to it. The folk at Samford will turn on me if they learn that I have tipped you off. I am telling you this, so you can protect yourself. What they are doing is not right. Please do not betray my confidence." Though he did not say it directly, he implied that the negative information about me may be going out through the administrative offices. I honored his request and began to search for a way to protect myself from those who apparently wanted to hurt me. I have always protected his identity.

Since I have mentioned the Samford administration, I must share the details of an event that may be the source of this ill will. In 1972-1973, Samford President Leslie Wright was the District Governor of Rotary District 681, which included Birmingham. When the Downtown Birmingham Rotary Club decided to establish the Birmingham East Rotary Club, I was selected to serve as charter president of that club. President Wright played a significant part in our club's beginning. However, he had allegedly promised some financial support from the District Governor's Office which our club never received. The directors of our club asked me to contact him and inquire if this was an oversight and ask if the funds were still available. Even though I inquired as diplomatically as I knew how, it was evident when President Wright and I talked that my inquiry upset him. Following that, he sent me a personal check for the amount that had been promised. I returned the check telling him that if the funds were not available from the District Governor's budget, our club had no desire to pursue the matter. I never heard another word from him, but all my dealings with him from that point forward were less than friendly.

In the January 1975 deacon's meetings, Jack Gadsen called for an executive session. The executive session meant that the pastor and other paid staff persons were required to leave the room. The pastor's office suite adjoined the room in which the deacons were meeting. I went to my office and stood close to a locked door that provided entry into the deacon's meeting room. Thus, I could hear most of what Jack said to the deacons as he made his case against me. After waiting for about thirty minutes while the deacons discussed his complaint, I went home. About an hour later, Oscar Lee Hurt, Chairman of Deacons, called asking if he could come talk with me and shortly thereafter, he and Danny Newman came to my house. He informed me that the deacons had voted to ask for my resignation. We then discussed some of the events in the meeting after I left. I told him that I would talk with him again the next day. He wanted me to give him my decision then, but I told him that I would have to think and pray about what I was going to do. He and Danny left, and I faced a long night of pondering my next move.

The next day I talked again with Oscar Lee and Danny. My answer to Oscar Lee was that there was more than one side to the issue. Jack had presented his side of the case and I wanted the deacons to hear what I had to say. If, after hearing me, they still felt that I should resign, I would consider their decision. I asked him to call all the deacons and request their presence at a special meeting the following Wednesday evening. He agreed to this and the meeting was arranged.

The church had thirty-six deacons. When we met the next Wednesday, thirty-five were present. I still have in my files the detailed notes that I used as I spoke to them. They follow in the same form that I used that night.
Message to Deacons January 22, 1975

I. I came to be Pastor, September 1, 1971.

    A. The beginning months of my service was that of trying to get my hand on the pulse of the church.
    B. I was aware that the church had suffered a tremendous shock in the loss of its previous pastor.
    C. I was not aware that no official statement or explanation had been given to the church concerning this matter.
    D. I discovered then and still find great discontent within the congregation that little or nothing official was said about the circumstances surrounding the pastor's resignation.

II. The Beginning of Service

    A. When I arrived, I discovered a hostile and discontented church staff. These persons were not angry at me, but angry about certain circumstances and at some individuals.
    B. l listened to complaints, tried to soothe hurt feelings, and pour oil on troubled waters.
    C. I sought to meet with various committees but was told that meetings were not being held. Then, I learned that meetings were taking place without my knowledge even though I had requested a meeting with the chairman or the entire committee.
    D. Not only was I being lied to, but this action revealed a conflict about the philosophy of leadership. I feel a pastor must have free access both to the chairman and the committee.
A committee can and MUST make its own decisions, but a pastor is responsible for pointing out how that committee decision will help or hinder the entire church program.
    E. To have every committee in the church going its own way, making its own decisions without regard for the total church program will bring chaos and conflict in the church fellowship.
    F. I have never had a completely friendly Personnel Committee. Certain members of the committee have felt it was their responsibility to either administer the affairs of the church themselves or question

every decision the pastor or staff member made. There have been times when this has been outright harassment.

G. Some committee members have agreed to a joint decision in the committee and then went directly to the church office and gave just the opposite instructions to those working there. Decisions were also made without consulting the entire committee.

III. The Tension Begins to Mount

A. When Reeves Sims became Deacon Chairman, he wanted a year of peace. I agreed to this, but there were those on the Personnel Committee who still insisted on administering the affairs of the church office.

B. It was during the last days of Reeves Sims' chairmanship that I discussed with him at my own initiative the advisability of making a move to another church.

C. I mentioned "putting out the fleece," i.e., sharing with my friends the fact that I might be interested in moving. Reeves agreed that I could do that and if the doors opened, it could be interpreted as the leadership of the Lord.

D. First Baptist Church, Gainesville, Florida visited. I was one of five candidates. They called Jerry Hayner, a friend and former pastor to one of the committee members.

Incidentally, First Baptist Church, Gainesville, is smaller than Ruhama, but I gave it prayerful consideration.

E. Larry Haisten became our Deacon Chairman. The Personnel Committee then consisted of Larry, Frank Hopson, Jack Gadsen, Reeves Sims, and the Pastor. It was unfortunate, but Larry's work kept him out of town much of the time. The suggestion to move came during this time.

IV. The Suggestion to Move

A. Reeves Sims came to me in the spring informing me that the other members of the Personnel Committee were unanimous in wanting to request my resignation. Reeves had opposed this but agreed to convey their feeling to me privately so that I would not be caught by surprise.

B. My answer was, "I am not happy about the way things are either but give me time to move and I will. In the meantime, I will work as hard as I can and try to do the best job that I can possibly do."

C. In June, after the Southern Baptist Convention, Larry, Jack and Frank requested a meeting with me and stated their feelings in regard to this matter. I gave them the same reply that I had sent to them by Reeves.

D. The idea of moving was not completely my idea. I do not like failure or defeat. But I thought moving ought to be explored since it had the possibility of God's will.

V. This Brings Us to the Effort to Move

A. I prayed about moving, talked with my wife about it, and prayed with her about moving.

B. I called Willis Bennett in the Office of Alumni Affairs at Southern Seminary in Louisville, made an appointment, and went to see him. The machinery has been set in motion. He cautioned me from the beginning that it would take time.

C. Biographical data has been put on file in Alabama, Georgia, Florida, South Carolina, Kentucky, Virginia, Texas, Tennessee and Missouri.

D. I enlisted the help of my friends: Dotson Nelson, Hudson Baggett, John McCrummen, Andy Tampling, George Bagley, Sam Granade, Jack Harwell, George Ingram, Bill Green, Knox Lambert, Bryant Strain, and LaFayette Walker. This is not a complete list.

E. I called James L. Sullivan in Nashville, made an appointment and went to see him. I spent two hours talking to him in his office. His advice was: "Do not resign with no place to go. Preach as good as you can. Visit hard. Minister to those who will let you. Work with those who will let you. Stay out of conflict and do everything you can to move, which includes praying about it. If I can help, call me. Use my name as a reference."

F. I called Duke McCall, president of the seminary in Louisville. Went to see him and got the same advice. He will help.

G. I talked with Darold Morgan with the Annuity Board in Dallas. Got the same advice. He will help.

H. Earlier, I went to Marion to see John McCrummen at Judson College. I received the same advice and assurance of his help.

I. I have spent much time in prayer. My message from God is: "Sit tight. Trust Me. I will work things out." Men, I am trying to do God's will trying to see if a door to another place of service is open.

VI. I Have Been Prepared to Rebuild the Staff

   A. Recently, when I was ready to bring a man before the Personnel Committee, I was informed that doing so would bring on a fight. Not wanting a fight, I backed off.
   B. But what about a fight? Who wins? No one wins in a church fight but the Devil. But sometimes evil must be faced. A church must purge itself of evil. The work of God is hindered by the presence and tolerance of evil.
   C. Ruhama could do without a fight, but if certain situations are not corrected, Ruhama will continue to decline.

VII. What Do I Want?

   A I would rather that we repent, forgive, love each other, and work together for the glory of God.
   B But if that cannot be, then I ask for time to move. This will involve my being in the pulpit of Ruhama. It is nearly impossible to be called to another church if you have no church.

VIII What Would This Involve?

   A. It would involve some compassion, patience, and restraint on your part.
   B. My ministerial career is at stake. No less than twenty thousand dollars of Cooperative Program funds have been invested by Baptists in my formal education. This does not include my personal investment or the investment of those who personally believed in me and helped me.
   C. I believe it would be wrong not to allow this investment to count for the most for the Lord.
   D. Ruhama has never fired a Pastor. To do so would give me a black eye as long as I live. But it would give the church a black eye until the Lord returns.

Conclusion: Give me enough time and I will move. I can do it and I will. I am convinced that it is wrong to put God on a time schedule. He simply does not operate that way.

As I concluded my remarks, I passed out a small ballot to each deacon that had the following on it: "I favor giving Brother McDonald the time he needs to move from Ruhama ( ) Yes ( ) No". The vote was to be by secret ballot. I asked each man to vote as God led him. When the ballots were returned, there were thirty-two "Yes" votes and three abstentions. The Deacon Chairman later informed me that the three officers of the deacons were the abstentions. It was never explained why the officers abstained, but for some reason they did.

When the meeting was adjourned, Jack Gadsen stormed out of the room saying, "We will never get rid of Ike. He will be here a year from now. If I have anything to do with it, I will see to it that he never gets another church." This was his swan song. He left the church shortly afterward along with some of his close friends. Though I could never prove it and did not try, I suspected some of this group of using their influence with persons whom they knew at Samford University to disseminate negative information about me. What I did not understand was that since I was trying to leave, why would they not let me go in peace? Why were they determined to discredit or destroy me?

Having won this battle, it was apparent to me that I had some time. Exactly how much I did not know, but I knew that I would have to increase my efforts toward moving. I began to get the word to those who were trying to help me. I was very aware that I had to do something to short circuit the negative information that was being shared so widely. After conferring with a few select friends, I decided to follow a piece of advice that kept coming my way. I had been advised to make an effort to return to Kentucky and do it on the basis of my previous record of service there. Willis Bennett thought this was a good idea, so we began an effort to get my name before vacant Kentucky churches.

It became impossible to promote any kind of program at Ruhama. The word was out that I had been asked to leave. It seemed that most folk were just waiting to see what was going to happen. The hate mail increased, as did the practice of vandalizing my reserved parking place at the church. Two spaces were reserved for the pastor. It was assumed that JoAnn and I would often come to church in separate cars. On Sunday morning I often arrived to discover the signs marked "Pastor" on those parking spaces had been spray painted with black paint and then roofing tar had been poured on top of the spray paint. It was an effort to hit me below the belt psychologically just before I had to preach. When that did not occur, I often came to my car after church to find that it had been covered with a mixture of Tempera paint and eggs. This happened so often that our sons would not go to the car after church if it had been vandalized. I was left to my own efforts to wash my car as clean as possible before the paint had been damaged. Roofing nails were thrown in my driveway at home, and there was a continuous stream of harassing phone calls.

The identity of the person or persons responsible for this harassment was openly discussed. I felt that Cass Johnson or some of his friends were the culprits, but I could never prove it. Johnson was a lifelong member of the church and a deacon. However, one Saturday evening my son Bryant and Martin Newman, the son of Danny Newman, decided to stake out the church parking lot and to see if they could catch the person vandalizing the parking places. They were able to hide behind some roofing materials which were stored next to the church building for use in the coming week. Cass Johnson drove up, left his car, and began to spray paint the signs. Just as he was opening a can of tar to pour over the signs, the boys confronted him. He became agitated and got in his car to drive off. When the boys tried to block him in, so he could not leave, he drove over the curb and left the scene.

The boys immediately came home and told Danny and me. We called two or three other deacons and the boys shared their story. Harold Knight, a deacon and a lawyer, was called, but he said he could not get involved because he was Johnson's lawyer. The police were called, but they said they could not cite anyone because they did not witness the vandalism. The boys met with the three officers of the deacons and told their story. A special meeting of the deacons was called to hear their report. Johnson refused to come to the meeting but sent a letter denying that the events took place. His story was that the boys were lying. He resigned his offices in the church, but the deacons voted to not to accept his resignations. The vote was not unanimous, but essentially the deacons decided that the boys' story was not true. I was instructed to go to Johnson and apologize for the behavior of the boys and to be reconciled with him. I agreed to go provided some of the deacons would go with me. Two of the deacon officers and two other deacons went with me to Johnson's home. We met and visited, but nothing was ever said about what had happened. I stood to depart and one of them suggested that we pray, which we did. Nothing had been said about the hate mail, the vandalism of the parking places, or vandalism to my car. It was an exercise in hypocrisy. But the word was out that Johnson was the culprit in terms of the hate mail and the vandalism.

As the summer of 1975 was ending and a new church year was beginning, I found myself facing Sid Smith, a new Deacon Chairman and Chairman of the Personnel Committee. His assignment was to obtain my resignation, and he became a constant source of harassment and ill will. Other members of the Personnel Committee were Oscar Lee Hurt, Coe Pinson, and Marvin Jones. They began demanding a weekly meeting with them in which I was to give a report in detail of what I was doing to find another place to serve. I refused to meet with them on these terms. They kept insisting and I kept refusing. At the request of the retiring Deacon Chairman, Oscar Lee Hurt, I did give a brief report to the deacons on July 16, 1975. Again, I have the notes used in making that report. Notice that I used very few names of people and no names of places knowing that to do so would not help my efforts. The July 16 notes appear below.

What have I done since late January and early February?

My friends with whom I had previously talked were made aware of the urgency of my need to move. Dr. Duke McCall and the Alumni Office at Southern Seminary have been quite active. Not a week has gone by that I have not made long distance phone calls, written letters, answered questionnaires, and sent biographical information wherever I could. My friends have been quite active also. I am doing everything I know to do to keep my word, but I have had no opportunity that resembled anything of the Lord's will. I have told my friends that I would be more than willing to take a smaller church or even accept a smaller salary providing there was some positive leadership from the Lord.

What is involved in moving? Why does it take time?

It is not considered proper for a minister to apply to a church. A direct approach would not be welcomed by most pulpit committees. A minister is at the mercy of his friends and interested parties to recommend him. A pulpit committee can easily have from thirty to two hundred (200) letters of recommendation. No two pulpit committees will work the same way. They seldom get in a hurry. You might get in a hurry or I might, but they usually do not. Negative reports circulating on the grapevine can close a door before it ever gets fully open. If a pastor has limited success or if there is a suggestion that there are problems, a committee usually will not investigate further.

What options are open to me and to you?

I could seek secular employment, but that is not desirable. Frankly, I would not even know where to look or how to start. To resign with no place to go would be the same as getting out of the ministry. I do not want to do this. I am considering the possibility of denominational work. Some have suggested that I go back to seminary, but I have no funds for that and would have no way to support my family. Several churches have my name now and something could easily break any day. I repeat my commitment to you that I will keep trying to move.

With this statement, my report to the deacons ended. You will notice that I gave the deacons no information other than my assurance that I was doing all I could to move. However, in early August I was contacted by Larry Pursiful, Chairman of the Pulpit Committee of First Baptist Church, Hodgenville, Kentucky. After some discussion, we agreed that I would preach for their committee and meet with them on September 3, 1975, at Bethany Baptist Church in Louisville where Lloyd Storment served as pastor. The next day after preaching for and meeting with the committee, I visited Hodgenville and returned to Alabama. Later, Larry Pursiful called and asked if the committee could visit my church in Birmingham. I agreed for a visit provided they would be as discreet as possible and not sign any visitor cards. They agreed to this and visited for a morning worship service. Once they returned home, they invited me to visit and preach for the church in anticipation of their recommending me to the church as pastor. At my suggestion, I made another trip to Hodgenville to discuss salary, benefits, and other practical matters related to making the move, none of which had been discussed prior to that time. Then my family and I visited Hodgenville and I preached for them on Sunday, November 9, 1975. They called me as their pastor on November 16, 1975 and I accepted their call.

On Sunday evening, November 16, 1975, Sid Smith and Oscar Lee Hurt insisted on meeting with me after the evening service. They informed me that the Personnel Committee was ready to recommend to the church that I be dismissed as Pastor. They knew absolutely nothing about my dealings with First Baptist Church, Hodgenville, and I had no intention of informing them. However, I told them that I would be willing to resign the church under certain conditions. The conditions were as follows:

1. I would resign either on November 23 or November 30.
2. My resignation would become effective December 31, 1975.
3. I would be permitted to take my twenty-five remaining days of paid vacation with all benefits paid during the month of December.

4. My family and I would be able to live in the pastorium until December 31, 1975, and if necessary longer with the extension being arranged with the Personnel Committee.

5. I would be paid for nine weeks of accrued vacation that I have not taken in past years. This payment would include salary and full benefits.

When I shared this with them, they agreed immediately, but said that they would have to confer with Marvin Jones and Coe Pinson, the other two members of the committee, to obtain their consent. I drew up this agreement in written form on November 21, 1975, for their signatures and mine. Sid Smith acted as though he was insulted by my insisting on his signing the agreement. I told him that it was a legal and binding document and that I had signed it. If he did not want to do what he had agreed to do, then we could start negotiating again. He immediately softened and said he would sign it and so would the others.

The document was signed, and I resigned on November 30, 1975. I told no one that I had been called by another church. In fact, my family and I did not tell anyone in Birmingham where we were going until after we had arrived in Hodgenville. I was convinced that if they knew, they would try to do me and my family harm in our new place of service. It was a sad ending to what had been a very hopeful beginning.

Often, I have been asked how I was able to conceal my dealings with the church at Hodgenville and our move there from the people in Birmingham. The truth is that I shared with no one but my wife and Lloyd Storment, my minister friend in Louisville, the details of my dealings with the Hodgenville search committee. Since we had family in Kentucky and had lived there a large part of our lives, a brief trip for family or for business was simple to conceal. And except for the weekend when I preached in Hodgenville, I was never gone for more than thirty-six hours. Once we made the decision to move to Hodgenville, I impressed upon our sons that those who were unfriendly to us, would try to do the family harm should they learn anything about what we were in the process of doing. It was our secret and we kept it.

I must say that I met and came to love some of the finest people that I have ever known in Birmingham. I made friendships that continue to this day. I also encountered some of the most duplicitous and ruthless people that I have ever known. I asked the Lord to help me to be forgiving and to keep me from being bitter. I do believe that He has answered that prayer. I did tell the church leadership that if they did not make some changes, there would come a day when they would close the doors of Ruhama. Sadly, that day came to pass near the end of 2003. I was invited to attend the last service, which I have called "the funeral of Ruhama," but chose not to attend. With all of my heart, I believe that those laymen who were determined to control and rule the church rode it like a dying horse into the ground. It was a sad end for a church with a great beginning and a long, eventful ministry.

Chapter 14

Early Hodgenville Years

The details of how I arranged to be away from my church in Birmingham to preach for an interview with the Hodgenville committee escape me, but I do recall that I did so without the Ruhama folk knowing what I was doing. I think I simply stated that I had to be out of town on personal business, which was true. It turned out that all of Louisville and Jefferson County was in turmoil because forced busing to desegregate the Jefferson County schools was beginning at the very time I was to be there. Coming into the city on September 3rd and leaving the next day gave me the opportunity to witness the police presence that sought to maintain order and the other forces demonstrating against what was happening. Both groups were making their presence known.

After speaking at Bethany on Wednesday evening and meeting with the committee, I was invited to come by Hodgenville on my way home the next day to see the church and community. My meeting with the committee and my visit in Hodgenville seemed to go quite well. I left with a positive feeling and with the assurance that I would hear from the committee soon. However, it was not until early October, about a month later, that I received a call from Larry Pursiful. When I answered the phone, he said, "Brother McDonald, this is Larry Pursiful." I responded by laughing and saying, "Hello Larry, I had about decided that I was not going to hear from you again." But he assured me that the delay had been caused by committee members being out of town and the need for them to work out some details in regard to calling a pastor.

When I asked if they were still interested in me, he assured me that they were. He stated that the committee wanted to visit my church in Birmingham and hear me preach in that setting. My response was that I would be happy for them to visit, but I had some requests about how they would conduct themselves during the visit. I requested that the committee divide so they would appear to be casual visitors, with no more than two of them sitting together and that they sit in widely separated places in the sanctuary. Further, I asked that none of them sign a visitor's card. Finally, I would prefer that none of them come to my office for a meeting after church. I would meet with them elsewhere, but not at the church. They agreed to all of this, but when they came, two of them did come to my office after church and visited briefly with me. Some of them brought their wives which made it appear that they just happened to be there for worship while visiting in Birmingham.

Later that week, I received a call from Larry Pursiful telling me that the committee had agreed to invite me to visit First Baptist Church Hodgenville and preach for the congregation in anticipation of their recommending that the church call me to serve as pastor. I told Larry that I would be pleased to do that, but that there were some practical matters such as salary, benefits, vacation, and housing that had not been discussed. I suggested that I come to Hodgenville again, meet with the committee face to face, and be sure that we had a clear understanding on these things. He said that a package had already been worked out and approved. I responded that I was glad to hear that, but I had not been informed as to the contents of the package and that I would not be comfortable with it until I reviewed it with the committee. He said that he did not know whether the church would pay my expenses for such a visit, but he would ask. When he called back, he gave me a date for the meeting telling me that my expenses would be no problem.

At that last meeting, we agreed that my family and I would visit First Baptist Church Hodgenville and that I would preach for the church on November 9, 1975, which is what we did. The church voted to call me as its pastor on November 16, 1975, and I accepted the call telling them that I would arrive in Hodgenville and begin serving the church on January 1, 1976.

The most recent history of the Hodgenville church had been openly shared with me during my discussions with the committee. The previous pastor had been gone about a year. He had become involved sexually with the church secretary and had asked that he be permitted to divorce his wife, marry the secretary, and remain as pastor of the church. The church had denied his request and asked for his resignation. He had resigned and appeared to have been reconciled with his wife. They had moved to Ohio but were unable to remain together and had later divorced.

This former pastor had developed an extensive counseling ministry along with leading the church to become involved in various social ministries. The daycare program was one of those ministries. Though the former pastor's sexual infidelity was commonly known within the congregation, I do not think the church leadership ever made any official statement to the church concerning the reason for his resignation. Since the church staff had been involved in these various ministries and had worked closely with the pastor, there were various opinions about these persons in terms of what they knew, when they knew it, and whether or not they supported the pastor in his immoral behavior. Many persons who had been closely associated with the former pastor in any way were viewed by some in the church and community with suspicion.

This was the second consecutive church where I was being called upon to succeed a pastor who was forced to resign because of immoral activity. I knew that I would be watched closely and that one of my first tasks would be that of trying to restore the tarnished image of the pastor. It was not going to be easy.

As my family was concluding our stay in Birmingham, we began to make all the arrangements for our move to Hodgenville, Kentucky. Hodgenville had only one traffic light and about 2,400 residents. There were fewer residents in the town than there were members of the church I served in Birmingham. I was elated, JoAnn was relieved, Philip was excited, but Bryant was steadfastly refusing to accept the move. He kept saying that he was not going and asserted that he would not stay if he was forced to go.

We made arrangements with a Hodgenville trucker named Tommy Wathen to move us. He was an experienced mover and did the best job of any mover that we ever used. We learned later that his home was almost next door to the pastor's home in Hodgenville. Assisting him was his wife, sister-in-law, and a couple of locals he had arranged to hire. They packed and loaded our belongings in two days and were on their way.

We left Birmingham on the morning of January 1, 1976 and arrived in Hodgenville late that day. I pulled our travel trailer with my Buick LaSabre and JoAnn pulled our small fishing boat with our Buick Century. We had arranged to give our German Shepherd dog, Smokey, some sedatives so he would sleep most of the way. He did not sleep much, but he was not too active. Smokey had been a gift from one of our Ruhama families who could no longer care for him. He was a wonderful pet.

We spent our first night back in Kentucky in a motel. We had parked the travel trailer and boat at our new home and drove the ten miles to Elizabethtown for a good night's rest. Early the next morning we met the movers in Hodgenville and began to give direction as to where our furniture might be placed as it came off the truck. Kentucky weather provided us with the welcome of a brisk wind accompanied by a cold rain.

I was disappointed when I discovered that though some painting and repairs had been done on the home we were to occupy, the house itself had not been properly cleaned. When I asked the chairman of the Church Property Committee why the house had not been cleaned and made ready for our arrival, he assured me that it had been done. I inquired who had performed the cleaning and he gave me the name of the family that he had hired to do the job. I met them later and realized that what was clean to them was much less than clean by most standards. I will never understand why he handled such an important job so poorly. It took us nearly a month for us to clean the house properly.

On a more positive note, I led the first service as pastor of First Baptist Church, Hodgenville, Kentucky, on January 4, 1976. There was a deacons' meeting at 8:00 a.m. that morning with breakfast provided, as well as an official church reception for our family that afternoon at the home of Larry and Pricilla Pursiful. It was a busy and eventful day.

The welcome and hospitality of the church and the Hodgenville community was warm and gracious. The following Sunday night the church had a potluck supper in our honor. We were given a traditional old fashioned "church pounding" which consisted of gifts for our pantry, freezer, and home. I was amazed at the number of gifts which the congregation provided, most of which were anonymous, useful, and thoroughly appreciated.

Later in the month, I met our across-the-street neighbor, Wathen Claycomb, the president of Lincoln National Bank, at Smith's Drug Store. We often drank coffee there. After coffee, Wathen asked if I had a few minutes explaining that he wanted me to accompany him to Middleton and Marcum's Dry Goods Store. I agreed to go with him. We entered the store and were greeted by the owner, Morgan Marcum, who was one of my deacons. Wathen told Morgan to get the best white dress shirt in the store and a tie to go with it. I picked out the tie and received it and the shirt as a "welcome to the town" gift from Wathen. He proved to be a great neighbor and friend the whole time I lived in Hodgenville.

At the first deacons' meeting on my first Sunday morning in Hodgenville, I met E. G. "Red" Sanders. He was a neighbor and served as Superintendent of Education for LaRue County. He asked me about my wife's teaching credentials and told me that he would find a place for her. As we walked out to our cars in the parking lot, he began to tell me about the accidental death of his middle son, Kelley, a few years prior to my arrival. We stood in the parking lot, in the cold, for nearly thirty minutes as he unburdened himself reciting the details of his son's death. When we departed for home to get ready to come back for Sunday School, he promised to find a job for my wife. This was a promise he fulfilled almost immediately; she was called to substitute teach the next day and taught in the LaRue County School System until she retired in 1998.

I stated earlier that one of the ongoing problems a pastor has to deal with is the church staff. Good staff members are difficult to find. Keeping them motivated is a continuing task. Dealing with the problems that they create or bring to work never seems to cease. I have known few staff members who had the ability to foresee the outcome, present or future, of their actions. While staff persons are a necessary part of ministry, they can also be a continuing burden to those supervising them.

Having made that observation, I found myself almost immediately having to deal with staff problems. The Minister of Music had submitted her resignation to the Church Personnel Committee shortly after I had accepted the call to the church. Instead of conferring with me, they had persuaded her to remain on staff on a part time basis. I would have preferred that she had been allowed to resign and depart, as her continuing presence later created a critical problem that put me in the position of being the bad guy when the Personnel Committee suggested that she conclude her services. I had tried to work with her, but she was not cooperative or responsible in her part time position. She blamed me for what happened and maintained a hostile attitude toward me all the time that I lived in Hodgenville. She returned to the Methodist Church where she had previously been a member.

Then the church secretary resigned during the first weeks of my tenure. She was very professional about it, stating that she and her husband were about to move to another city and that the timing of her resignation had nothing to do with my arrival. After interviewing several candidates, we decided to employ Patsy Cundiff, a member of Buffalo Baptist Church and wife of Mike Cundiff who had grown up at First Baptist Church. Patsy proved to be an excellent choice. She kept her church membership at Buffalo but was loyal to our church serving as church secretary for about ten years. She resigned when her husband accepted a job and moved to Munfordville about thirty miles away.

The next staff problem had to do with the church's daycare ministry which was in operation when I arrived. The daycare coordinator had resigned, and the Early Childhood Education Committee met jointly with the Church Personnel Committee to decide on a replacement. An older lady in the church, who had worked in the church nursery for several years, applied for the job. However, both committees felt that Joyce Priddy, currently a member of the daycare staff, was better qualified for this position. Joyce was offered the job and accepted it. The older lady took the committee decision personally, became quite angry, resigned her church nursery position, and held me personally responsible for the committee's decision. I had been present when the committees met but had no part in the decision because I was totally unfamiliar with the daycare program or the personnel involved in its daily operation. The older lady refused to accept those facts, gave me grief, and opposed my ministry until the day I resigned.

My ministry in Hodgenville seemed to be typical of that in a small, county seat town. The county had about 12,000 residents and was a bedroom community for Elizabethtown, Ft. Knox, and Louisville. The major employers in the county were Nationwide Uniform Corporation, the LaRue County School System, the LaRue County Government, and Sunrise Manor Nursing Home. The county was mostly an agricultural society but had few full-time farmers whose income was solely from farming. There were three banks and three funeral homes in the county. Everyone seemed to know most of the people in the county, and there were few if any genuine secrets.

Early in my ministry, I sensed that without major growth in the town and county, we would not experience much growth in the church. However, I gave a lot of attention the Sunday School and committee structure of the church. The Sunday School attendance had declined over the past several years. With a continuing effort, attendance increased from below 200 to an average of about 240, but we were unable to sustain that over a long period of time. Though I did not quit promoting attendance, it became apparent that under the existing economic conditions we would do well to maintain what we had.

When I arrived in Hodgenville in January 1976, there was a thriving retail community on all four sides of the downtown square. In less than ten years all of those businesses had closed. These businesses included two dry goods stores, a hardware store, a furniture store, a five and dime store, plus other associated small businesses. There was a Chevrolet dealership located on the square that closed about five years later. Thus, the entire retail community on the city square disappeared. A small shopping plaza had been established in the northwest corner of town, but none of those businesses relocated there.

A few businesses that were not on the square did relocate to other parts of the town in newer buildings. I inquired among several of my fellow pastors in other central Kentucky small towns and learned that similar decline was everywhere.

During my first five years in Hodgenville, I began and completed the requirements for my Doctor of Ministry degree at Southern Baptist Theological Seminary in Louisville, Kentucky. This was my third degree from the seminary having previously earned the Bachelor of Divinity and Master of Divinity degrees. JoAnn also completed her Master of Science in Education degree which she had begun earlier at Samford University in Birmingham. She lacked six semester hours when we moved but completed those hours during our first year in Hodgenville. Then she began work on her Rank I Certificate for teaching which requires as much work as a doctorate but is not a degree program. At one time, every member of our family was involved in college or graduate studies.

My Doctor of Ministry studies provided many interesting experiences. Three other pastors in the Elizabethtown area were enrolled in the same program: Lawrence Phipps, Terry Wilder, and Wayne Hayes. I was about twenty years older than these men, but we became good friends and usually ate together once a week. While none of us were ever in the same seminars, we encouraged, advised, and helped each other. Wayne Hayes moved and had to interrupt his studies. When he began them again, I became his Field Supervisor and guided him through his remaining studies plus the writing of his doctoral thesis. These friendships have been a treasure over the years.

The Doctor of Ministry degree program was designed by the various seminaries to provide additional professional studies in a degree-earning setting for ministers who were actively pursuing their careers. Seminars were offered in one-month "J Terms" in January, June, and July when the seminaries were not in regular academic session. Many pastors could use either their vacation time or were given this time by their churches to pursue these studies. Each seminar required the reading and written review of about twenty-five to thirty books before the seminar began. Other intense research and study was done while the seminar was being conducted. Several PhD students took some of these seminars and complained that they were much more demanding than their regular PhD seminars.

The degree program was presented to us as being about sixty percent practical and forty percent academic. However, it turned out to be about ninety percent academic and ten percent practical. Being friends with many of the faculty, I made some suggestions as to how the program could be made more practical, but that was to no avail. Academic communities have a tendency to be set in their ways and reluctant to change. My suggestions were politely endured but not accepted as being worthy of implementing any change.

I did all my studies in July because that was not a busy time in my church. Since I lived about sixty miles from the seminary, I would be in my pulpit each weekend and often returned to lead the Wednesday prayer meeting. I was fortunate that I never had other responsibilities that interfered with my studies. When it came time to write my thesis, I did most of that between ten o'clock at night and three in the morning. It took about six months of steady writing to get the thesis ready for the final copy. I finished just as my deadline was approaching and received the degree on December 18, 1981. It is interesting that President Duke K. McCall's signature is on every one of my seminary diplomas. My academic studies beyond high school spanned thirty-two years yielding a BAE on June 7, 1954; a BD on May 16, 1958; an MDiv on January 23, 1970; and the D.Min. on December 18, 1981. These college and seminary studies were continuous from September 1949 through May 1958. The last two seminary degrees were earned in blocks of time in the late 1960s and late 1970s.

During my last doctoral seminar, I learned that seminary professors James Blevins and Alan Culpepper were going to lead a group of students on a Holy Land tour shortly after Christmas. Seminary credit could be earned if one made the trip and completed the academic work. After discussing this study tour with James Blevins, T. A. Prickett and I decided to petition the faculty for permission to take the trip and apply the hours earned toward the last four hours of our Field Supervision. The faculty approved our request and we began making preparation for the trip. When Red Sanders learned of my plans, he went into the community and solicited enough contributions to pay a large portion of my expenses for the trip.

This Holy Land trip proved to be a great experience for me. It was my second trip overseas and my first trip to the Middle East. We had a good mixture of students and mature pastors in the group. Several persons whom I had known in Alabama were also in the group. Seeing the land in which Jesus lived and where most of the story of the Bible events took place caused the message of the Bible to come alive for me. The tour was worth at least a year's study in the seminary classroom and maybe more. I received insights into the Biblical message that would have escaped me had I not visited the scenes where the events took place.

I learned when I returned home that though I had requested and received faculty approval to apply the hours earned from the Holy Land trip toward my Field Supervision requirements, Verlin Kruschwitz, my Field Supervisor, would have no part in the agreement. I had kept him informed of my actions, but he steadfastly refused to agree that I did not have to fulfill all of the remaining requirements for that last four hours of Field Supervision. It was not until after I had made the trip and completed the academic requirements involved that he made me aware of his disagreement with my arrangements with the seminary faculty. After a lengthy discussion concerning the permission granted by the seminary faculty, I saw that I had no choice but to do as he required. I do not think he ever saw my point of view. He kept saying, "Ike, you need to do the things that are required in this last four hours of study." I did as he insisted but always felt he was unreasonable in the demands that he was making. It was not until much later that I learned the negative interpretation that he placed on my actions.

With the completion of my Doctor of Ministry degree, there were predictions that I would soon leave Hodgenville. A small minority had opposed my being involved in the program of study. They had stated that I was simply using the church and that now that I had received the degree, I would take the first opportunity that came and leave. I confess that I did not understand their negative attitude. Some of my fellow ministers had been encouraged by the congregations they were serving to pursue these studies, and their churches paid the expense of the studies. Plus, their churches celebrated with them when the degree was conferred. I did not have that experience. Some did begin to address me as Dr. McDonald when they learned that I had received the degree, but that was about all the recognition that I received. I had long before decided to remain with the church at least two more years just to prove my critics wrong.

It was always my belief that a minister had a responsibility to the community beyond his service to the church. In every place where I served since seminary graduation, I have been a member of a civic club. In Calhoun, I was in the Jaycees. In Paducah, I was in the Optimist Club. In Birmingham, I was a charter member of the Birmingham-East Rotary Club, serving as Charter President of the club. When I came to Hodgenville, I was invited to join the Hodgenville Rotary Club and served as Vice President and President of the club. While serving as President, we observed the fiftieth anniversary of the club and provided community leadership for raising the funds to purchase the "Jaws of Life" rescue equipment for LaRue County. Our county did not have this equipment which was greatly needed in dealing with the increasing number of auto accidents in our area. It was a fun experience for me. I have always enjoyed being a Rotarian and continued my membership in the organization when I left Hodgenville.

Evangelism has always been the heartbeat of ministry so far as I was concerned. In nearly every church that I served, we set baptismal records or challenged the records that existed. Using the Sunday School as the organization for evangelistic outreach is how Southern Baptists built the strong denomination that we became, linking our evangelistic outreach to a strong mission program at home and abroad. Every revival that I led in the churches where I served was promoted through the Sunday School. Not every revival was a success in reaching the lost and reviving the church, but that was the goal.

To my knowledge, Hodgenville had experienced only one spirit-filled revival in its history. It had been a community event held at the local fairgrounds in the late 1940s when Lloyd Cloud was pastor. Angel Martinez had been the evangelist and there had been numerous conversions as a result of the effort. I was told early in my tenure that the Hodgenville church was a revival church. These words were probably meant to encourage me as at the time I was preparing the church for a revival. However, I found the very opposite to be true. We could do everything necessary to prepare the church for a revival, but the event would come and go without any noticeable impact on the church or the community. Parents would literally stand between me and their children not granting me permission to talk with them about their relationship with the Lord. There seemed to be a prevailing skepticism about the value or the lasting spiritual impact of a religious revival in the community. Contrasting this attitude was the desire on the part of many in the church and community for God to do something that would make things better for the community. Yet there seemed to be strong underlying skepticism that anything of this nature would occur.

Reviewing this experience, I offer the following observations as to why the community lived with this frame of mind. This was a small, close knit community. Everyone's history was an open book. There were few if any secrets. People knew who was honest and who was not. They knew who had a drinking problem, who was unfaithful to their spouses, and who had fathered or given birth to children by someone other than their spouse. They were aware of any immoral activity that had taken place or might be taking place. In short, everyone had a picture window view into the happenings of everyone's life whether it was good or bad. While they may turn a blind eye to negative or immoral activity, accepting it or making allowances for it, they never quite got over the gut feeling that such things were not right in the eyes of God. And they were always wondering if any changes a person might make for the better were genuine or how long they would last. There was a prevailing skepticism as to what changes God could bring in human lives and how long they would last if He did.

My conviction is that this kind of attitude is unbelief. It is the same kind of unbelief that Jesus encountered when He returned to His hometown of Nazareth "and did not do many mighty works there, because of their unbelief" (Matthew 15:38). I believe this attitude put a spiritual wet blanket on much of what I tried to accomplish during my years at Hodgenville.

Further, there was a tolerance of and acceptance of human frailty within the community that never failed to amaze me. A person could be guilty of some grievous infraction or follow a way of life that was totally unacceptable by most standards, and people in the community accepted these persons as if there was nothing wrong. Occasionally, the subject of someone's questionable lifestyle would become the subject of discussion over coffee at the local drug store. Jokes were often made about these folk and their lifestyle.

When I asked LaRue "Mose" Hamilton, one of my more honest and trusted sources, why these persons of questionable character received community acceptance, he replied by telling me a story out of the political world. It seems that a Republican was criticizing a Democrat for being tolerant of another Democrat whose misdeeds were well known. The Republican asked, "How can you defend him? Don't you know that he is nothing but a son of a bitch?" To which the Democrat replied, "Yes, I know that, but he is OUR son of a bitch!"

I conclude these observations by quoting the words of Alexander Pope:

"An Essay on Man"

Vice is a monster of so frightful mien
As to be hated needs but to be seen;
Yet seen too oft, familiar with her face,
We first endure, then pity, then embrace.

Among the questionable lifestyles present in Hodgenville was that of homosexuality. I learned after arriving in the community that several of our citizens, male and female, were practicing homosexuals. Many of them were in the church. This discovery came during my first year as pastor at First Baptist Church. I had begun a series of sermons based on the book of Romans. One does not go very far in Romans before encountering Paul's teaching about sin and rebellion which contains a condemnation of sexual sin including homosexuality. My sermon was delivered in the late 1970s when many prominent people in the entertainment world were coming out of the closet, announcing their homosexuality. Further, they were encouraging others to join their ranks. I chose to speak a realistic word to the young people of the church, pointing out that the homosexual lifestyle was not Christian, just as any sexual activity outside of marriage was not Christian. I encouraged my hearers to avoid all sexual sin, especially the sin of homosexuality, noting that it was severely condemned in the Bible.

My stance ignited a lively discussion within the church and community. Since our morning services were broadcast on a local radio station that enjoyed wide coverage, comments and discussion came from every direction. It was then that I learned that a homosexual community existed in Hodgenville and some alleged homosexuals were our church members. Further, the community being aware of this, had given a quiet acceptance of these people and their practices. The reasoning behind their acceptance was that most of the homosexuals came from good, prominent families and they were good people.

My conflict with the homosexual community came to a head when I was made aware that they wanted me to endorse the homosexual lifestyle. My feeling was that they were more than welcome in the church provided they would remain celibate and not practice or promote homosexuality as a normal way of life. If this position seemed too demanding, I reminded them that the same standards were applied to the heterosexual community. Unmarried people were expected to remain celibate and married people were expected to remain faithful to their mates. The Bible teaches this protocol and I felt I had no right to deviate from it.

To say that my words ignited a firestorm of discussion, opposition, and resentment in the homosexual community and among their supporters would be an understatement. I had never before encountered the kind of opposition and hostility that came as a result of my stand. This group was small, vocal, and actively hostile. They worked to undermine everything I tried to promote in my ministry the entire time I served the church. Several of them would find ways to abuse me verbally, laying on me an old-fashioned barnyard cussing as often as possible. I tried to accept their reaction as part of the perils of the territory, but I must say that on occasions it was all I could do to maintain my composure. I confess that I had faced angry and hostile people before but never to the degree that this group displayed on a regular continuing basis.

After leaving the Hodgenville pastorate and community, I have had many discussions with friends from within and without the community concerning this situation. I have observed that I have never known of a place that produced so many homosexuals per capita as did Hodgenville and LaRue County. I have never had an informed person who was familiar with the community who disagreed with my observation. It is a phenomenon that is hard to explain.

In spite of this pocket of opposition, I enjoyed a reasonable acceptance and respect in the LaRue County community. I made friends in and out of the church and ministered with reasonable effectiveness to the total community. As I indicated previously, when you serve the largest church in a small, county seat town, you are often called upon to minister to everyone who resides within its boundaries. It goes with the territory.

I have never enjoyed conflict. However, I have had to deal with it everywhere I have served. My nature is that I am not one to allow people to run roughshod over me. I always occupy the ground upon which I stand. There are those in every community and church who seem to think that the preacher is fair game for their negative actions. They try to take advantage of his good nature. Such an attitude usually sets the stage for conflict.

I had been in Hodgenville for about four years when the Personnel Committee decided to review my salary and compensation package. Red Sanders was on that committee. He proposed putting me on my wife's medical coverage through the school system and dropping my family medical coverage through the Southern Baptist Annuity Board. This proposal would save the church much of the expense of that coverage. However, Mr. Sanders did not appear to grasp the fact that should my wife cease to be an employee of the school system, my family and I would have been without medical insurance. Further, insurance coverage through the Baptist Annuity Board was part of the agreement I had with the church when I came to be pastor and it could be transferred from one church to another. When I tried to explain this to Mr. Sanders, he either he did not grasp what I was saying or was so intent on saving the church some money that he did not see the seriousness of such a change for me and my family.

After some discussion with various committee members about this, I had told them that Mr. Sanders' proposal was unacceptable to me and that I would not agree to it. I thought the matter had been dropped until a few days later when I was visiting Cortland Cox, the high school principal, in his office. Mr. Sanders came in and had hardly entered the room when he turned to me and asked, "When are we going to have another meeting and get this insurance deal worked out?" I replied, "We aren't going to have another meeting and I am not going to agree to it being changed." My reply apparently struck the wrong chord. Mr. Sanders raised his voice and became noticeably angry, asking, "Don't you want to save the church some money?" My reply was that I was "not interested in saving the church money, but rather more interested in providing for my family as we had agreed when I came to serve the church."

By this time both of us had lost our tempers. We were standing toe to toe shouting at each other. After a few harsh exchanges, I said, "You are not going to step in my face to get your way as you have everyone else around here." Mr. Sanders replied that I had less than a spotless record in terms of getting along with people. Our voices kept rising in volume and the two or three people in Mr. Cox's office who had initially been present had left quickly. Mr. Cox spoke up and insisted that we try to calm ourselves. Both of us left the school. I was angry and humiliated that I had lost my composure and participated in an angry shouting match.

I went home and nursed my embarrassed ego. When JoAnn arrived, I told her what happened. She was not too sympathetic with my plight and told me that I could not afford not to try to make peace with Mr. Sanders. I told her that she was more than right. I did not sleep well that night.

The next morning, I drove out to the Board of Education offices. When Mr. Sanders saw me enter, he told me that he did not want me coming in with any apologies. He went on to say that I had meant everything I had said and that he was more than offended by my words. I stood in his office and listened to what he had to say. Then I told him that I had come to apologize for losing my temper and embarrassing him and others at the school. I stated that when people are angry they often say things that they don't really mean. I told him that I was in hopes that we could mend our fences and get on with what had been a most pleasant relationship from my point of view. I stated that I bore him no ill will.

He in turn informed me that people often mean what they say when they are angry. However, he said that he did not intend to quit coming to church or quit giving to the church. During this conversation, he had not looked directly at me. Finally, as our conversation continued, he began to look at me occasionally. Neither of us sat down. We stood in his office with his desk between us. Finally, I told him that I did not want to take up too much of his time. I felt that I owed him a word of apology and I hoped that he would feel that I was sincere and accept it. I thanked him for hearing me out. As I prepared to leave, I reached across his desk and offered my hand. Without looking at me, he reached out and shook my hand. I thanked him again and left.

The next Sunday, true to his word, Mr. Sanders was in his regular seat in church. I was as miserable preaching that day as I can ever remember. But we both made it through the service and as best as I could tell, both of us put the bad experience behind us. It may not have been textbook Christianity, but it was the best we could do at the time.

Chapter 15
Late Hodgenville Years

Having completed my Doctor of Ministry studies at Southern Seminary, I got the feeling that the church and community took a wait and see attitude in regard to how long I would remain in Hodgenville. I must admit that I was open to going to another church, but I had turned fifty years of age and that factor began to limit my opportunities. I prepared a new resume and had it professionally printed. I arranged for what I thought was a good group of references, but I had little response to any of my efforts to move.

I confess that I was comfortable in Hodgenville. Problems within the church were not numerous. Our growth would wax and wane. It was not possible to maintain any sustained growth in our Sunday School. Looking back, I am convinced that our existing buildings prevented any lasting growth. In time past, it was possible to crowd people into close quarters, but as our people had become more affluent and accustomed to better, more spacious buildings, they were less than eager to be crowded into older buildings. We seemed to have settled into just going from week to week without much change. I chose not to push too hard for progress sensing that the people were happy and were not wanting to do a great deal more than they had been doing.

Earlier, I indicated that the previous pastor had developed a counseling ministry. That ministry included group counseling. Many believed that it was in the context of these counseling sessions that improper relationships developed. This mindset had its effect on any formal counseling work I might have been called upon to do. In fact, I noticed early in my time at Hodgenville that few came to my office seeking counsel.

However, I soon noticed a pattern of informal counseling that developed and continued during my entire tenure. Being a people person, I often joined a group who drank coffee at Smith's Drug Store early in the morning and in the middle of the afternoon. Following that, I would make several stops at the various businesses in town before returning to my office. Since I was walking from one place to another, I often met people on the street and engaged in brief conversations with them. After some months and many such encounters, I realized that those who wanted to talk with me were timing their meetings with me on the street. As we exchanged greetings, a short conversation would follow in which the counsel they sought could be given. It all took place in the public eye. Few may have realized what was happening other than what appeared to be a greeting and a brief conversation, but counseling was taking place and no one's reputation was being threatened.

During this time, I was invited by Southern Seminary to serve as a Field Supervisor in the Doctor of Ministry program, making me an Adjunct Professor. I guided Wayne Hayes and Robert Sutton through their Field Supervision and assisted each of them in writing their doctoral thesis. This last help was not required, but they both received excellent grades on their thesis. I worked closely with faculty members Larry McSwain and Alan Culpepper in supervising these students.

As my work continued at the church, an active youth ministry came into being. The most effective of the part-time youth ministers was Mike Ficco from Paducah. Bob Kersey, a staff member of First Baptist Church Paducah had taken Mike under his wing when Mike was a teenager. Mike had gone to Murray State University and had worked at First Baptist Paducah during the summers and on his school breaks. Bob told me that Mike was enrolling at Southern Seminary and would make us a good youth minister.

Our Youth Committee interviewed Mike and gave him the job. He proved to be everything Bob Kersey had said and more. He had a lot of charisma and good people skills. Our youth ministry flourished under his leadership. However, God had called Mike to preach and he wanted to serve a church in that capacity. After about two years, I recommended him to a rural church nearby that called him to be their pastor. He was gracious in asking me to preach at his ordination at First Baptist Church in Paducah. Unfortunately, Mike and his infant son died in a tragic accident a few years later. He had married and was serving a church in Alabama at the time of his death.

There were several other part-time staff members before the church chose to employ a full-time person who would be the minister of music and youth. A committee was appointed, and the search began. This resulted in calling Steve Coldiron as Minister of Music and Youth. His family was from Kentucky, but he had grown up in the Detroit area. He served well for about eighteen months and then became disenchanted with ministry in a small town. Steve was able, but he was moody and abrasive with some of the congregation. When conflict arose between him and persons in the groups with whom he had to work, I tried to counsel him about his people skills but to no avail. He believed that others were totally at fault.

Steve was called to another place of service. When he left, we were not on the best of terms, but I had tried to support his work and keep him out of conflict with his opposition. His complaint to me was that he did not receive an adequate increase in his salary and he was unhappy with my informal review and evaluation of his ministry. My evaluation and review of his work was positive, but it did contain strong suggestions about avoiding conflict with his critics. Steve had natural gifts for ministry, but he had much to learn about working with people.

Our next and possibly the best staff member with whom I ever worked was Barbara DeCoursey from Franklin, Indiana. Barbara was a Southern Seminary graduate and a talented church musician who possessed great people skills. She came to serve as our Minister of Music and Youth. She was a loving, caring person and everyone loved her. I never had to bail her out of trouble or conflict. She worked long and hard, to the point that I often had to tell her it was time to go home and get some rest. When she discovered that the church had hand bells, she organized a hand bell choir. JoAnn and I played in the bell choir until we left the church. After more than three great years on our staff, Barbara went home to Indiana to marry the love of her life.

One additional thing about Barbara; we paid her the same salary that we had paid her male predecessor. Some of our people grumbled that we could have paid her less because she was a woman, but I would not hear to that. She did the job, she did it well, and she deserved fair pay.

Our next staff venture involved some changes in the position. We voted to call a Minister of Education and Youth and a separate part-time Minister of Music. This arrangement proved to be effective and we experienced some growth in our congregation, but problems developed. It seems that part of the congregation never had been able to relate to more than one staff person at a time. They chose to support either the pastor or the staff person. It was an adversarial, love/hate relationship. I never understood this attitude, but that is the way it demonstrated itself.

We called Houston Hall as Minister of Education and Youth and Charles Roberts as Minister of Music. All went well for about a year, but Houston and Charles began to be friendly with those who opposed my ministry. Much of this opposition came from the homosexual community along with their family and friends. It is always a signal of trouble brewing when a staff person becomes overly friendly with those who are critical of or hostile to pastoral leadership.

I chose to confront this problem directly soon after I saw it developing. My critics had led Houston to believe that he could become pastor of the church if he would help them get rid of me, and Charles became his ally in this endeavor. I talked with them both about what they were doing and informed them that if they continued, the next throats to be cut after mine would be theirs. They rejected my counsel and I told them that loyalty was a two-way street. If they persisted in being disloyal, they would be on their own. I would neither support nor protect them. They still would not listen to my counsel. I stepped back and let them do their dirty work. Within less than a year both were forced to leave.

Unfortunately, when there is a negative departure of church staff no one wins and many are hurt. Both of these staff members also participated with some of my opposition in an event in which it was made to appear that I had misappropriated church funds. Since I never touched church funds, had no check writing authority, and had no authority to disperse church funds without church approval, and since no money was actually missing, these charges were absurd. But the story circulated through the church and the community. Few believed the story, but when you are accused, even if it is a false accusation, it calls your character into question. I chose the high road of continuing to hold my head up and go forward praying that truth would prevail, and it did.

During all of this upheaval in the church, we experienced one of those Spirit-filled revivals that occasionally comes to churches. I had worked hard preparing the church for the revival and praying that this one would be different. Dr. E. Kevil Judy, a retired minister, from Henderson, Kentucky, was our evangelist. We spent a great deal of prayer time getting ready for the revival, and God heard our prayers. There were professions of faith in every service. Parents, who had previously stood between me and their children not wanting me to talk with them came bringing their children to my office or called asking me to come to their homes and counsel with them. Children, teenagers, and adults made professions of faith. There were many other decisions as well. This was one of about three or four genuine Spirit-filled revivals that came to the churches that I served during my entire ministry.

An outgrowth of this revival was the facing of some of these internal problems by the congregation. Our deacons began to see what this internal conflict was doing to the church. They met informally without my knowledge and took public action coming to the front of the church at the conclusion of one of our services stating their approval and support of me personally and of my ministry as their pastor. I credit this action to the leadership of Cortland Cox, who remains to this day the best deacon chairman with whom I ever served.

One of the things that I developed during my stay at Hodgenville was an effective way of presenting a children's sermon. I saw a demonstration of how best to do it while visiting the First Presbyterian Church of Orlando, Florida, where my cousins Joan and Joe Stine are members. Their associate pastor presented a children's sermon which proved to be the exact method for which I had been searching for years. He took the major theme of the message for that day, condensed it into language for the children, and in the space of about three minutes shared it with them. It was a powerful event catching the attention of both children and adults. It previewed the message that would follow. When I began doing this in the services at Hodgenville, it seemed so natural to me that I wondered why I had never thought of doing it that way before. It proved to be enjoyable and effective for everyone involved. My previous children's sermons had been so ineffective that I had stopped doing them.

During the previous ten years at Hodgenville, a natural order of events continued to take place in our family. Paul, Bryant, and Philip all completed their college studies and were working in areas of their choosing. Paul was trying to make it in the entertainment world. Bryant had married Leslie Hazelip of Franklin, Kentucky, and was working for Western Kentucky University while pursuing his master's degree. Philip had begun teaching in the Hardin County School System and was working on his master's degree. Then, Bryant went to work for Key Oil Company and moved to Owensboro to operate a bulk oil plant. JoAnn had become chairman of the Business Department in LaRue County High School.

Both of our mothers were advancing in age, becoming less able daily to take care of themselves. JoAnn often went to London, Kentucky, on the weekend just to be sure that her mother's needs were being met. She and her sister, Bobbie Rush, had their hands full trying to take care of an aging, strong willed mother who was fast becoming physically unable to care for herself.

My mother's condition was rapidly deteriorating. In conversations with my brother and stepfather, we began trying to make plans as to how we could provide for her needs. Her short-term memory began to fade. Often, she could not remember when she had last seen my stepfather, who had just left her that morning to go to work. We finally decided along with her physician that when she had another episode that sent her to the hospital, we would try to make the transition to nursing home care for her. Later, she developed a severe case of shingles that weakened her to the point that nursing home care was the best option for her. She went directly from the hospital to the nursing home.

I made five trips from Hodgenville to Lake City during the first year my mother was in the nursing home. After a day or two visit, I would leave early enough to see her at the nursing home and then depart for Kentucky. I would cry and pray all the way to Atlanta or Murfreesboro. That is when I did my grieving and when she died four and a half years later, I had no tears left. I thanked God when my sister-in-law, Burma Sue, called to tell me that she had gone to be with the Lord. My mother was a good woman, a wonderful mother, a devout Christian, and she loved me and my brother without reservation.

During this time JoAnn and I had the happy experience of becoming grandparents. Bryant and Leslie had decided to leave Owensboro. He sold his part in the oil business that he had developed, and they moved back to Bowling Green. Leslie went to work as a dental hygienist and Bryant was hunting a job. Then we learned that Leslie was expecting their first child. It proved to be a trying and exciting time. Leslie was pregnant and working while Bryant was looking for a job. He pursued many opportunities and was hired by State Farm Insurance just before their first son, Adam, was born. Bryant began his job with State Farm Insurance in Murfreesboro, Tennessee, just a few days after Adam arrived. They moved to Murfreesboro as soon as Leslie could care for herself and Adam. It was the end of a trying time for them and the beginning of a new opportunity in their lives. JoAnn and I were excited grandparents.

Staff positions for Minister of Education and Youth and Minister of Music were waiting to be filled. Search committees were appointed so that we would not lose the ground that we had gained in recent months. There was some grumbling about the fact that we had not been able to keep staff much longer than two to three years. I knew that when we called a person right out of seminary, they were looking to move on to larger churches which would offer them greater opportunity to minister. It was unrealistic to expect to keep staff for a long period of time, but my critics continued to blame me when a staff member departed. They claimed that no one could work with me for much more than three years. False stories from the past were dredged up and a spin put on them that cast me in the most negative light possible. Most of these stories were total fabrications.

I spent more time than I should have trying to refute the false negative stories that were being told. Finally, I decided to move on with what I was trying to do. If people wanted to believe lies, I could talk until doom's day and it would not change their minds. It was not possible to chase down and correct every negative story being circulated.

What I failed to realize was that First Baptist Church Hodgenville did not have a history of long pastorates. In fact, one of my deacon friends told me that the church wanted a pastor to come and stay about five or six years and move on. He would be tolerated up to about eight years, but after that, the church wanted him to leave. I was at that time well into my twelfth year and had already overstayed my welcome in the minds of many. I have since suspected that the reasoning in the minds of the people was that the longer a pastor stayed, the more he knew about the congregation and the community. It was impossible not to know both the negative and positive side of most people's lives. There are few genuine secrets in a small close-knit town or county.

In retrospect, I see a pattern of information sharing which continued until the day I departed. People would come to me sharing the negative and/or positive history of a person or a family. In turn, someone else would do the same thing about another person or family. Even when I asked people not to tell me stories of this nature, they would often continue on ignoring my request. The longer one stays in a church and community, the more he comes to know about the people. The church family was aware of that fact.

I made a point of not allowing any person's negative past to influence my relationship with them. I did not allow the past to limit a person's opportunity to serve or work in the church. After all, the good Lord has given all of us more than a second chance. Further, one becomes aware that some people have conflicts that make it impossible for them to work in a positive way with another person. I was careful to arrange that people with conflicting personalities were not put on the same committees. Often the lay leaders on the Nominating Committee would be aware of these conflicts and would handle it without my help. There were always those who wanted to serve in what they saw as being the more influential positions in the church but who had neither the ability nor the spiritual character that those positions demanded. When people with these aspirations and limitations were discussed, they were always given some place to serve, even though it was not in the position they desired. I continue to believe that my actions reflected stable and mature leadership.

Previously mentioned were our efforts to grow a stronger Sunday School. Arthur Flake, the father of Baptist Sunday School work, taught that "Your Sunday School will take the shape of the building in which it meets." He was right. Our buildings were all pre-1960 construction and were not adaptable to the programs designed for the 1980s and 1990s. Though the church had been able to maintain better attendance back during the 1950s through the 1960s, we were not able to match what they had done. However, we did provide a strong youth and music ministry. When Barbara DeCoursey became our Minister of Music and Youth, these areas flourished.

Barbara DeCoursey had worked at Ridgecrest Baptist Assembly in a youth program called Centerfuge prior to coming to work for us. Upon arriving in Hodgenville, she began to promote the idea of taking a group of our youth to a week at one of the Centerfuge encampments. I became involved in this effort and went with our youth four different years. We went to three different locations and found the experience to be helpful in growing and strengthening the spiritual lives of our young people. Also, several different parents took time to go as chaperones. I still have some of those who were involved in these groups tell me how much those times we spent together meant to them.

It was during this time that Patsy Cundiff, who was serving as our church and financial secretary, announced that her husband had taken a job with the school system in Hart County and they would be moving. She was resigning her position with the church. She had served our church in this position ever since I first came to Hodgenville, having done so effectively and with great dignity. Her departure put us in search for someone to take her place.

After the interview process, we decided to offer the job to Betty Vance, a member of the Buffalo Baptist Church and a lifelong resident of LaRue County. Betty was experienced, mature, and a most capable person. She was and remains one of the best and most efficient persons with whom I ever worked.

The last Minister of Music with whom I worked at Hodgenville was a young lady from Alabama named Angela Warren. She was a music student at Southern Seminary, an excellent musician, a tireless worker, and gifted with great people skills. She continued the music ministry without appearing to lose a step in the transition, and everyone seemed to enjoy working with her. She became engaged to a young man named Paul Harrington, a flutist and a member of the Louisville Orchestra. About a year later they married. Later, Angela left to serve a church in Louisville.

When Angela came to serve our church, I had a conversation with her about her desire to be ordained. She assured me that she was not seeking ordination. I explained to her that a majority of our church would not favor ordaining a woman in any capacity. However, I did point out that a small minority may be willing to ordain a woman. We left it at that, but, a few months before she left our church, she came to me asking if I would request that the church ordain her. I reminded her of our previous conversation and told her that I would not make such a request because it could upset a majority of our people and possibly bring about a serious breach in our fellowship. I went on to tell her that I was not opposed to ordaining her, but she came to us with the understanding that she was not seeking ordination. I pointed out that we were already dealing with some serious problems and that we did not need to create another one. She was not happy with my response, but she accepted my decision.

We were still left with the vacancy for education and youth. Again, a committee was appointed, and a search began. This search led us to John Jackson, the son of Gene and Mary Jackson, who had been members of the church for most of their lives. Gene had a history of being involved in conflict and of physically assaulting people both in the church and community. When I came to the church, he came to me sharing some of this story and promising me that he would control his temper and other outbursts which had been a problem over the years. The church later ordained Gene as a deacon, and he served without being a problem until his son came on staff.

John Jackson and his family were living in Alabama at the time we called him. He had shared with his pastor, Lawrence Phipps, a close friend of mine, that he had been called to the ministry. He was in his late thirties and had never been employed anywhere for an extended period of time. When members of the church heard that we were considering him for our staff position, several persons advised me not to bring him on staff. They all told me that Gene and

Mary could not be realistic when it came to their children and that to bring John on staff would be nothing but trouble. I responded saying that I had discussed with the parents and they had assured me that they would never dream of causing problems for me or the church. I have since wished that I had listened to those warnings. The church did call him to serve, but it was a very poor vote. The people knew the family history.

The arrangement we worked out with John was that he would be our minister of education and youth, but he would be free to take up to six hours per semester at Southern Seminary. His classes were to be on Monday which would not interfere with his service to the church.

I did everything I could to prepare for John's arrival, even arranging a five and a quarter percent loan through a special housing deal sponsored by the Commonwealth of Kentucky and a local bank for his purchase of a home. But whatever was done for him never seemed to be enough. I do not think I ever heard him express gratitude for anything done for him or his family.

Both John and his parents broke every agreement and promise that they had made to me and the church. Gene reverted back to his bullying ways trying to intimidate and threaten everyone who appeared to question John's activities in our church. Many felt that it was but a matter of time before Gene attacked me physically. He tried to intimidate me, but I never let him feel that I feared him or what he might do. He was the typical bully who would not attack anyone who showed no fear when faced with his bullying tactics. He would announce what he planned to do in deacons' meetings but never carry out his threats. He would bring a TV camcorder to a deacons meeting pretending to record the proceedings. He personally pushed the church into buying a new bus for the senior citizens group. The bus was purchased, but the church never approved the purchase. He did everything he could to undermine my leadership and create division within the church. The senior citizens group in the church became a small but vocal group whose favor John and Gene constantly courted in an effort to solidify John's position and to weaken my leadership.

One example of Gene's bullying episodes had to do with Howard Sandidge, then serving as deacon chairman. Gene would bait Howard with sarcastic remarks whenever Howard was present. One afternoon Howard and I were having coffee in Smith's Drug Store. Gene came in and joined us. Everything was pleasant until we all began to leave. Gene made a personal remark to Howard which Howard answered in kind. Gene had opened the door as if to leave, but he turned, grabbed Howard by the lapels and began threatening him. By then I had grasped the open door with my left hand. I saw Gene draw back his right fist and start to hit Howard. I grabbed Gene's right arm with my right arm and insisted that he turn Howard loose and go to his car. Howard kept telling Gene that if he hit him, he would sue him. I separated them and sent both of them to their cars. Someone later told that I ran when all this happened, but a witness in the drug store said, "You are wrong. The preacher broke up the fight and sent both men to their cars."

The situation at the church became so tense and heated that it was almost impossible to have any kind of meeting without the threat of violence. One Sunday, Bobbie Brownfield placed some reserved signs on parking spaces in the church parking lot next to his funeral home. Bobbie had permission to use the church parking lot when no church activities were in progress. Gene arrived, removed the signs, and took them with him to his Sunday School class. When Bobbie entered the class and asked Gene for the signs, class members had to step between the two in order to keep them physically apart. Gene is alleged to have threatened his Sunday School teacher causing the teacher to take a leave of absence from the class for several weeks. Several men in the church came to me advising me to be careful not to be drawn into a brawl with Gene. My response was that I did not think that he had the courage to assault me. I was right; he never did.

In a deacons meeting, Bobbie McDowell moved that the deacons recommend that the church ordain John. I was opposed to this action but was in no position to stop it. I could have fought it, but the battle would not have been worth the cost to me personally or to the church. Also, my opposition could have delayed the ordination, but it probably would not have prevented it. We set the date for the ordination and invited Lawrence Phipps to preach the ordination sermon. The ordination service was nice, and Gene came to me later thanking me for the way it was handled. I sincerely regret taking part in the ordination. If John was called of God, he has yet to demonstrate any evidence of such a call.

John began to openly criticize of me. He told Lawrence Phipps that he intended to do all that he could to end my ministry at Hodgenville. He aligned with my critics in the church who kept telling him that with me out of the picture, he could become the pastor. He began to go through all the church records trying to find some sort of evidence that I had done something wrong. In doing this, he crashed our church computer system more than once.

Some of our church leaders asked me if I would agree to go with them and John to a seminary faculty member who was skilled in giving counsel when staff relationships seemingly could not be resolved. I agreed, and we went, but John continued to insist in that meeting that I was unfit to pastor the church. He refused to agree to even try to work through any disagreement. It was an exercise in futility.

As circumstances became more strained every day, Angela Harrington stated to Betty Vance that this conflict was ridiculous. She went on to say that if John and I were Christians, we should get together, forgive each other, and get on with the Lord's work. Hearing that, I decided to have a heart-to-heart talk with Angela. As best I could, I tried to explain what the problems were and tell her that efforts had been made to work out differences, but that John had refused. I warned her to be careful not to get drawn into the conflict and that even if she stayed out of it, she could become the victim of those who were after me. She was nice, but I could tell that she did not grasp the seriousness of what I was telling her. Later, after I had resigned, Gene became verbally abusive to her. She tearfully confided to Betty Vance that "Brother McDonald warned me this would happen, but I did not believe him."

During all of this time, I had been faithfully circulating my resume to churches that I felt might consider me. Some of these churches sent committees to hear me, but I was having no success in terms of getting a second or third interview or in being invited to visit a church in view of being called to serve as pastor. I was under the impression that it was the age factor, but I learned later that negative information about me was being shared with these committees. I cannot blame them for wanting to avoid any leader who appeared to be the source of unrest within the congregation he was serving. While it was true that there were problems within the church, it was not true that I was source of those problems. However, it is almost impossible to separate one's self from the problems if you are the pastor of the church.

These were extremely tense and difficult times for me and my family. All of our sons had moved out and were no longer living with us, but they were not unaware of the events that were taking place. JoAnn and I were in the midst of this turmoil every day. There was an immense amount of gossip, all of which was almost totally untrue, or the truth was so distorted that it was not recognizable. I was still making every effort to find another place to serve only to be frustrated at every turn of events. Had I known the outcome, there are some things that I would change, but hindsight is always clearer than foresight. It was as the Bible says, "We walk by faith, not by sight" (2 Corinthians 5:7).

Chapter 16
Hodgenville: Concluding Months

In late 1989, it became apparent to me that my working relationship with the church was not improving. In fact, it was getting worse. The gossip mill was working overtime within the church and the community. John Jackson and his family were actively portraying themselves as victims. I was being portrayed as one who was holding the church back and mistreating staff members. Those who wanted to see me leave were telling everyone who would listen that I was the problem and that things would not improve until I had departed.

On two separate occasions, an influential church member sent word to me by two different persons proposing that if I would take a six-month sabbatical and not return to serve as pastor, he would see that my salary was paid in full for those six months. I politely declined the offer each time indicating that I was not for sale and that when I left it would be on my own terms.

Finally, this person came to me personally with the same offer. I gave the same answer that I had given the messengers. I was polite. In fact, I was never rude at any time. But there were occasions when this person was visibly upset with me. The issue between us as I saw it was that of control. When my response to this person's directions were not positive, our relationship quickly became adversarial. While I tried to avoid an adversarial relationship, it appeared to me that this person became angry and our relationship which I had thought was mutually friendly and respectful became less than that. I made a genuine effort to avoid such conflict, but it appeared to have no positive effect. This casualty of church conflict is one that I truly regret. However, I am convinced that though I may share some responsibility for the outcome, I was not totally at fault. I did try to maintain a positive relationship, but my efforts were rejected.

As things continued to deteriorate, I decided to confront the problem head on. I went first to the deacons on November 5, 1989. My message to them follows:

MESSAGE TO THE DEACONS

Let me begin by saying to you that what I am about to do I have never done before. I have been in the ministry since I was fifteen years old. I have been a pastor since I was eighteen years old. But tonight, I am walking where I have never before walked. Indeed, I had hoped and prayed that I would never have to come before you this way. But I believe it is necessary.

We have problems in our church fellowship. They are problems that refuse to go away. They are problems that demand a solution.

I have worked, prayed and tried to do everything I that I know to do, hoping that we could get a positive spirit going within our church. It seems that every time we appear to be ready to turn the corner and establish a positive spirit, something happens to short-circuit the effort and we lose ground instead of gaining it.

One of the things that seems to be hurting us is a number of rumors that are circulating within the church and community.

There is hardly a day that goes by, but that I hear that we are having secret meetings in which we are planning to fire John. It may be that such meetings are being held, but if they are, I have not been a part of them nor do I know anything about any such meetings.

Before John's ordination was recommended to the church, several deacons pointed out that numerous statements were alleged to have been made by him to the effect that (1) he did not wish to be ordained; (2) that he did not wish to be ordained by this church; (3) that he preferred to be ordained in Oneonta, Alabama by the same church that had licensed him to the ministry; and (4) that he did not want me to have any part in his ordination.

When our deacon chairman discussed this with me, I suggested that the deacon officers and the pastor meet with John and discuss his desires. Since the issue was his ordination, we wanted him to be in agreement with what was to take place, to be happy about it and to be a willing participant.

We did meet with John for an hour and ten minutes. We asked him the following questions:

(1) Do you want to be ordained?
(2) Where do you want to be ordained?
(3) Is there anyone in particular that you would like to participate in it?
(4) Will it be all right to work out the date and get back to you on that?

When the meeting was concluded, we all left in what appeared to be good spirits. Yet, some of you were called and told that John was upset because he had been mistreated in the meeting.

Recently, the Personnel Committee met, and a minority of its members expressed a desire to change the way we develop the church budget. The Chairman of the Deacons, the Chairman of the Personnel Committee, the Chairman of the Stewardship Committee, and the pastor met and discussed this. It was decided not to change the basic way we develop the church budget. That decision was shared with the Personnel Committee. Yet, it is being told that this was another meeting to plan to fire John.

The rumors continue to circulate, and they are polarizing our people. Some are alleged to support John while others are alleged to support the pastor. This is tearing our church apart. It is being talked over the phone, on the street corner, in the coffee shops, and everywhere. It has nearly killed any evangelistic effort that we try to make. People will join a church where the Lord is loved, worshipped, and where the members love and speak well of each other. But few people will join a church where a fight is raging or where a fight is imminent.

In a recent meeting of the Personnel Committee, the issue of voting by ex officio members came up. Ex officio committee members were voting when I became your pastor. They have continued this practice since that time. Our by-laws make Robert's Rules of Order the parliamentary system by which we conduct our meetings. Roberts Rules of Order plainly state that ex officio members have the right to vote if they are members of the organization that they serve.

Yet it has been told repeatedly that what was done was out of order. I spent two hours after Prayer Meeting Wednesday night trying to answer the questions of an upset church member who had been told numerous rumors, none of which were true.

If it is possible, I feel that we need to try to find the source of these rumors and encourage the person or persons involved in spreading them to stop this behavior.

There are other incidents: The purchase of the church bus; the manner or method by which this was done has caused more problems than the bus itself.

Last year's church budget; interference with my supervision of John; harassment of W. D. Burden, Forest Gilpin, and the pastor over the replacing of the associate teacher of the Victory Sunday School Class; this became so bad that Brother Gilpin resigned the class and refused to teach it for a number of weeks; the Drug Store incident between two members of our church which the pastor witnessed.

There continues to be a constant feeding of the rumor mill that puts the pastor and other church leaders in the role of the "bad guys". This is undermining the confidence and trust level that the church has in its spiritual leaders.

Jesus quoted from the Old Testament to describe one of the methods of Satan in terms of undermining spiritual leaders. Satan's method is "to strike the shepherd and scatter the sheep" (Mark 14:27); the circulation of gossip, rumors and untrue stories about your leaders always does great harm to the fellowship of the church.

In I Corinthians 1:10-17, Paul speaks of a method and issue that was being used to divide the Corinthian church. Sadly, it is the same method and issue that is being used in our church.

Every pastor that I know wants his people to love and respect him. I am no exception to that. But I want our people to love Christ and His church more than they love me. It is the Lord that we serve and worship. No man deserves our love and loyalty more than Christ. He is to be first. And we must love the church which is the body of Christ.

When we choose sides and support men, we begin to devour and destroy ourselves. That is what is being promoted in our midst and it must be stopped.

What can we do? We cannot afford to do nothing. This is a spiritual problem and it will not go away.

The early church in Acts faced its problems, prayed about them and took corrective action. This is what took place in the case of Ananias and Sapphira (Acts 5:1-11). It is also what took place in Acts 6:1-7 when deacons were given the job of restoring a broken and disturbed fellowship.

Together, I want us to work out some course of action which we can prayerfully support and follow.

Again, I repeat that our problem is a spiritual problem. When hearts are right with God and one another, we can focus on the greater task of winning our community and world to Christ.

Your questions, discussion, and suggestions are in order. If at any time you want me to leave the meeting so that you can continue your discussion, I will be happy to do so.

I remained in the meeting briefly. Little discussion took place. I asked to be excused and left. The meeting did not last long after I left. When I talked with some of the deacons later, they indicated that little was said and nothing substantial was accomplished. It seemed that no one wanted to face the problems or attempt to resolve them.

Having taken the problem to the deacons and sensing that they were not willing to face the issues and take some positive, redemptive action, I decided to take the second step - that of placing the problem before the church. I chose to do it the following Sunday, November 11, 1989, during the morning worship service. Since we had a live broadcast of the service, I took a tape of one of my previous sermons and asked the radio station to end the live broadcast with the choir special and then to play my taped message. I felt that it would be in poor taste to broadcast any problems related to our church fellowship over the air.

The message I delivered was entitled "Calling the Church to Prayer." The text was Philippians 1:3-11. Having read the text, I explained that I had chosen to do that day what I have never done before. However, it was being done out of a sense of duty to my divine call to the pastoral ministry and my love for the people at First Baptist Church Hodgenville.

I acknowledged that since I was calling the church to prayer, asking that each one put aside petty grievances and seek the forgiveness of those whom they might have wronged in the past, it was my duty to do the same, which I did as best I knew how. Since our problems as a church were spiritual, we, each and every one, needed to confess that before God asking His forgiveness and help as we sought to heal His church in Hodgenville. The congregation was then invited to leave their seats and gather around the pulpit area for prayer.

Concluding that invitation, I said, "Understand that you are not being asked to come forward to pledge your support to a man. You are being asked to come forward to pray for yourself and your church. If you love the Lord and you want to see His will done in and through this church, then gathering here at the front is a small price to pay to see His will be done here on earth as it is done in heaven. I invite you to join together here for prayer."

The response to this message and appeal was almost totally positive. People left their seats, gathered down front, came up on the pulpit area and filled the aisles. I called on the following people to lead the group in prayer suggesting a subject for their prayer, but not limiting them to that subject only: John Jackson, praise; Howard Sandidge, thanksgiving and petition; Roy Long, forgiveness; Donald Rock, love; Lou Bingham, unity. For the benediction, I read I Corinthians 13 and dismissed the congregation.

I had been standing on the right side of the pulpit and as I turned toward my left I saw John Jackson standing about eight feet away. He put his head down and turned away from me as if to leave. I asked him to wait and I went over and embraced him. He accepted my effort but seemed totally uncomfortable. I would have been uncomfortable too had I been him because he never stopped spreading rumors or doing all he could to undermine my pastoral leadership of the church. As I prepared to leave the sanctuary, John's father, Gene Jackson, confronted me and said, "Preacher, that is the worst abuse of a pastor's power that I have ever seen." I replied, "Gene, I'm sorry you feel that way." His words told me that the Jackson family had no intention of stopping their efforts of sowing discord and of trying to remove me from the pastoral leadership of the church. I closed the church doors and went home.

During the time that this internal turmoil had been taking place, I had been actively trying to get other churches who were looking for a new pastor to consider me as a possible candidate for their pulpit. In one of those churches, a friend whom I had known in Paducah was serving on the search committee of his church. When I walked out into the service Sunday, November 11, 1989, he and his wife were present. I felt that even though what I was doing was a positive effort to resolve issues in our church, it would have a negative impact on him and his church. I was right; I never heard from him or his church after his visit with us.

Things settled down and became quieter after I called the church to prayer, but I had a sense that it was only the quiet before the storm. We had the usual Thanksgiving and Christmas activities. Nothing unusual happened. John

Jackson and his family continued to curry the favor of the senior citizens group. When the seniors had a meal at the church, I would attend and eat with the group, but I was about as welcome as an illegitimate child at a family reunion. Some of the seniors were polite and welcoming, but they were in the minority.

I continued to circulate my resume' but was having little success. Word seems to get out when there are problems within a church, and the blame usually is placed on the pastor. Lay people generally assume that if the pastor is a good, capable leader, there will be no problems. This assumption is not true, but that seems to be the way it works in the mind of the laity. I made regular trips to the Alumni Office at Southern Seminary and kept them supplied with copies of my resume', but that proved to be futile. I stayed in contact with the Church-Minister Relations Office in Kentucky and several other state conventions, but again that proved to be ineffective. Persons in leadership in these state convention offices will not incur any risk in terms of helping someone even if they know that he is a gifted and capable leader. They lead you to believe that they will be of help, but they are a Church Relations Office rather than a minister's advocate. The minister is left on the outside looking in.

What a person needs when he is in the position in which I found myself is a very active advocate who will leave no stone unturned in terms of working in his behalf. I did not have that kind of advocate even though I had many friends who were willing to send my resume' to churches that were searching for a new pastor. Most pastors are so busy keeping their own ship afloat that they have little time to devote to helping a fellow pastor. I think most of them want to be of help, but lack of time and "know how" hinders their efforts. Some promised to help but never did.

There were several facts about moving that I later found to be evolving. When I first entered the ministry, it was considered inappropriate for a person to apply for an open position. You needed someone to write a letter recommending you and include your resume' with the letter. But now it is acceptable for a person to make direct contact with a church and to apply for an open position. Also, I had been told not to resign with no other job offer in hand. It was the old "a bird in hand is worth two in the bush" philosophy. Add to that the assumption that a preacher without a church must have something wrong with him. He must have done something wrong or proved to be a poor leader in his previous church or he would still be employed.

However, all of those guidelines were changing. Also, I learned that a minister is often judged by the church he is serving. If the church projects a negative image or has a questionable reputation, that can keep a pastor from being considered for a position. Sometimes having no church to serve is better than having one that projects a poor image. I recall at least three search committees that came to visit me and were turned off by the negative vibes they picked up in the visit. Two churches sent committee members who already had a negative impression of my church. They reported that the candidate was fine, but he was in a poor environment. Thus, they went on to consider other candidates.

Finally, there was the fact of denominational politics. In the late 1970s, the Southern Baptist Convention was taken over by a group of far right-wing fundamentalists. This group had always existed in Southern Baptist life, but the more mainline, center-of-the-road Baptists had kept them out of any position of power or influence up to that time. Most of the pre-1970s Baptist leaders were college and seminary trained and theologically conservative, but they were not fundamentalists. Since I was college and seminary trained, I naturally fell into the group that was pushed out of power and influence. While I have never seen any list of acceptable or non-acceptable ministers, I have been told by those who are supposed to know that such a list did exist. Mostly, the list was alleged to have excluded those who were college and seminary trained and/or were unwilling to follow the political leadership of the fundamentalists. I was included in that group along with nearly fifty percent of the pastors that I knew in Baptist life. The fundamentalists were highly organized and motivated. They worked hard at keeping people like me out of any influential pulpit and they were successful.

I found myself cut off from being able to move out of a difficult situation and facing increasing opposition from a small but highly vocal minority who would stop at nothing to oust me from my job and place of service. My opposition did not come from the best people in the church, nor were they the best people in the community. The sad thing about all of this was that the good people in the church chose to remain aloof from the conflict. Most of them said and did little or nothing to support me in the face of unjustified criticism and attack. I think most of them had seen similar circumstances before. They saw the pastor as expendable. If he resigned and left, things would settle down for a while. They had to live in the community with those who opposed him. He could leave, but they had to stay. It was their way of making peace with highly disagreeable circumstances.

The concluding months of my service as Hodgenville's pastor in 1990 were filled with escalating conflict that took place in various committee meetings. As an ex officio member of each church committee, I met with the committees and had always been expected to give some direction and leadership in the committee work. However, I soon found that members of the committees had been enlisted to oppose any leadership that I sought to give. Open conflict and verbal abuse began to take place in some of the committees. While this was usually done by only one committee member, the other members of the committee sat by quietly and said nothing. At this point in time, I knew how to choose my battles and I began to sidestep any conflict that arose, but the pattern of opposition soon became quite obvious.

I realized quickly that my opposition had enlisted those whom they could influence on the various committees and were following a plan of open opposition to my leadership. Further, they were sharing their negative influence wherever they could get a hearing. Most of these people had never been involved in the ongoing leadership of the church, but most aspired to be in leadership positions. However, the church had always declined to offer them their desired places of service. I had little to do with it.

By the end of the summer of 1990, I began to hear rumors about a possible vote on my tenure. Stuart Singleton came to me and asked me to request that the church take such a vote. I knew that was a set-up and told him that I would never agree to such a thing. John Jackson's daughters began to tell their friends that the church was going to vote me out and make their father the pastor of the church. Word came to me that a petition requesting my removal as pastor was being circulated among the members for their signatures. I knew that the by-laws stated that it would take a seventy-five percent vote in favor of my dismissal for me to be terminated. I did not think that my opposition could get that kind of support.

We did not have an evening service on the first Sunday of September 1990 because of the Labor Day holiday. I learned the next week that there would possibly be a call for a vote on my tenure at the next church business meeting scheduled for September 12. We had a deacon's meeting scheduled after the evening service on Sunday, September 9. When the evening service was over, and the deacons went to their meeting room, they found about fifteen people waiting in the room demanding to meet with them. The deacons at first refused to meet with the group, then they agreed to meet with them in the Fellowship Hall after the deacons had a chance to meet separately.

It became apparent that much of my opposition in the church was aware of what was about to happen because the group had increased to about thirty people by the time the deacons entered Fellowship Hall. Some of my supporters had heard what was happening and they came into the room also.

The spokesman for the group was Robert Seth. Jewel Throw had the copy of the petition which fifty-six families had allegedly signed asking that I be terminated as pastor. Howard Sandidge was the deacon chairman but was not effective in the meeting due to his hearing problem. There was conversation in the room, with several people trying to speak at once, plus the confusion of background noise, thus making it difficult for him to hear. Lonnie McCugh, who was ordained both as a deacon and a minister, stepped up and suggested that the group give the signed petition to the deacons and allow them to contact each family to determine the level and nature of their discontent. Robert Seth said that was not necessary and the group refused to give the petition to the deacons. Jewel Throw began to read the list of signatures. I stepped close to her looking over her shoulder as she read. All of the signatures that she was reading were in the same handwriting. I recognized the handwriting as that of the reader, Jewel Throw. I was familiar with her handwriting because she had written numerous letters to the church. Lonnie McCugh continued to make his case for allowing the deacons to deal with the matter in a quieter, more direct and peaceful manner, but the group would not agree to this.

However, the crowd was demanding immediate action. When asked what complaint the group had against the pastor, those who responded said, "Brother McDonald has been here too long." No one said that I did not visit, that I was a poor pastor, that I could not preach, that I had neglected to minister to members of the church, that I was dishonest, that I was immoral, or that I had represented the church poorly in the public eye of the community. In my opinion, their complaint meant that I had been there long enough to know more than they wanted me to know. Many in the group would nod in agreement when someone voiced this complaint. When I quietly reminded one member of the group that he had assured me that he would not participate in such a meeting, he replied, "I'm here because my mother wanted to come. I came to give her a ride home." My observation is that a woman's skirt is always a convenient object behind which to hide. I found it interesting that Gene and Mary Jackson were conveniently out of town this particular weekend.

After about an hour, the meeting began to wind down. My opposition would not surrender the petition to the deacons, and the deacons would not agree to recommend that I be terminated. I have always believed the petition was a ruse. Jewel Throw had probably made a lot of contacts in an effort to get people to sign it. However, since the names I saw were in her handwriting, I believe I am safe in assuming that when people listened to her or pretended to agree with her, she simply listed their names with or without their consent or signature. Why else would she and her group refuse to hand the document over to the deacons, so they could contact those who allegedly had signed it? I cannot remember exactly how the meeting was ended, but it did end, and people began to leave. The next day, I met with the deacon leaders and we agreed to call a special deacon's meeting for Tuesday evening.

All eighteen deacons attended the Tuesday evening meeting. After Howard Sandidge explained that I had requested the meeting, I was asked to speak. I thanked the men for being present and told them that I was hoping that we could find a solution to the problems within our fellowship. I explained that I wanted to ask them two questions and requested permission to ask and get an answer verbally from each man. They agreed to this procedure. My first question was: "Do you believe that my resigning as pastor would solve the problems within the church?" I faced each man and asked him to give his honest, heartfelt answer. Each man answered, "No." My second question was: "Do you personally want me to resign as your pastor?" Again, each man was asked individually to respond. They all answered, "No." With this response, I told them that as leaders of the church, we must come up with some workable plan to restore fellowship and bring peace within the congregation. There was a minimum amount of discussion, but no decision was made by the group. We dismissed the meeting and went home.

When I arrived home, I discussed with JoAnn what had taken place. Then I said, "There may be a vote tomorrow night, but I think I will survive it." She asked, "Well, what about the vote the next business meeting or the one after that?" I thought about that briefly and said, "You are not happy in these circumstances, are you?" She replied, "No, and you aren't either. There is no reason for us to stay where we are not wanted and where opposition makes your work impossible or ineffective. These people who oppose you are not going to give up and quit." I said, "If I resign with no place to go, the chances of my ever being a pastor again are slim to none." She said, "That may be true, but it would be better than living like this. We have lived on my salary before. We can do it again until God provides another place of service for you. Something will work out."

When JoAnn and I finished talking it was nearly 11:00 p.m.; I picked up the phone and called Howard Sandidge, Donald Rock, and Lonnie McCugh, three of our deacon leaders. I told each of them that I wanted them to call a meeting of the Personnel Committee and Finance Committee before the Church Business Meeting the next day. My request was for them to work out whatever severance package that they could agree on and in return for that, I would give them a letter of resignation that would be effective Saturday, September 15, 1990. This meant that I would not go back into the pulpit again. Each of them tried to persuade me not to do this, but I told them that I had decided to take this action and my decision was final. They all reluctantly agreed to my request.

Wednesday was spent trying to get my thoughts together in terms of writing a letter of resignation and letting some of my friends know what was happening. A call to Howard Cobble at Severns Valley Baptist Church was in order because he had been privy to several conversations with those who were unhappy with my leadership. Howard agreed that a quiet departure was better than a bitter fight. There was no good to be gained in splitting the church. I also called Bill Marshall, the Executive-Secretary of the Kentucky Baptist Convention. He was out of the office, but his secretary said he would return my call the next day.

Later in the day, I called our youngest son, Philip, and explained to him my decision. He was upset over the unfairness of the entire ordeal but said he would be at our house as soon as his school responsibilities were over. By the time he arrived I had composed my letter of resignation and had it ready to give to those whom I had called. The text of the letter follows:

September 12, 1990

First Baptist Church
200 South Lincoln Boulevard
Hodgenville, Kentucky 42748

Dear Members of First Baptist Church:

For more than fourteen years it has been my privilege to serve as your Pastor. I am grateful for the trust that you expressed as you called me to this office and for the support you have given me over the years.

I am submitting my resignation to you as your Pastor effective September 15, 1990. I thank you for the good years that we have shared together, and I pray God's blessings on you in the future.

Sincerely,

Isaac B. McDonald

Philip drove me to the church shortly before the Church Business Meeting was to begin. A larger crowd of people than usual was gathering and entering the church. I went to the church office and found the three men whom I had called the night before and gave them my letter of resignation. They began to tell me what was going to be recommended to the church in terms of a severance package. I stopped them and told them to tell me about it after it had been approved by the church. Then I left. Gene Jackson was standing outside on the sidewalk. It was obvious that he was quite upset. I think he was also aware that with my departure, his son, John, would not last long as a church employee.

Philip and I drove back home where JoAnn met us, and we went for a ride. We did not return home until after nine o'clock. By then the meeting at the church was over and most folk had gone home. I did find several notes from people who had come by the house and failed to find us at home.

We had a call from one of our friends who shared with us the action that was taken at the church. Lonnie McCugh had read my letter of resignation. Robert Seth had moved that it be accepted. Jewel Throw seconded the motion. The motion was passed by a vote of 84 for and 49 against.

The church then approved the following severance package which was recommended by the deacons and Stewardship Committee:

1. Dr. McDonald is to receive sixteen (16) weeks base salary beginning with the week of September 17-21, 1990.

2. All annuities (retirement) in arrears to be paid plus and additional six (6) months to be paid, beginning with the bill for October 1990.

3. Six (6) months health insurance to be paid, beginning with the bill for October 1990.

4. Dr. McDonald will have use of the parsonage until June 1, 1991.

With this action another chapter of my life was coming to a close. I was about to enter into an entirely new experience, but I was at peace. All the stress of a sad and tragic event in my life was giving way to the anticipation of a new opportunity that God would provide. I was certain in all of my uncertainty that I would not run out of opportunities.

Chapter 17
Unemployed: What Every Minister Fears

Since entering the ministry there have been three times that I have been without a place to serve. During my first year and a half in college, I would have enjoyed having a church, but I was probably not mature enough to handle the responsibility. However, in December 1950, I was called to serve the New Oak Grove Baptist Church near Alachua, Florida. Having served that church for a little more than two years, I was called to two half-time churches. They were Athens Baptist Church and Mt. Zion Baptist Church, both located in Columbia County Florida, near my home of Lake City. I served those two churches for one year and was called as pastor of Ft. White Baptist Church, also in Columbia Count where I served until I resigned that pulpit in late August 1954 to enter Southern Baptist Theological Seminary in Louisville, Kentucky. I entered my second period of being without a pulpit during my first year at the seminary and did not serve as a pastor again until September 1955 when I was called to serve the Shady Grove Baptist Church in Franklin, Kentucky.

Having resigned First Baptist Church, Hodgenville, Kentucky, I was again among the unemployed. Being unemployed is what nearly every minister fears, and I had lived with this fear for years. However, I was not fearful at that moment; I was relieved to be out from under the strain of a troubled church and a stressful pastorate.

There were several tasks at hand. I had to continue making contact with my friends, letting them know that I was available for pulpit supply, an interim pastorate, or another pastorate if a church would be interested in calling a fifty-eight-year-old unemployed preacher. I had books to pack, a new resumé to prepare, and a host of other things that would keep me busy over the next few months. It was an exciting time, but it was a time filled with uncertainty. I was literally walking where I had never walked before. Several of my friends had been down this path and were kind enough to call to offer advice and words of encouragement. I still have the list of those who called during the first weeks after I resigned my church. Some of those have been repaid with a call from me later in their own ministry when they went through a forced termination.

Earlier, I had called Bill Marshall, the Kentucky Baptist Executive Secretary, but had failed to reach him. However, he returned my call before the week was out and was helpful in putting me in touch with some persons who later helped me get into some interim pastorates and some pulpit supply. I realize now that he knew it was not going to be simple or easy for me to get a call to another church, but the interim route would open an avenue of service as well as income though it would be greatly reduced from what I had received as a pastor.

Writing these words, I am able to look back and see clearly some of the great hurt that was visited upon my family as the result of what was happening to me and my wife. All three of my sons were devastated by the turn of events. I encouraged them more than once not to become bitter or angry at the church. We all agreed that what happened was neither right nor Christian, but we all realized that our lives must not be shaped by events that we felt were unjust or undeserved. One of the things that I prayed for was that the Lord would help me not to become an embittered or angry old preacher. I believe the Lord has answered that prayer.

JoAnn and I made a point of being out of town the weekend after I resigned at Hodgenville. We visited with her sister and brother-in-law in northern Kentucky and attended worship at Florence Baptist Church. When I got back home, I began preparing my resumé and started sending it to persons who were willing to help me find a new place of service. I met with Lloyd Storment, Bill Hancock, Wayne Hayes, Larry McSwain and the pastor at Bryant's church in Murfreesboro, Tennessee. All my friends seemed eager and willing to help me, but all they could do was suggest my name or share my resumé with a search committee or a church seeking an interim pastor. I knew it was going to be an uphill battle.

One of the greatest surprises to me was that many pastors whom I had known over the years appeared to be avoiding me. Close friends did not do this, but those who had been acquaintances and perhaps a little more than just "speaking friends" were noticeably not willing to spend much time in my presence out in public view. I believe that my situation triggered an anxiety reaction within them. Namely, that if they got too close to me or spent much time with me, what happened to me might just rub off on them.

I am aware that my leaving First Baptist Church, Hodgenville, was a forced termination. While it is true that I resigned of my own free will, it would have been a struggle to hold onto my position as pastor of the church. I was neither fired nor voted out of my position, but a small group made it impossible for me to continue in that role and be effective or happy. When this happens to a minister, a cloud of suspicion hangs over him in the minds of many as to what he might have done to cause such a reaction to his ministry. The truth is that often the minister has done nothing to precipitate the situation other than carry out his ministry and fulfill his duties. People are fickle. They get tired of you. They remember a decision you made with which they did not agree. Or they decide they want a change in leadership. A campaign of murmuring begins and often grows to the point that it is impossible for the minister to continue effectively. Hence, the minister resigns and leaves. It is never a happy or a desirable experience, but still, it happens.

What I faced in the months leading up to the Christmas and New Year season was going to be a complete change of pace. I did not have to promote the annual Lottie Moon Mission Offering or make plans for the celebration of Advent or Christmas. The time spent from the event of my resignation in late September 1990 until the Christmas and New Year season was pretty much routine. All I had to do was send out resumes and hopefully find a place to preach or a church that was searching for a pastor which would give me a second look. A few opportunities to preach came my way, but no churches with vacant pulpits came calling. In spite of that, I did manage to be optimistic about the future.

I worried about JoAnn. She had seen me, and the boys hurt, and she could do nothing to relieve that. Further, she was still teaching school in LaRue County which brought her in contact with people from the church who had been unsupportive. Supportive people were around, but both of us would rather not have to come in contact with those whose presence aroused negative memories. I knew that she was strong, that she was a survivor, but I was aware that such circumstances were taking a toll on her. However, there was nothing that I could do to relieve the stress she faced each day. Both of us seemed to quietly resolve to face whatever the future brought us and deal with it on a day to day basis. There was little else we could do.

We worshipped in several churches but made no move to settle anywhere. A small group of the leaders at First Baptist Church who had served faithfully with me had been made to feel unwelcome. They were in the process of leaving the church. Several others had already left and gone to other churches. Those who had been leaders met at the home of Michael and Nada O'Bryant. While we did not meet with them, I did encourage them to stay together and form a new congregation. After several meetings, none of which we attended, they decided to follow my advice.

I do not recall much that happened during the Thanksgiving and Christmas season in 1990. I do know that we were able to spend more time with our family because I did not have any church responsibilities. We did not attend any worship activities at First Baptist Church. We did not want to be a distraction, nor did we wish to convey the message that we missed being there. It was a genuine relief to be out from under the pressure. And to be truthful, though there were many whom we would have enjoyed seeing, there were some whom we never wanted to see again. The latter group had been rude, untruthful, deceptive, and vicious along with having attacked us without a justifiable reason. There was nothing to be gained by further contact with such persons.

Our continuing relationship with First Baptist Church Hodgenville has been one of keeping our distance and maintaining our absence. None of the McDonald family has been in a worship service of the church since my resignation. I have participated in only two weddings and two funerals in the church since I resigned. The locks on the doors were changed the week after I left, the implication being that I was a threat to take something from the church that was not mine. I had to ask for a key to go back into my office to pack and remove my books and other possessions. Our name was removed from the mailing list and never restored. I have received no written communication from the church of any significance. The church did not make any attempt to give us a farewell reception or to celebrate our time of service in any way. For a time, I strongly resented this kind of treatment, but I have dealt with my feelings and it no longer disturbs me. JoAnn and I did decide to do nothing that would embarrass the church or put the church in a negative light while we still occupied the parsonage. We have extended that practice until this day and it will continue.

Two persons that I remember being very supportive throughout my search for a new opportunity were Dick Bridges at First Baptist Church Bowling Green and Bill Hancock at Highview Baptist in Louisville. Unfortunately, both of these men went on to experience forced terminations themselves, so their efforts were brought to an untimely conclusion. Lloyd Storment in Louisville remained a stalwart and supportive friend, as did Lawrence Phipps in Alabama. On the local scene, Larry Vance, Pastor of Vine Grove Baptist Church, and Dewey Keys, Pastor of East Rhudes Creek Baptist Church, were the only ones who were openly supportive.

I met Bill Hancock for lunch in Louisville on January 17, 1991 and talked with him about my options. I left several copies of my resumé with him. January 17 happened to be the fortieth anniversary of my ordination to the ministry. I went home and vacuumed the house before JoAnn got home from school. She arrived shortly after five o'clock and I told her that it was not too cold for us to take a walk if we would go immediately. When we returned from our walk, I was experiencing some discomfort in my upper chest and arms. I began to suspect that I was in the early stages of a heart attack. I told JoAnn and she suggested that I call my doctor, Bill Handley. I had trouble reaching him, but after several calls, I was able to make contact. He urged me to come immediately to the Emergency Room at Hardin Memorial in Elizabethtown. Unknown to me, JoAnn had called the local EMS. They responded by going to almost every house in the Hamilton Acres subdivision before coming to ours.

As we watched the EMS team go from house to house, I told JoAnn to get our car out of the garage and drive me to the hospital. As inept as the EMS team appeared to be, I did not want to trust them to make the trip. They pulled up to our driveway as we were pulling out and I told them that we were on our way. They said that was dangerous, but I told them we would risk it and we did. It felt like she drove about ninety miles per hour all the way.

Making our way to the hospital, I was aware that my situation could take a turn for the worse. I told JoAnn that if I did not make it she was to take her time in making any major life decisions. She promptly told me that she did not want to hear that kind of talk. I then began to pray telling God that at fifty-nine years of age, I was too young to die. I asked the Lord for three things: first, I asked Him not to let me die; second, I asked not to let me become an invalid; and third, I asked that I not have so much heart damage that I would be unable to work. I renewed my pledge to faithfully serve with whatever remaining days He would give me just as I had tried to do since He called me to preach. All of my prayer requests were answered that night.

When we arrived at the hospital, the triage nurse wanted to interview me, challenging my statement that I was having a heart attack. I brushed her aside and started down the hall to the Emergency Room Nurse's Station. Bill Handley was waiting for me and he took over, getting me into a treatment room and starting the diagnosis procedure. JoAnn was busy giving the necessary information to the admitting clerks. After several minutes had passed, I noticed that the triage nurse was still standing at the foot of my gurney. She had followed me all the way into the Emergency Room and into the treatment room. I asked why she was still there, and Dr. Handley smiled and told her that it would be all right for her to leave.

After what seemed like just a few minutes, I asked Dr. Handley if I was having a heart attack. He replied that I was in the early stages. I then asked if he was going to administer the TPA clot busters. He replied that he was in the process of ordering that at that very moment. He then told me that he would like for a cardiologist to see me, but the doctor he would choose was not on call. When he told me that Dr. Lon Keith was his preference, I told him to call Dr. Keith and tell him that I had asked for him. He did, and Dr. Keith was at my side within an hour. It seemed to me that all of this took place in about fifteen minutes, but JoAnn assured me that it took about an hour.

They moved me to the Coronary Care Unit and hooked me up to all the monitors and machines. The TV was on. It was the night that the United States invaded Iraq for the first Gulf War. I lay there and watched it off and on all night long. Only once during the night did the nurses rush in to check on me. I had been asleep and woke up as they entered the room. I could tell that I was having problems, but they passed, and the rest of the night was peaceful. Shortly after 5:00 a.m. JoAnn stepped into the doorway and said she was on her way home to get ready to teach school. She had been there all night. I had told her to go home, but she had chosen to stay.

I went to the hospital on Thursday evening. Early Friday, I learned that I would be having a heart catheterization on Monday. Since the weekend was approaching, I was going to spend it waiting in the Coronary Care Unit. The time did pass quickly. I had a few visitors; most were family. Philip stayed close. Bryant and Leslie came. Paul stayed in Louisville since JoAnn assured him that I was doing well, and his work schedule was demanding his presence. Dick Bridges came up from Bowling Green. I was surprised at how few of my minister friends showed up, but it was the weekend and they all had to work. I learned later that several of them did come by but limited their visits to JoAnn and my family.

Near noon on Sunday, I was moved out of the Coronary Care Unit to the Progressive Care Unit. It seemed like the floodgates were opened to visitors. There were people walking the halls that I either did not know or barely knew who came into my room and wanted to sit and visit. I thanked several for coming telling them I did not feel up to having company, but they stayed anyway. I finally asked a nurse to put up a "No Visitors" sign. However, everyone assumed that the sign meant all but them. Stuart Singleton came in, threw himself across me in the bed in an attempt to hug me and began apologizing for what he had done to bring about my departure from the church. I told him his presence was unwanted, inappropriate, hypocritical, and insincere. I asked him to leave. To this day, he is the only person who opposed my continuing as pastor of the church, who has made any kind of an apology for what they did, a fact that I find that both interesting and sad.

Dr. Keith had scheduled my heart catheterization for early Monday, and it was done near noon. With the procedure completed, he told me that he would be up shortly to discuss the results with me. He did not come to my room until nearly 9:00 p.m. that evening. When he arrived, JoAnn was there. On a paper towel, he drew a diagram of the heart along with the blood vessels leading to the heart. Then he began to show me the blockages that he had found. I had two that were ninety percent blocked, two others that were eighty percent blocked, plus two or three that were seventy percent blocked and maybe more. Then he said, "You have a significant decision to make." I said, "I have already made the decision. If you were me, where would you have the surgery done and who would you choose to do it?" He replied, "I would go to Jewish Hospital in Louisville, and I would choose Dr. Layman Gray as the surgeon." I asked, "Would you arrange for that as soon as possible?" He replied, "I will." JoAnn had been quietly observing all of this. She spoke up saying, "This is a big decision. Is surgery the only way?" I replied, "With this much heart disease, if I don't have the surgery, I will be risking having another heart attack within a year which could either end my life or make me an invalid." She looked at Dr. Keith and he said, "He's right." So, from that moment on, I was on the fast track for heart bypass surgery at Jewish Hospital in Louisville.

On Tuesday morning, Dr. Keith came by and told me that I would be going that day by ambulance to Jewish Hospital. I told him that I felt well enough for JoAnn to take me to the hospital, but he said, "It is simpler this way, trust me." Late Tuesday afternoon I was transported to Jewish Hospital in a run down, rough riding Ford ambulance which had little heat. It was a cold, gray, January day and I was beginning to get cold by the time we arrived. I heard one of the EMS crew who was getting me admitted tell the admitting nurse that I was a diabetic. I was surprised since I had never been diagnosed as a diabetic. I immediately challenged what she had said. She insisted that I was a diabetic. I informed the admitting nurse that I had never been diagnosed for diabetes or treated for the disease. She agreed to make that notation on my chart. I was getting an education in how medical mistakes are often made.

Jewish Hospital in Louisville had the reputation of being on the cutting edge of medical care in the area for treating heart disease, so I was totally surprised to see how rundown the facilities appeared. I spent about an hour in the corridors on a gurney. Then I was carried to an area of the hospital which was alleged to be for patients being admitted for possible heart surgery. It was in the basement with no apparent outside light. Beds were old and uncomfortable; other equipment seemed to be falling apart. I began to wonder if I was going to end up in the same condition. Later, I was transported to the X-ray department for a chest X-ray. When they appeared to have finished, the technician came back and informed me that we had to repeat the procedure. I asked why and was told that my lungs were so large that they could not get them all on one X-ray photo. Though no one told me, I assumed that all my years as a runner and a physical fitness enthusiast had kept my lungs in good condition.

I shared with the hospital staff my surprise at seeing the facilities in such poor condition. They told me another section of the hospital was in the process of being remodeled for heart patients. Sometime during Wednesday, I was moved to that part of the hospital. The smell of fresh paint and glue for new carpet was almost overpowering. I could not believe that patients who had just had their chests opened for heart surgery and for whom coughing was a painful experience were being exposed to such conditions, but they were. The new rooms were larger with bigger windows, and the outside light was refreshing.

The news of my presence and approaching bypass surgery in Jewish Hospital began to spread. Friends from home and Louisville began to come by or call. It was interesting to see who came and who did not. Late Wednesday, I saw Verlin Kruschwitz, my fellow pastor and doctoral studies field supervisor, walking down the hall. I called out to him, he stepped into the room and told me that he would return after visiting another patient. We had a good visit when he returned, but in retrospect, he appeared to have something else on his mind. After praying with me, he left. I did not see him again until several months later when he was in Baptist Hospital with a blocked heart artery.

Early Wednesday evening, Dr. Layman Gray came by and told me that he had been able to study the results of my tests by Dr. Keith and that my surgery had been scheduled first in line for Friday morning. He explained that since I was stable when I arrived, they had placed me in the first available slot. He said that I would have at least three, maybe four bypass grafts and that he did not anticipate any problems. Dr. Gray was quiet, thorough, and personable. I was at ease being in his care.

Thursday was a day of preparation for the next day's surgery. Family and friends began to come in near mid-afternoon. Lawrence Phipps, my pastor friend from Alabama, arrived late in the day. He explained that one of his men had given him his credit card and told him to catch a plane and come up and stay until he was sure I was going to be all right. He was back early the next morning with Larry Vance and a host of friends and family. All stayed until I was out of surgery and about to be out of intensive care. My three best friends from high school, Tommy Ramsey, George Ferree, and Morris Williams, called Thursday evening as did my brother and other family members from Florida. My wife's sister and her husband, Bobbie and Ralph Rush, came and stayed with JoAnn.

All I remember from Friday, the day of the surgery, was the first shot to get me ready to go and later waking up in the recovery room. JoAnn said I sat on the side of the bed and told dirty jokes until Lawrence Phipps and Larry Vance led in prayer, then I had them repeat the prayer just to be sure it would take. It must have because I came through with no problems. I remember JoAnn and the boys coming into recovery and the nurse telling them I was waking up. I had a tube in my throat and one hand was free enough to wave, so that is what I did. When Paul came in, the sight upset him, and he did not come back until I was out of intensive care.

While writing this I asked JoAnn about the details of some events related to my surgery and stay at Jewish Hospital. She went to some of her records and handed me a day-by-day account she had kept of what took place before, during, and after my surgery. I had forgotten that she had kept a running account of events along with a list of those who either visited or called to inquire about me. As I looked over her list, I discovered that some whom I thought had not checked on me had, in fact, done so. It was humbling to read the list of those who called or came by. As always, I am and continue to be grateful for my friends.

Most of my visitors on Saturday were family. Since I was still in Intensive Care, visitors could come in only at certain times. Lawrence Phipps came by early telling me that he had to catch a plane back to Alabama. He had prayer with me and left. Philip came in a little later and I motioned for him not to leave. I was tired of being alone. A small TV was available, but I insisted that it be turned off. I could not stand to listen to it. I slept off and on most of the day. Family members came and stayed briefly and left. I do not remember being in pain. Since I had a breathing tube in my throat, I either communicated with hand signals or wrote brief notes to the nurse or my visitors.

I have referred to JoAnn's notes which she kept on a calendar from day to day. She says that the respirator tube was removed on Saturday. I thought it was not removed until early Sunday. However, by early Sunday both the respirator and catheter were removed, and I was feeling much better. Before noon I had been moved to the Transitional Care Unit and was up walking around pulling my intravenous unit with me. It felt good to be on my feet. I was told that as soon as I could urinate I could be transferred to the new unit which had just be remodeled for heart surgery patients. I drank water and soft drinks, but nothing produced the desired kidney action. I finally persuaded them to give me some decaffeinated coffee and that did the trick. I was soon upstairs in better surroundings.

Having moved to the new unit, I could now have visitors and they began to arrive in a steady stream. Friends from the Louisville area, church members from Hodgenville, minister friends, and a host of others came. Many came that I did not expect to see, but it was refreshing to have them drop by. Among my visitors were hospital personnel responsible for checking on my progress and who encouraged me to walk and do a variety of exercises. They were surprised that I could do most of the things they suggested with no adverse problems. I think my excellent physical condition made all that possible. Add to that the fact that I was determined to recover from the surgery and get on with my life. I walked the halls, visited the stairwells for brief step climbing, did the breathing and chest exercises, and all the other things that were suggested. I experienced little pain or discomfort.

No one, however, had prepared me for the after effects of the anesthesia. I could hardly bear the smell of any perfume, cologne, or other cosmetics. Often when a nurse or female aide came into the room I found myself relieved when they left. I could not even use aftershave lotion for nearly three months. It was that long or longer before all effects of the anesthesia were out of my body.

Being in a hospital setting where others have a responsibility for your welfare can be a life changing event. It seemed to me that every female aide or nurse in the hospital came by every day on every shift to inspect the condition of the incision from which the graft for my bypass was taken. It began in my groin and continued downward below my knee. My private parts were always exposed, and I know they all sensed my discomfort. They were always apologetic, and I tried to make the best of it with humor saying, "You can look if you promise you won't laugh." Polite humor often helps one to get through delicate circumstances.

My hands and arms had been used for various intravenous medical treatments and bore the marks of that activity. It was several weeks before all evidence of that disappeared. Not only that, but my complexion was ashen and pale from the experience. It was several weeks before I began to look like I was really alive and healthy. Further, my medical event took place in the dead of winter when there was little sun or weather warm enough to get some sun. I was pale as a ghost much longer than I wanted to be.

Most of the doctors that I saw after the surgery were those doing a residency in cardiology. On Tuesday after my surgery on Friday, two resident physicians came by and removed drainage tubes in my chest and the electrical leads for an external pacemaker. The procedure was painless except for the removal of the top drainage tube. I complained to the doctor that had he warned me, I could have been prepared for the pain. He apologized and explained that often patients had no pain with the procedure. Then, as they conferred, they agreed that I was doing so well I could go home. Those words were music to my ears. I immediately went to the nurse's station and told them that when Dr. Gray made his rounds I must see him. I had been in the hospital twelve nights and was eager to get home to my own bed, so I could get a good night's rest.

The nurses kept assuring me that they had given Dr. Gray my message, but he did not come by until late Wednesday. He explained that he wanted his patients to stay six days after surgery; if I would agree to stay that night, I could go home tomorrow. It was nearly 6:30 p.m. at that moment and JoAnn was still in Hodgenville, so I had little choice but to agree to one more night of disturbed sleep. It is not possible to get much rest when you are in the hospital. The staff is constantly checking on you, there is always some noise from somewhere, and some lights are always on. In retrospect, I think Dr. Gray knew what I wanted and rather than having to insist that I stay just played the waiting game. That being the case, it worked out just the way he planned.

Early in the week after my surgery, I received a call from the business office at Jewish Hospital. The person who called informed me that they had checked with the SBC Annuity Board with whom I had my medical insurance and had been informed that my insurance had lapsed for nonpayment of premium. I informed the caller that to my knowledge that was not the case but that I would check and get back to her. First Baptist Church Hodgenville had agreed to pay my insurance for six months beginning with the October 1990 payment. Had no payment been made, I could foresee some trying times ahead.

Taking a few minutes to get my wits about me, I decided to call Billy Buchanon, a church member who worked for the Cadillac dealer in Elizabethtown. When I explained the situation to him, he asked for phone numbers for the Annuity Board offices and for my account number. By that time, I was upset. Concluding our phone conversation, I told Billy that if the premium had not been paid to "just bring me the keys to the church because I am going to own it." Billy laughed and said, "Don't worry, Preacher, we'll get this worked out." Later in the day, Billy called me and said that after a tense conversation with the church secretary in Hodgenville and several calls to the Annuity Board, the check for my premium payment had been found on the desk of an Annuity Board employee in Dallas. I have often wondered since this event whether Jewish Hospital could have handled the matter differently, but I guess what happened was best. However, it did put me through a lot of stress.

On Thursday, January 31, 1991, JoAnn came to check me out of the hospital. They had a nutrition class for her which she attended. Roger and Betty Hunt from Paducah came to visit and stayed with us until they wheeled me out of the hospital to our waiting car. I was dismissed near noon and we headed home. We stopped at Wendy's in Elizabethtown for a sandwich and brought it home for lunch. When we got back in the house, we discovered that the plate of food JoAnn had prepared for my supper the night I went to the hospital was still in the oven where she had put it when I told her I was having a heart attack. It went immediately into the garbage. The sandwich from Wendy's was chicken which I would be eating plenty of in the future.

Friends and family called or visited until near our normal bedtime. I slept well but woke up several times. Rest was not going to be a problem at home. All I had to do for the time being was to get back into a routine and let my body heal as quickly as possible. I did not know how long it would take, but I was determined to get back to my old self as soon as possible. While I did not realize it then, not having the responsibility of a congregation hanging over me during this time made my recovery easier and much quicker. The blessings of life often arrive in strange clothing.

I have always believed that out of every experience of life, there are things to be learned. My heart attack and surgery caused me to realize how much my family loves me. We had always been a family that expressed our love verbally and physically. I had never doubted that any of them loved me. However, in the things my wife and children said and did during this crisis, I came to sense a love and commitment from each of them which was and continues to be much deeper than I had sensed before. We are all much closer, more loving, and more expressive of our love than we were before this happened. While I would never want to go through any of these events again, I will always be grateful for the doors of realization that opened for me and hopefully for them. I believe with all my heart that being loved by those whom you love is one of life's supreme blessings.

Chapter 18

Interim Pastorates: The New Adventure

February 1991 began with me at home recovering from heart bypass surgery and trying to regain my physical strength. Since it was still winter, I was confined to home and did the suggested exercises in the house. They consisted of simple physical exercises, walking through the house, and breathing exercises to keep my lungs clear.

Numerous friends called or came by. Several people from the church visited, called, or sent flowers and food. Family members called almost daily to be sure that all was going well. I began to keep a daily account of all this activity in the appointment calendar in which JoAnn had kept notes on the earlier events of my hospitalization and surgery. It is surprising and inspiring to look back and read all the notes that were made about what happened during this time.

Within a week after leaving the hospital, I began to get out of the house for some exercise and contact with people. JoAnn and I would often go out to the high school and walk in the halls after she got home from work. The building was open for night classes and other activities, so many in the community went there to walk when it was too cold to be outside.

One of the pleasant and unexpected surprises that came our way in early February was a visit from John and Barbara Jones. John's younger brother, Jeff, and I had bought a house together about five years earlier. It was a good frame house that was located behind the Catholic Cemetery in Hodgenville. We had purchased the property on speculation thinking we could sell it later for a profit. We had sold it on contract several times only to have the buyer leave after several months of living in the house. The rent was used to pay on the mortgage against the house. As luck would have it, a buyer had come forward with the money to purchase the house and it had been sold. John and Barbara came to see us and brought the check for my share in the house. This was a totally unexpected but highly welcome windfall. It came just as compensation from the church was ending. JoAnn observed that it was interesting that the sale of the house came at this particular time in our lives. We both took it as a sign that the Lord would continue to take care of us, and He has.

Early the next day I went to Lincoln National Bank, deposited the check, and paid off the note for the money I had borrowed to purchase my last automobile. The note being paid proved to be the last money that I borrowed from that bank. Within six months we had purchased a house in Elizabethtown and we began banking at First Federal Savings Bank where we financed the purchase of our first home. Moving from one bank to another can take a little time, and we tried to make the move as smooth and unnoticed as possible. We did not want to send any negative messages to the banking community or to anyone in this small town, nor did we wish to send a message that we were cutting our ties in the community. We had good credit at the bank in Hodgenville and we wanted to end our relationship on the best terms possible.

In early February, there was a constant stream of people either coming by the house or calling to check on how I was doing. I was exercising more each day and becoming stronger. I began to go by Smith Drug Store for morning coffee with the men with whom I had visited each weekday for several years. The spirit of friendship and congeniality within that group continued unabated. I eventually conducted funerals for several of them or members of their families even though few of them belonged to the church that I had served. Most all of them proved to be good, faithful, loyal friends.

Two of our visitors in early February were our backdoor neighbors, Irene and Woodrow Arnette. We had been close to the Arnettes, who were members of our church, but they seemed to be less and less willing to continue a relationship. JoAnn was upset, and I was disappointed. Woodrow Arnette and Wayne Dobson were alleged to be the two men who changed the locks at the church shortly after I resigned. I felt this act was unnecessary and sent a negative message throughout the community. I have never learned what precipitated their action, but it caused us to wonder how they could have been so friendly before and suddenly behave in such an unfriendly way once I ended my service to the church. The Arnette's visit in early February was friendly, but close contact with them ceased. It became as though we had never been friendly or had a close relationship. There were some families who reacted this way, but most of the church families have continued to be warm and friendly.

Near the end of February, I began to participate in public gatherings. When the Kentucky Baptist Evangelism Conference met in Elizabethtown the last of February, I attended. One of my friends, Russell Bennett, saw me, shook his head and remarked, "Man, I thought lightening was fast." He was surprised that I was up and going so quickly after my surgery, but I felt good and my strength was gradually returning.

Early in March 1991, the group that had left First Baptist Church Hodgenville rented space in the old Farm Bureau Building. They had met for several weeks at the home of Michael O'Bryant. They began meeting in this rented space and would do so for several months. Later, they purchased twenty-five acres on the south side of town just beyond the Lincoln Parkway. It proved to be an excellent location, and the church has grown over the years. I led midweek prayer service for them a few times but never spoke in a worship service during the early days of the church. One of the deacons, Creed Gardner, wanted me to become pastor of this new congregation, but I discouraged that by saying, "I don't think you want to bring that up. Don't you think I have served my sentence in LaRue County?" He did bring it up, but other leaders in the church thought it best to call fresh leadership. I agreed with the decision and would not have accepted the church even if they had called me. It was best for me to move on to other opportunities.

Since I was actively seeking work, I continued updating my resumé. JoAnn suggested that I enlist a new group of references. She then told me that one of my references had been "poisoning the well" by giving me a poor reference when an inquiry had come to him. Lawrence Phipps had discovered this fact while serving as chairman of a search committee for a denominational job in Alabama. Lawrence had shared this in detail with JoAnn when he came to Louisville to be present for my surgery. When he had evidence of the deception of my reference person and my surgery was scheduled, he had waited for the outcome before taking any action. However, he strongly insisted that I enlist a new group of references.

Learning this, I called Lawrence and he told me the story. The guilty party was Verlin Kruschwitz, who had been my field supervisor in the doctoral studies at Southern Seminary. He had also been a fellow pastor, serving a church in a neighboring community. He had given me a negative reference by phone and by letter in response to a formal inquiry. When Lawrence came to Louisville, he called Verlin and confronted him about what he had done. Verlin at first denied his actions but then tried to justify them by telling Lawrence that in his opinion, "Ike was lazy." Lawrence then said, "Verlin, that may be your opinion, but if you had an ounce of integrity, you should have told Ike that you did not want to be a reference for him. You lied to him and you have betrayed his confidence. In essence, you have stabbed him in the back." Lawrence stated that the conversation ended on that note.

However, Verlin did write a letter to the search committee in which he made general statements about knowing me. He concluded by stating that I was recovering from bypass surgery and that I should be able to return to work. I have the letter in my files. The date on the letter is the day after my surgery. JoAnn noted in her record that he had called her at Jewish Hospital on that day to check on my condition. Lawrence and I both concluded that he may have been trying to cover his tracks. It is a sad story of betrayal and duplicity.

For some time, I considered going to Verlin and confronting him about his actions. I wanted to know why he did it. He had nothing to gain by what he did. However, after discussing the event at length with Sidney Maddox, I decided that a confrontation would accomplish nothing, so, I let it go.

I tell this story, part of which appears in an earlier chapter, to point out that life events do have consequences. Strong differences of opinion between strong personalities would best be resolved. Unresolved conflict can simmer and bear a bitter brew. It can destroy a relationship.

In early April, I led the prayer service for the Parkway Baptist Church. This was my first time to speak publicly after my surgery. All went well. I had no problems and I felt good about the experience.

In late April, I received a call from Louis Franklin, a deacon in Dawson Springs Baptist Church, Dawson Springs, Kentucky. He explained that the church was without a pastor and they were seeking someone to serve in the interim. We agreed that I would visit, speak for them, and explore the possibility of my serving the church as their Interim Pastor. I spoke for them on the first Sunday of May. The church called me as their Interim Pastor and I began the following Sunday. It was a relationship that would last exactly one year.

The agreement with the Dawson Springs congregation was that I would serve from Sunday through Wednesday leading the worship and prayer services and doing any pastoral ministry that I felt was in order. If a church committee needed help or guidance, I would provide that at their request. I would stay in Dawson Springs in housing provided by the church. They would pay me a salary and mileage for my car plus any other professional expenses which might be incurred. An elderly widow in the church had an apartment in her home which was not occupied at the time. She made that available and I stayed there for about three months. As I was sharing these arrangements with JoAnn, she asked, "How old is this widow?" I replied with a smile, "She is 89 years old." It was the truth and that ended the discussion.

Once in Dawson Springs, I learned that Lewis Franklin was Deacon Chairman of the church. He was a pleasant man with whom it was easy to serve. The relationship with the Dawson Springs Baptist Church proved to be a healing experience for me and for the church. The previous pastor of the church had resigned under pressure from a group who felt his effectiveness had ended. He had identified this group and turned his supporters against them. His actions had divided the church with some in each group refusing to speak to each other. Some wanted to nurse their negative feelings while others wanted to find a way to move forward. My first few months were spent listening to the stories of various people while encouraging them to be forgiving and to get on with the Lord's work. I began a visitation program with the deacon of the week. It gave us a chance to do something positive for the church. As we ended our evening visitation, we often talked about whatever the deacon had on his mind. Usually, I listened to his story about what had happened in the church and then we discussed the deacon's vision for the church in the days ahead. These sessions ended with prayer. It proved to be a healing event for the deacon and the church family.

Slowly but surely, I began to sense that the church was coming together and beginning to look to the future. Since Dawson Springs was a small town, I began early on to try to fit into the community. There were groups that drank coffee each morning and I joined them. Several people were out early each morning walking and getting exercise. Since I was still recovering from heart surgery, I went to the various walking sites and joined the walkers for that early morning routine. I did not share my health status or the fact that I had undergone surgery until near the end of my time with the church. But I did let them know I was on a low-fat diet and that I was trying to control my weight.

The church and the community responded quite positively to my ministry. They were a loving church. Even though they had seen ministers turn out to be less than they should have been, they always treated me with respect. Their attitude did much to restore my self-confidence as a minister. I do not recall one negative response to my ministry the entire time I was in Dawson Springs.

During the months following my surgery, JoAnn and I began trying to make plans about where we would live once we moved out of the parsonage. We looked at the possibility of buying or building a home in Hodgenville. We looked at housing in Elizabethtown. Since we had never owned a home and did not know what the future would hold in terms of my working, we looked at all the possibilities. We knew that the end of May was coming, and we needed to make some sort of decision. When we were unable to find a place to buy, I went to Earl Jones for advice about renting the parsonage until other arrangements could be made. He suggested that I to talk to Bobby Heady, the deacon chairman, and see if we could arrive at a rental agreement until we were able to arrange for other housing. Bobby and I agreed on $325.00 a month for rent with a weekly refund should we vacate the house with time left in the month.

Near the middle of June, our son Philip called and said he had found a house in Elizabethtown that he wanted us to see. The house was in the Terrace Hills Subdivision and had been on the market for several months but had not sold. When we arrived to look at the house, we found that no landscaping had been done and the house had little curb appeal. It had three bedrooms and two full baths on the main floor. It had fourteen hundred square feet of living space, a full, unfinished basement, and a two-car garage. The builder had originally put the house on the market for $74,000.00 but had reduced it to $69,000.00. The realtor kept telling us that the builder was needing to sell the house. When JoAnn said she thought the house would do, I made an offer of $64,000.00 dollars. The realtor took the offer to the builder and we began negotiating, finally agreeing on $67,500.00. We signed the agreement and went to the bank for financing.

When we applied at First Federal Savings Bank for a loan, we found that we knew several of the bank officers. They were aware that we were wanting to move as quickly as possible. Our loan was approved in near record time. We had the closing and found ourselves with a house payment that was less than the rent we were paying in Hodgenville. Blessings were continuing to come our way. I returned to Dawson Springs planning on coming home the next weekend and starting the moving process. Never mind the fact that due to my recent surgery, I was not supposed to lift more than thirty-five pounds.

What happened next remains one of the great surprises and blessings of my life. My wife's sister, Bobbie Rush, and her teenage daughter, Tamara, came with their van as soon as I left early Sunday to return to Dawson Springs. They began packing and moving items that they could get into their van and ours. That continued through Monday. On Tuesday afternoon, several friends gathered with pickup trucks and one panel truck that Creed Gardner had borrowed and moved the rest of our belongings to our new home. Those helping with the move were Mike and Nada O'Bryant and their son Kevin; Donald and Roberta Rock; W. D. and Mae Burden; Creed and Anna Mae Gardner; and our son Philip. The job was finished around 2:00 a.m. Wednesday. I received a call from JoAnn around noon Wednesday telling me to come to our new home in Elizabethtown when I returned that evening. I arrived home at 11:30 p.m. and found all our furniture in place. It looked like we had been living there for months. JoAnn observed that we had moved and once again and I had managed to contribute little to the event, which was a long-standing wifely observation.

On the Sunday morning after our move to Elizabethtown, I was preparing to go to Dawson Springs. When JoAnn told me that she would probably attend Parkway Baptist Church, I suggested that she move her membership to the church and move mine by proxy. With those instructions, we made our move from First Baptist Church Hodgenville, thus ending a fifteen-plus-year relationship. It had been mostly good with a few disappointments, but we were at peace with the direction we were going.

Our move to Elizabethtown proved to be one of the best decisions we ever made. It is a nice community, located in the middle of the state with highways that give ready access to most of Kentucky. With this location, I have been able to serve a number of churches within a hundred-mile radius of my home. We lived in the Terrace Hills Subdivision for about four years before moving just outside Elizabethtown on Rineyville Road which is also known as Kentucky State Highway 1600.

In early May 1991, just as I had settled in at Dawson Springs, Lawrence Phipps called me from Enterprise, Alabama. The search committee for the Director of Missions job in Coffee County, Alabama, was inviting me to visit them for discussions about becoming their Director of Missions. Lawrence wanted me to come to Enterprise, meet with the committee, and see if we could arrive at a working agreement.

From the beginning, JoAnn was opposed to even considering the job. Our previous experience in Alabama had left her with a firm resolution to never return to the state except for a brief visit and she meant brief. However, out of courtesy to Lawrence, I felt we should go.

The opportunity had several negatives. The Coffee County Association had located its offices and residence in one of the smaller towns of the county. The Director of Missions was required to live in the home. Lawrence had tried to get this changed because he knew that I wanted to own my own home. Further, the opportunity for JoAnn to teach school was limited. In fact, it did not exist. There were people standing in line for all available teaching positions.

We made the trip to Enterprise and met with the committee. Lawrence saw to it that we were well entertained. On Sunday afternoon, I spoke in one of the churches to a packed house of messengers from every church in the association. They voted unanimously to offer me the position. As JoAnn and I left the sanctuary prior to the vote, she said, "Oh Ike, you had them eating out of your hand." I replied, "That may be true, but I feel the Lord has other plans." We visited with Lawrence and his family that evening and early the next morning. Then we departed for home. I was anxious to get back to Dawson Springs and JoAnn was anxious to get out of Alabama. I did not accept the job, but JoAnn's feelings about Alabama had nothing to do with my decision. Neither of us felt any positive leadership from the Lord about returning to serve in Alabama.

We returned to Kentucky and I continued to serve at Dawson Springs. As the summer was ending I moved out of the widow's home to the home of John and Faye Ray. John was a deacon in the church. John and Faye had a large home and I had the upstairs as my quarters. The Ray family proved to be wonderful people and they were helpful to me as I served the church.

As with nearly every church that I have served as Interim Pastor, the question arose as to whether I would consider becoming the Pastor. I met with the Dawson Springs search committee on two occasions. The salary they offered was less than JoAnn was making teaching school, and they wanted us to move into the church parsonage which was located next door to the church. Both of these conditions were totally unacceptable to me, and I told them that I could not serve them effectively under those conditions. Thus, our talks ended, and they moved on to consider other candidates. While I would have enjoyed serving the church, it remains my conviction that the Lord was not calling us to sacrifice what He had already provided in order to do that. Furthermore, the Lord was at that time leading me into a new career as an interim pastor, a role in which I have served effectively.

My tenure as Interim Pastor at Dawson Springs Baptist Church concluded on Mother's Day 1992, exactly one year after I began serving them. The church was gracious and generous to me and sent me on my way with a lovely reception and other festivities on my last Sunday with them. I will always treasure this experience because they restored my confidence as an able pastor and leader. No congregation has ever been more gracious and kinder to me as I departed than this one. Friendships were established there that continue to this day.

Several months of inactivity went by in terms of preaching and interim opportunities. I filled pulpits occasionally, but no chances to serve as an interim came my way. However, in early spring of 1993, as I attended a board meeting of the Western Recorder, Frank Hatfield, a member of the group, began telling the group that his church had just lost its pastor and was in a quandary as to where to turn for a possible interim leader. I quickly reached into a file containing copies of my resumé and handed one to him, assuring him that I could solve their problem. He seemed somewhat surprised but took my resumé telling me that he would give it to the proper people. After returning home that evening, I called him to learn whether he needed more information about me. In that conversation, he told me that his wife was the chairman of the committee charged with filling the pulpit or finding a suitable interim pastor. He assured me that she would contact me before the week ended and she did.

Frank Hatfield was a member of First Baptist Church, Shepherdsville, Kentucky, about thirty miles from my home. I soon learned that the church had forced the pastor to resign because of his numerous alleged moral and ethical failures. What I did not know and learned later was that the church had agreed to a severance package for the former pastor that caused them to fear that they could not pay an interim an adequate salary. They offered such a ridiculously low salary that I first told them that their offer would not even cover the cost of driving to and from Shepherdsville. Mrs. Hatfield listened to my response to their offer and told me that she would go back to her committee and get back to me. She returned with a much improved but still low offer. I suggested that I come preach for them a week or two and then we could see if we could come to agreeable terms. She agreed to this and I began filling the pulpit.

After a week of working with the church, the Interim Search Committee came to me with an offer that was still low, but which contained a mileage expense that was reasonable enough to allow me to serve without doing so at my own expense. After I had served them for a few months, I discovered that they had not been honest with me in terms of their church finances. They were in much better financial condition than they had indicated. I do not think that the Hatfield family was aware of the financial condition of the church, but I remain convinced that the other leadership of the church was aware, and they simply wanted to fill the pulpit as cheaply as possible.

I served First Baptist Church Shepherdsville for about a year. I found the church to be dysfunctional and cynical in terms of relating positively to a pastor or church staff. While it is true that they had endured several pastors and staff who were much less morally and ethically than they should have been, they dealt with these events by placing all pastors and staff into the same group, unworthy of respect or fair treatment in their eyes.

It was no surprise to find that the entire church staff was frustrated and demoralized. I spent an inordinate amount of time keeping the church staff focused and in a positive frame of mind, a procedure that had to be done every week and sometimes more than once a week. While I do not wish to imply that the entire church family was dysfunctional or that there were no good people in the church, there was much more of this negative, cynical element in the congregation than I have encountered elsewhere. Nevertheless, there were also some wonderful Christians in the Shepherdsville congregation. They were faithful, encouraging, and willing to sacrifice that the church might move forward. This dynamic continues to be one of the strangest mixtures that I have encountered in my entire ministry.

As my tenure at Shepherdsville was drawing to a close, I was contacted by a committee from the Bloomfield Baptist Church. Their pastor had retired, and they wanted to talk with me about coming to serve as their interim pastor. To my surprise, they came to Shepherdsville the next Sunday to hear me preach and then took me out to lunch. We agreed that I would visit and preach for their church, and if the church agreed to call me as interim pastor, I would consider serving them. In this meeting, we discussed the pastoral duties I would be expected to perform, salary, mileage, the time I would spend on the church field, and whether my theology would be acceptable to the church family.

I was their pulpit guest the following Sunday. They had a fellowship supper before the evening service. When the meal was concluded, we went to the church sanctuary for a question and answer session which lasted nearly an hour. Finally, Roy Wiggington stood and stated that he felt I would be an acceptable choice as Interim Pastor. He moved that the church call me for that position. The Chairman of the Search Committee presented to the church the agreement we had discussed previously. It was the same as we had agreed upon except they recommended that I be paid fifty dollars more per week than they had earlier suggested. In all my years in the ministry, that had never happened before. I knew immediately that serving this church was going to be a positive experience.

My time at Bloomfield Baptist Church was extremely pleasant. The people were warm, were friendly and responded positively to my leadership. The Pastor Search Committee asked for my help on two occasions, both having to do with the man whom they called to be pastor. As they were about to agree on a candidate to bring before the church, they asked to me review the biographies of several persons and rank them in the order of which I felt would be the best person to lead the church. I did as they requested and was disappointed when they chose the weakest candidate in the group as the person whom they wanted to bring before the church.

The Search Committee sought my help a second time when a storm of objections arose within the congregation while they were in the process of having the candidate visit, preach, and answer questions from the congregation. I tried to assist the committee in dealing in a positive way with these objections, but I told them that with so much negative reaction, it would be wise to withdraw the candidate from the process and go on to another person. They would not consider this option. The result was that the church called the man as pastor, but it did not prove to be a happy, healthy, or positive relationship. He later left the church to form another church nearby and took some of the membership with him. However, I have since learned that the church appears to have recovered from this negative experience and is doing well.

When one concludes an interim pastorate, it is seldom possible to step into another place of service immediately. Such was the case when I left Bloomfield. But within a matter of weeks, I had an interview scheduled with the Bardstown Baptist Church. Then the Northside Baptist Church which was still a mission of Severns Valley Baptist Church in Elizabethtown called and asked me to meet with them. I scheduled both interviews for the same day. I met with the Bardstown committee in the late afternoon and the Northside committee later that evening. Neither interview seemed promising, but after meeting with the Northside committee, I called the

Bardstown committee and asked them to withdraw my name from consideration. However, I did not have positive feelings about my meeting with the Northside committee.

Howard Cobble had recently resigned as pastor of Severns Valley to accept a church in Georgia. After he left, the Missions Committee, which was made up of an equal number of members from Northside and Severns Valley, began to assume a more active oversight of the work at Northside. Conflict soon developed between the person serving as pastor of Northside and the Missions Committee. The deacons at Severns Valley became involved in this conflict. The outcome of this conflict was that the Northside pastor resigned and left. Thus, a strained relationship developed between the Northside congregation and the Severns Valley congregation.

When Howard Cobble left Severns Valley, the church had appointed Tim Clark, its Minister of Education, to be the Acting Senior Pastor of the church. This action meant that I had to interview with the Missions Committee and then be approved by Tim Clark before either congregation would vote on calling me as Interim Pastor. What I did not know at the time was that Tim Clark had received negative information about me from the Hodgenville area and he was skeptical about my suitability for this place of service.

It was some time later that I learned that my good friend Raymond Ward had gone to Tim Clark on three occasions and recommended me as one who could effectively lead Northside Church. On the last occasion when Raymond talked with Tim, he told him that if they would give me for the job for three months and if it did not work out, he would personally pay my salary for that amount of time. Still, it was with some misgivings that Tim offered me the job.

After a final meeting with the Missions Committee, an agreement was reached. Clarence Vertreas, Bobby Thompson, and Ed Hodges gave strong support within the Missions Committee. These men never wavered in their support of me the entire time I served the church. They never interfered with my leadership and were stalwart supporters through some difficult and trying times. Fortunately, for all parties concerned, my entire time of service proved to be a most positive experience. The church grew and stabilized while my leadership skills were vindicated and appreciated.

During my service at Northside Church, I was officially on staff at Severns Valley Baptist Church, which meant that I attended staff meetings there and had that church as a support resource for the needs of the Northside Church. I reported regularly to Tim Clark and worked closely with Linda Polley and other staff members. Every member of the staff proved to be supportive.

One of the first and major problems which I had to confront was to clarify the relationship between Northside, the mission church, and Severns Valley, the mother church. As the mother church, Severns Valley held title to the land on which Northside was located and the church buildings. The indebtedness on the property was in excess of a half million dollars. If the monthly income of Northside was not sufficient to make payment on the note, the mother church had funds budgeted to make the payment. Some within Northside were insisting that the mother church simply give them title to the property and let they do with it as they wished. However, there were title restrictions on the property as well as economic realities which would prevent such action. Further, Northside did not have the financial strength to meet the note payment each month.

After conferring with various church leaders, the donor of the property, and the church legal counsel, a business meeting of Northside was called. I acted as moderator of the meeting and shared with the congregation my findings. I stated that the title to the property was held legally by Severns Valley, the mother church; that Northside did not have the financial resources to retire the indebtedness even if the mother church chose to give them title to the property; and finally, that there were restrictions within the deed stating that the church had to continue as a Southern Baptist Church. This last statement caused some immediate discussion because there were those within the Northside congregation that wanted to make the church non-denominational. As moderator, I explained that Northside Baptist Church was a Southern Baptist Church and that it would continue as such. If a person could not accept these conditions, then it would be wise for them to seek a church in which they could be comfortable.

After a brief discussion, I shared with the congregation that when Northside ceased to be a mission of Severns Valley, the mother church would give them a clear title to the church property. Such action was the common practice of Southern Baptists. The mother church had no intention to do otherwise. The meeting was adjourned shortly after these statements were shared with the congregation. While everyone was not satisfied with the outcome of the meeting, a large problem was put to rest. Some persons did leave the church but returned after several months stating that they were more than willing to be members of a Southern Baptist Church.

Several deacons from Severns Valley were present in this meeting as observers. They did not enter into the discussion, but they did report back to the deacons of Severns Valley the proceedings of the meeting. Word began to filter back to me that they had complimentary things to say about how I moderated the meeting. From that moment forward, any doubts within the Severns Valley leadership about how I would handle problems or lead Northside seemed to fade away. All the doubt and questions that had arisen in their minds as a result of negative talk flowing out of Hodgenville seemed to be a thing of the past. I can truly say that it was nice to be redeemed in the eyes of those who have had doubts about my ability and credibility.

I served Northside Baptist Church as Interim Pastor for fourteen months. JoAnn and I had moved our membership to the church during that time. I talked with Ronny Raines, whom the church called to be pastor, while he was in the process of dealing with the church. I found him to be a committed and capable leader. However, once he became pastor, he always seemed to be ill at ease when I was present though I was careful to avoid creating any problems for him. For that reason, JoAnn and I soon moved our membership to Severns Valley Baptist Church. Thus, we began a new and different experience.

Once we became members of Severns Valley Baptist Church, we were careful to keep a low profile in the church, not wanting our presence to create any impression other than that we came each week to worship. We were friends with Al and Ruth Rider who were the teachers of a co-ed senior adult Sunday School class. They kept inviting us to the class and we began to attend. I explained to Al that having a retired preacher in the class could cause problems, but he assured me that it would not, and it never did. The class had a discussion group format and the Riders, and the class members often asked for my input. When the Riders had to be away, I often taught the class. At least once every year, we had the entire class in our home for a meal or a social event which became a welcome and enjoyable event.

This account of these first places of interim pastoral ministry has been shared in order to provide the reader with an overall picture of what takes place during this type of service. No two churches are exactly the same, and all churches, like people, have distinct personalities. In many ways congregations are the same because of the human factors involved, but in other ways they are quite different. The interim pastor must draw upon his experience and training as he carries out this kind of ministry. It often is very much like serving as pastor of a church. However, one must always be aware of the fact that his service is temporary and not long term. My longest tenure was fourteen months while the shortest was one month. At the writing of this account in July 2016, I have served twenty-two congregations as interim pastor. Most of these churches were within one hundred miles of my residence and one was as close as three miles.

In August 1998, JoAnn retired as a public school teacher. Her sister had retired the previous year and Bobbie's husband, Ralph, retired about a month earlier than JoAnn. All three had been in public school education. The sisters decided that it would be nice and exciting to spend some of the winter months in Florida, thus escaping the cold and gloom of Kentucky winters. Since their mother, Hazel Ensslin, was in a nursing home in northern Kentucky, they wanted to be close enough to drive home in one day should her needs require it. A careful search of the internet focused on the panhandle of Florida and led them to the small town of Seagrove, Florida, on the Gulf Coast, about halfway between Panama City and Destin. They found a rental house that was large enough to accommodate both families. We spent January and February of 1999 in Seagrove with the Gulf of Mexico at our back door.

These months were exciting. We ate fresh seafood in the local eateries, shopped in the consignment shops and large malls in the area, played golf during the day, and dominoes at night. We visited and ate with other Kentuckians who were also spending the winter in the area. It was a fun time. Going home after two months seemed almost too soon. Thus we began our winter stays and happy times in Florida.

Beginning our third year of snow birding, we rented a beachfront condo in a new facility in Seagrove. It was a second-floor condo with three bedrooms, three baths, and a large balcony facing the Gulf of Mexico. We were to spend two winters there with each of us sharing the master bedroom one of those years. It had space enough to have company so some family as well as friends could come to visit us.

Shortly before our winter trips to Florida, both of our mothers had gone through a serious decline in health resulting in their moving to extended care or a nursing home facility. My mother had experienced short term memory loss and after a bad case of shingles went to a nursing home in Lake City. JoAnn's mother had fallen and suffered back injuries that made it almost impossible to walk. She had gone to an extended care facility in northern

Kentucky. Later, she suffered a stroke and went to live in Baptist Convalescent Center in Covington, Kentucky.

Both of our mothers were in nursing homes for nearly five years. My mother was hospitalized with pneumonia a few weeks before her death in April 1994. Most of our family gathered in Lake City for her funeral which was held at Parkview Baptist Church. I did not preach her funeral but did conduct the graveside service at Mt. Carmel Baptist Church Cemetery where many family members are buried. Later, when her youngest sister, Mary Sue Young, died, I conducted her graveside service at that same cemetery.

During the years 1994 through 1999, several significant events took place. We bought a larger house on the edge of Elizabethtown and sold our first home which was in town. JoAnn retired from teaching school and we began our winter stays in Florida. Near the middle of December 1999, JoAnn was diagnosed with early stage breast cancer. Though this diagnosis was a surprise, both of us accepted it and faced the fact that surgery was necessary. We made plans for surgery following Christmas, but JoAnn's mother died unexpectedly on Christmas night 1999. Hazel had been in a nursing home for nearly five years as a result of a stroke. We believe that she had another stroke on Christmas Day and quietly slipped away during the night. Hazel's funeral involved as many of the family as possible. All of her five grandchildren plus one great grandson served as pallbearers. Her oldest grandson, Paul, sang "Amazing Grace" at the conclusion of the main service which was conducted by her pastor, Terry Lester. I conducted the graveside service. The weather was cold and snowy.

Immediately following Hazel's funeral, we rescheduled JoAnn's surgery for December 30, 1999, which was my birthday. The good news was that the doctor removed the cancer with a lumpectomy. The bad news was that radiation plus a regimen of drugs was the recommended follow up. We remained in Kentucky for about four weeks and then joined Bobbie and Ralph Rush in Seagrove for the remaining time of our winter stay. When we returned home from Florida, JoAnn received twenty-nine radiation treatments at Hardin Memorial Hospital. Even though she insisted that she was able to go alone, I went with her for every treatment. The therapy sapped her strength. I do not think that she would have been able to make it alone the last week. It was a long time before she regained her strength. We rejoice in the fact that the cancer has not returned, and we have moved on with life.

Chapter 19

Interim Pastorates: A Continuing Saga

For nearly a decade and a half, my ministry consisted of serving either as an interim pastor or simply that of filling various pulpits on a week to week basis. I served several churches from one to three months. While these congregations may have considered me their interim pastor, my service was hardly more than that of a supply preacher. In conversations with their search committee members and other church leaders, it was apparent that none of them wanted any input from the outside. This attitude probably was the result of a desire to maintain control, a distrust of outside sources, or a sad mixture of both. Had these churches been willing to accept outside counsel, many problems that needed to be faced could have been dealt with and possibly resolved.

Near the last third of this time of my ministry, JoAnn, Bobbie Jean, and Ralph Rush, all retired from public school education. Our two families began going to Florida for January and February to escape the cold and dreary Kentucky winters. Doing this would change the way I served as an interim pastor and it would ultimately bring an end to that ministry. What I am about to share will cover those last years of ministry.

Our first winter months spent in Florida were January and February. Later, we stretched that into ten weeks and finally into a full three months. If I was serving as an interim pastor when it came time to go south, I arranged for a retired seminary classmate, Dr. John Al Miller, to serve these churches while I was away. Dr. Miller's wife, Eloise, was from Elizabethtown, and when he retired they had moved there. He was highly effective and was well received in every church. He proved to be a great supporter.

I was serving the Bardstown Junction Baptist Church, just south of Shepherdsville, when time came for us to go south for the first time. The church was aware that I would be away for two months and they graciously accepted the ministry of Dr. John Al Miller. This arrangement worked well, and I found the church in excellent condition when I returned.

The congregation at Bardstown Junction Baptist Church was mostly working middle class people. To my knowledge, there were no persons of wealth in the church. Some were school teachers, and a few were supervisors where they worked. They were hard working folk who loved the Lord and wanted their church to grow and prosper in the Lord's work. They had asked their previous pastor to resign simply because he had neglected the duties of leadership and service as pastor of the church.

I served this church nearly a year. They responded positively to my leadership. There was never a moment of conflict that developed between us. The church came out of its state of depression and we enjoyed a time of continuing growth and positive fellowship while I served them. They called a pastor who has served them well for over a decade. I look back on this as one of my most effective and successful interims.

Shortly after concluding my service at Bardstown Junction, I was asked to serve the Immanuel Baptist Church in Glasgow, Kentucky. This church had been formed by a group of ultra conservative members who had left Glasgow Baptist Church because of theological differences. The separation had been friendly, but each group believed that it was for the best. The retired former pastor of Glasgow Baptist Church had been serving as the interim pastor before I came to serve in that position. He continued to attend Immanuel the entire time that I served as their interim pastor.

When I first began my interim ministry, I had heard about The Center for Congregational Health, an arm of the Pastoral Care Department at Baptist Medical Center, Winston-Salem, North Carolina. This group provided special training that would equip and certify a person to serve as an interim pastor. However, the cost of this training had been beyond my means. Later, while serving Immanuel Baptist Church in Glasgow, church leaders learned of my desire to take this training. They encouraged me to register for the seminars and paid the entire cost. I completed the training and was certified by the Center to serve as an Intentional Interim Pastor.

My service to the Immanuel Baptist Church had begun in late summer and was concluded a few weeks after I returned from our winter stay in Florida. Again, Dr. John Al Miller had served the church during my absence. His ministry was well-received. The church called a pastor shortly after I returned. Serving this church allowed me to form some lasting friendships which I treasure.

Following other brief tenures at a group of rural churches, I concluded my interim ministry at Rineyville Baptist Church, Rineyville, Kentucky. This church was located just three miles from my home in a growing, middle class community. The previous pastor had been there about eleven years. His ministry had been reasonably effective but filled with conflict. He had not been a good match for the church. He had followed a pastor who had served the church for more than twenty years and had retired. It was a hard act to follow.

There were several obstacles to an effective interim ministry. However, I sought to work through and around these and began lead the church through the program which was designed to prepare them for the calling of a new pastor. A lay group joined me in leading the church through these activities. Many of the things we did were designed to achieve a healthy fellowship and to prepare them for the future. A number of those who served with me in this preparation for the future were church leaders. Some were members of the Pastor Search Committee.

Months later, negative information came informing me that several of the people working with me and serving as church leaders or on the Pastor Search Committee were working behind my back on an entirely different agenda. I felt that if their efforts were carried out, the church would be split. In fact, I felt that a church split was imminent. I could see no way to avoid such an event.

With these facts in hand, I conferred with trusted friends and family members. Everyone suggested that I withdraw immediately from this toxic situation. It was late in the week. I wrote a letter of resignation which would be effective when read. I went to the church on Sunday and led the two morning services. At the close of the second service, I read the letter and told the congregation that when the benediction was pronounced, my service with the church was ended. As JoAnn and I walked out of the church, someone asked what I was going to do. My reply was, "I'm going to Disney World." And with that we were gone. The church split that I feared would happen began that evening, and within two weeks a final breech had occurred.

After leaving the Rineyville Church in early January 2005, JoAnn and I went home not knowing when or where we might go. We had decided not to return to the panhandle of Florida because weather conditions were not consistently favorable. We felt that we could deal with poor weather at home and avoid the cost of expensive rent. However, that was about to change.

Being a Florida native, I was blessed with having relatives scattered all over the state. Choosing to winter in west Florida gave me the opportunity to visit with and renew relationships with my mother's two remaining sisters, Mary Sue Young and Hallie Sperry. Both aunts lived in Panama City, which was about thirty miles from Seagrove, where we stayed. Aunt Mary had never married and had spent most of her adult life in Panama City. She had also been a surrogate mother to Aunt Hallie's two daughters when they were growing up. Aunt Hallie's oldest daughter, Mary Hollie Ostrander, had moved back to Panama City from Atlanta when it became apparent that her mother and aunt needed someone to look after them because of age and declining health.

These two aunts passed away during the four-year span in which we wintered in the area. I am grateful that I could visit with them and renew our relationship during this time. Aunt Mary had asked me to serve with Mary Hollie as co-administrator of her estate. She had a will and her affairs were in order. Also, she had asked me to take possession of her ashes after cremation and dispose of them as I saw fit. I had agreed verbally to do this, and Mary Hollie was aware of this. After the cremation Mary Hollie discussed with me what we should do with the ashes. I told her that there was one grave site left in the family plot in Mt. Carmel Cemetery at Lake City. We agreed to inter her ashes there.

On the day of the funeral, we drove to the Mt. Carmel Cemetery. My brother, Ralph Hardee, had prepared a small, deep hole in the grave plot. I conducted a brief graveside service in the presence of family members Mary Hollie Ostrander, Bill and Lou Harrell, Ralph and Burma Sue Hardee, JoAnn, and a few friends. Aunt Mary's ashes were interred in a grave plot joining her father, mother, two sisters, brother, and brother-in-law. Having done that, Mary Hollie and I carried out the remaining conditions of Aunt Mary's will in perfect harmony. Mary Hollie and I remain close as always.

In late February, Bobbie and Ralph Rush called to tell us that they were meeting some friends in south Florida for a winter cruse. They had stopped in Venice, Florida, to visit briefly with other friends who lived in the Venice Municipal Mobile Home Park. While there, they talked with Jim Brown, the park association president, about the availability of a mobile home unit that they could purchase for use in the winter. Most residents of the park were winter residents, and many were Kentuckians. Jim suggested that they check with him after their cruse. When they returned, he had a unit ready for sale and they bought it.

Early evening on the day of their purchase, Bobbie called JoAnn and told her what they had done. She was so excited about their purchase that JoAnn casually suggested that they look around to see if another suitable unit might be available. Early the next morning, Bobbie and Ralph began to walk through the park and noticed a man placing a "For Sale" sign in his window. They knocked on the door, went in, found it to be acceptable and called us on the spot. The owner quoted a price and we told him we would get back to him soon. This transpired on a weekend and we had several phone conversations with Bobbie and Ralph about the property. I told JoAnn that I did not want to purchase a unit where I did not own the land. Residents of Venice Municipal Mobile Home Park do not own the land. Further, I felt that the price was more than we should invest, but I said nothing to JoAnn about that.

Over the weekend, we continued to discuss whether we wanted to consider the opportunity to buy in Venice. I set a price in my mind as to what I felt we should pay for the property. On Monday, the owner of the property called Bobbie and Ralph saying that he had misquoted the price. His new price was exactly what I had set in my mind but had not shared with anyone. We talked to the owner who agreed to hold the property until we could get there late Wednesday or early Thursday. We arrived in Venice on Wednesday afternoon and agreed to the purchase on Thursday morning. It was a whirlwind event.

Jim Brown was a native of London, Kentucky, having grown up just a few blocks from JoAnn's home. After a tour of duty in the U.S. Navy, he had moved to northern Kentucky and worked for the railroad as a locomotive engineer most of his adult life. As president of Venice Municipal Mobile Home Park, he knew the procedure for transferring property and utilities. He was kind enough to lead us through this process and helped us greatly as we began to settle in our new winter abode.

We stayed in Venice long enough to complete the property transfer and to take possession from Clayton and Catherine Brown, the previous owners. They left all furnishings except their bed. We bought a bed, had it delivered, spent about two weeks in our new winter home, and headed back to Kentucky.

The Sunday after we purchased our winter home in Venice, Clayton and Catherine Brown took us to Sunday School and worship services at First Baptist Church Venice. We enjoyed their company, the class, and the worship service. We continued to attend there when we were in Venice. However, we soon began to see evidence of extreme fundamentalism in both the class and worship services. At first, we were able to tolerate these conditions, but it became increasingly difficult for us to worship in this atmosphere. We often came away from church angry and upset.

We decided to visit the Venice Presbyterian Church located next door to our mobile home park. We felt at home immediately. We sang from hymn books, the music was worshipful, the pastor was young but able and gifted in the pulpit, and the people were warm and friendly. Early in our visits there, I saw one of my seminary classmates whom I had not seen for fifty years. He was kind enough to introduce me to the retired ministers' group in the church, and to help me become involved in the various church activities. It was a breath of fresh air for the McDonald family. Many of our park residents were members of churches back home, but few attended church while in Venice. However, many Kentuckians were Baptists and worshiped regularly at Baptist churches while in Venice. Venice Presbyterian Church proved to be a perfect fit for us. Everything about the church seemed to meet our spiritual needs. The retired ministers group included Baptists, Presbyterians, Methodists, Reformed, and others. We were invited to participate in the worship activities and ordinations of the church. It continues to be a happy and healthy relationship.

We quickly became a part of the mobile home park culture. Both of us made friends from many places. We participated in the social activities of the park. Each year various state groups would put on a monthly supper with some entertainment. These were fund raising events with the profits going to the park social committees for upkeep and continuing activities. JoAnn and Bobbie gave leadership for seven years for the annual Kentucky Night. I served as the master of ceremonies for most of those years. We played bingo, several card games, and golf. Ralph and I became regulars in a "happy hour" group of Pennsylvania men that met each week. When the two of us hosted this group, our wives insisted on providing the finger food and other tasty morsels which became legendary with the group. Later when we moved to another park, these men insisted that we continue to meet with them and we have.

Though I did not seek such a role, I eventually became the unofficial chaplain of the park. It took a while for folk to learn that I would accept them as they were and not be judgmental. I often found myself in religious discussions dealing with and listening to questions that people struggled with daily as they sought to relate to God. Requests came for me to visit park residents in the hospital or pray for family members back home who were either sick or facing some sort of crisis. Since we had an "over 55" age requirement for park residency, death was a common event. Early on we began a yearly memorial service for park residents who had died within the last year. I always presided over that event.

The next ten years passed quickly. We would go to Venice in early October and return home just before Thanksgiving. Then, we would return to Venice right after Christmas and stay until after the first of April. Waiting until then allowed many of the "snowbirds" to depart and thus relieve the traffic congestion on I-75 North. On our trips south and north, we always drove to Lake City, Florida, and spent a day or so with my brother before continuing our trip. It gave us a nice break plus a good family visit.

Spending four to five months of split time away from Kentucky, my opportunities for supply preaching and brief interims back home were becoming less frequent. Most churches seeking a preaching and visiting interim did not seem to be open to someone serving them for a few months and then leaving. Further, to promote such an arrangement would take a continuing daily effort. The various Baptist leaders also seemed less interested in helping keep my name before the churches. Thus, I backed away from self-promotion, began to devote my time to other things, and accepted the opportunities that came my way.

Over a span of about five years, I underwent three different surgeries. The first was hemorrhoid surgery followed three weeks later by prostate surgery. These first two were done at Hardin Memorial Hospital by Dr. Marshall Johnson and Dr. Steven Vaught.

The third surgery was also done by Dr. Johnson, but it took three separate trips to the emergency room plus multiple tests to determine that my gall bladder needed to be removed. Even after the tests, Dr. Johnson was not certain that my gall bladder was the problem. However, once he got into the surgery, he found that my gall bladder was more severely diseased than the tests had indicated. One difficulty with diagnosing my problem was that previously I had undergone bypass heart surgery. The pain that I experienced with each gall bladder attack was not typical of gall bladder pain. Attending doctors always seemed to focus on my previous heart problem. Once my gall bladder was removed, the problems that I had experienced disappeared.

For several years JoAnn had complained that her eyesight was not being corrected by the prescription glasses that she had received. I had a similar experience and had undergone cataract surgery on both eyes in October 2000. My eyesight improved dramatically almost immediately. I kept encouraging her to get a second opinion from an ophthalmologist rather than an optometrist. When one of the members of our Sunday School class told about her successful cataract surgery at St. Luke's Eye Clinic in Tarpon Springs, Florida, JoAnn decided that she would go there.

Since Tarpon Springs was about an hour and a half north of Venice, we arranged to stop by there on our way down in October. We discovered that St. Luke's is in fact a large eye hospital with multiple services available for every eye problem that might be medically treated. After seeing several doctors and spending most of the day in consultation, it was confirmed that JoAnn did need cataract surgery. It was scheduled for late December, but later moved forward to early January because of the Christmas holidays.

JoAnn had cataract surgery on both eyes in early January. However, she complained that she was not seeing much better than before the surgery. When the doctor examined her eyes after the surgery, he concluded that she had a retina problem and referred her to a retina specialist. We continued to make the trip from Venice to Tarpon Springs almost weekly. After much consultation and multiple tests, JoAnn underwent retina surgery. It failed to provide her with improved eyesight. Though she could see well enough to read, drive and work at her computer, she was disappointed with the outcome and so was I. JoAnn's ability to adjust to circumstances has always amazed me. She still does all the things she did before her eye surgery, but at a more deliberate pace.

Chapter 20

Going Strong, But Counting Down

In the spring of 2012, JoAnn and I began to discuss our need to live near one of our children should a medical crisis or the need for long term care arise. Our closest son was about sixty miles away, the next was ninety miles away, and the last was one hundred fifty miles away. They would be too far away to be commuting to help care for us should we need them. Though we were happy in Elizabethtown and had many friends there, we knew that it would be wise to move closer to one of our sons.

First, we talked with our sons and came to the agreement that since Philip was the least likely to move, we should consider moving to London. Everyone agreed that such a move would be the most practical. The only sticking point was that as JoAnn grew up in London, her life's ambition was to leave and never return as a resident. However, she had been away more than sixty years and both London and Laurel County had changed in many ways. As we weighed all our options, JoAnn said that she was willing to return.

We had barely made that decision when Philip called telling us that his across-the-street neighbor, Gary McDaniel, had approached him saying that his son was selling the house that he had recently built next door to his father. Gary had bought the house stating that he wanted to choose the neighbors who would be moving next door. He asked if Philip thought we might be interested in buying the house and moving to London. He shared with Philip a reasonable price for the house and lot. We told Philip to tell Mr. McDaniel that we would come look at the house and talk with him about a possible purchase.

The house was a three-bedroom brick home with two baths. Two of the bedrooms were very small. It had 1,600 square feet of living space, one walk-in closet, nine-foot ceilings, hardwood floors, and a two-car garage. We were at that moment living in a house with 2,000 square feet of living space on the main floor, two bathrooms, five walk-in closets, 1,650 square feet in the basement with 1,200 square feet finished, plus a two and a half car garage, a front porch, and a large rear deck that was partly under roof. Moving into a much smaller home was not going to be easy, but the house in London had possibilities. Also, it was almost directly across the street from Philip's home.

Gary McDaniel agreed to hold the house with no deposit or down payment until we could sell our home in Elizabethtown. We made the deal on a handshake and went back to Elizabethtown to sell our home and prepare to move.

Arriving back home, we began to pack things that we could easily move. Philip bought an enclosed trailer with which he made at least four trips moving our belongings which he stored in his second garage. Extra furniture and anything that would give the house the appearance of clutter was either moved, sold, or donated. Once things were cleared out, we hired an independent appraiser to give us some idea of the value of the house and lot.

Having determined the approximate value of our property, we chose three realtors and asked them to look at our home and tell us how they would proceed to sell it should we choose to list it with them. Danny O'Brien of Rainbow Realty was our choice and we signed a listing agreement with him on Wednesday shortly after noon. The next Wednesday shortly after noon he returned with an offer. We knew the prospective buyers. They were Donald and Betty Vance from LaRue County. Betty had been my secretary for about three years when I was pastor of First Baptist Church Hodgenville. Their offer was slightly less than we were prepared to accept. I asked Danny to call Don and tell him what we wanted. He did, and Don agreed immediately to accept our counter offer. The sale was a done deal.

Though he never stated it directly, Danny O'Brien had been dealing with Don and Betty Vance for some time looking for a home that would be acceptable to them. Once he secured the listing from us, all he had to do was to call them, show them the house, obtain their agreement to buy, and most of his work was done. He was kind enough to split the real estate fee equally between both of us, which was a fair and generous act. He was a good person with whom to work.

The purchase of our home in London went smoothly, and on September 21, 2012, we arrived in London to occupy our new home. Though we were close to Philip's family physically, the closeness has never appeared to be a problem for us or them.

When the movers began to move our furniture into the house, it became obvious to us that if we got rid of half or our belongings, we still would not have enough room to live comfortably in this house. After much discussion, we agreed to add a larger master bedroom and bath with a large walk-in closet, as well as a covered deck at our back door. This work was to be done in the spring and summer of 2013.

On our first Sunday in London, we attended First Baptist Church where Philip is a deacon and where his family are members. We transferred our membership, thus beginning a healthy and happy relationship with the church family and its leaders. Our pastor, Dr. Terry Lester, has since retired. He was gracious to us, inviting me to fill the pulpit on occasions when he had to be away and to lead the mid-week Bible Study in his absence. Since his departure, I have filled the pulpit several times. The church family has been positive in response to my preaching and teaching. Their attitude of respect is encouraging, humbling, and inspiring.

JoAnn has renewed friendships with former classmates and those who were part of the community. It is always interesting to be in a group and have several persons recognize her and engage her in conversation about their past associations. Her mother, Hazel Ensslin, lived in London until her health failed in the early 1990s. She had moved to northern Kentucky to be closer to her younger daughter. Hazel was a friendly, outgoing person, and we hear Hazel stories almost every week.

The construction of the addition to our house began in the spring of 2013. We had hired an architect, Bret James, to draw plans, but we were unsatisfied with them. We returned to him for additional help but came away frustrated. This is not to say that he was not good at his trade, which he was and is, but somehow his suggestions and our desires never meshed.

However, our builders were a different story. David Kelley and Lee Jones seemed to understand early on what we wanted. They worked from the basic plans and we added or changed things as we went along. Their suggestions as well as their work were more than we could have asked for. We would often confer on what they were about to do, and the finished product was what we desired or more. We occupied the new addition in late September 2013 and felt at home immediately. Once we were settled, we made our seasonal departure for Venice.

Our residence in Venice Municipal Mobile Home Park spanned ten years. We had briefly discussed moving but had made no conscious decision to do so. Bobbie and Ralph Rush had also mentioned selling but never said a word about moving to another park. However, several privately-owned parks in the area had recently been sold, and the residents of those parks soon faced rising rents causing them to either sell their units at a loss or to simply abandon them.

Venice Municipal Mobile Home Park had once been part of a military base during World War II. The property on which the park was located had been conveyed in trust by the US Government to the City of Venice. However, the Federal Aviation Association still exercised a final say in the administration of the property. Also, the Venice City Council appointed the Airport Board which, allegedly, directly administered the park. Park residents never saw any of these persons. Along with these circumstances, questions began to arise in our minds about the future of the park. Since residents of the park did not own the land on which their units were located, any hint that the land might be sold caused some anxiety, and some of the city leaders did occasionally mention this possibility.

Near the end of March 2014, Bobbie and Ralph came by and told us that a family member of one of the park residents had asked them if they would sell their unit. They asked for a day to consider this, arrived at a selling price, and the person agreed to purchase their unit immediately. It happened in less than a week's time.

Prior to this event, I had gathered information about the cost in terms of moving to nearby Venice Isles Estates. Several of our friends lived there and had helped me gather the information I was seeking. The initial cost would be more, but you owned the land. The amenities that the park offered were outstanding, plus the fact that the monthly fees were much less, and the park could not be sold without permission of the resident owners. It was just what we were looking for.

We put our unit in Venice Municipal Mobile Home Park on the market and sold it in about two weeks. This freed us to begin looking for a place in Venice Isles Estates. Bobbie and Ralph decided to relocate there also. They found a place and made an offer which was accepted. We began looking but were slow to find what we wanted. Since Bobbie and Ralph had plenty of room in their new home, we moved what we were taking with us to their place and stayed there until we found a suitable unit. JoAnn found our new unit shortly after the "For Sale" sign appeared. We called our realtor and were the first ones to look at it. We made an immediate offer and learned an hour later that it had been accepted.

However, it took nearly a month to complete the legal and financial details of our purchase and to take possession. We stayed in Venice until that was done. As soon as we got the keys to our new residence, we began to move our belongings from the Rush home to ours. In less than a week we moved in, did some cleaning, took an inventory of repairs and changes that we needed to make, hired someone we knew to do that work, and departed for our Kentucky home. It was near the middle of May and the Florida summer was already heating up.

Back in London, we had many tasks waiting on us. There were family obligations, yard work left over from construction, preparation for summer events for grandchildren, and getting ready for the absence of our son, his wife, and oldest granddaughter soon departing for a brief visit to Europe. We were to be in charge of a ten-year-old granddaughter and her older brother back home from his first year of college. Add to that their collection of pets, three cats, three ducks, one dog, and one rabbit. It turned out to be an interesting and fun summer.

In our new Kentucky home, we continued to rearrange furniture and the separate office areas we both occupy. I had donated a large portion of my professional library to the new Baptist Seminary of Kentucky, but I still have more books than I need, and I continue to find more books in the used book stores in south Florida, adding to our space problem. Being a lover of good books, I find it difficult to part with a volume once I have it.

When I began writing this account of my personal journey, I did not anticipate it being this long or that it would take more than a decade to complete. Since my junior year in high school I have been writing, most of it being focused on academic work. One of my college majors was English, which was not planned but perhaps was the result of divine guidance. One does not survive in the pastoral ministry without being able to express one's self by the written and spoken word. While serving as a pastor, I wrote at least two new sermons each week, articles for the church paper, and a Bible study for the middle of the week. In the beginning, I had no idea of how much writing I would be doing.

Early in 2014, My oldest grandson, Adam, came to me with a request to write a weekly blog for a motivational and inspirational website that he and a friend were in the process of developing. My contribution was to be a weekly devotional of about 350 words designed to be read by young professionals. It had to be brief because of their limited time. It was to be Bible based so that any truth they gained could be applied to their daily activities. I agreed to give it a try, and I have written about fifty articles which appear on his website under the title of "Monday Morning with Ike." These articles are also appearing on the website of First Baptist Church, London, Kentucky. This experience for me has been demanding and enjoyable. It appears that at age 86, I am not done yet.

Seeking to bring these memoirs to a conclusion, I confess that I am at a loss as to exactly how to accomplish that task. My life is obviously not over, but I am aware that I could depart this earthly scene abruptly should God choose to call me to my eternal reward. There are, however, a few brief things that I want to say before this volume is concluded.

Both JoAnn and I are deeply grateful that we have been allowed to live into our ninth decade while maintaining reasonably good health. We enjoy being able to spend some fall and winter months in Venice, Florida. Our doing this has been an unexpected blessing of our senior years. Our Florida time and the relationships that we have formed have been a blessing to both of us.

Our church experience in Venice and in London has blessed us both immensely. Attending and being a part of a Presbyterian Church in Florida has given us an appreciation of a wider world of fellow Christians and the spiritual journey that we all share. The congregation and pastoral staff of First Baptist Church London has been accepting as well as encouraging. Our gifts and calling have been accepted and affirmed, allowing an opportunity for expression and continuing service. We could not have found a warmer or more encouraging fellowship than what we have experienced there.

Having lived into my mid-eighties and enjoyed reasonably good health, the medical community assures me that I will probably live into my early nineties. That would be nice if I could continue in good health, be able to care for myself, not be a widower, and die quietly in my sleep. Since none of those arrangements are in my hands, I am trusting the Good Lord to see to it that some of this does come to pass. I will be fortunate if any or all of these wishes are granted.

Several of my mature Christian friends have observed with me that it is much easier to look back and see the guiding hand of God in our lives than it is to look ahead and see where He is leading us. My experience says that is true. In retrospect, I am keenly aware that God has persistently nudged me in the direction that He wanted me to go. Often, I have resisted and questioned His reasons and judgment. But He never failed or abandoned me. In the end, He did for me what was best and right. In my best efforts, I could never have arrived at this destination in life without His blessings and guidance. If there is good to be found in me or my doings, praise Him. If there is blame or failure, let it fall on me. But even where blame might be placed, or failure be found, God's grace has bailed me out and blessed me once again. To Him be the glory, honor, and praise forever. Amen and Amen.

> We are travelers on a journey,
> Fellow pilgrims on the road
> We are here to help each other
> Walk the mile and bear the load.
>
> I will hold the Christ-light for you
> In the night-time of your fear;
> I will hold my hand out to you,
> Speak the peace you long to hear.
>
> "The Servant Song" by
> Richard Gillard
> © 1977 Scripture in Song

Author's Afterthought

Having written, rewritten, proof read, and revised this document several times, the author has an observation which could possibly be of interest to the readers. This is especially true should they be pastors or staff persons involved in congregational ministry.

The several chapters that tell the story of ministry to local congregations all contain philosophies of and accounts of ministry in a real live situation. The stories tell of working with people in large and small groups as well as personal, one-on-one encounters.

Out of this story, the author observes a philosophy of administration and ministry emerging that is down to earth, practical and people centered. While the story has not been written for this purpose, the author is aware that this has happened.

That being the case, he feels that in a practical way, students of as well as practitioners of ministry could profit from reading these stories of ministry in a local church setting.

Readers who may share this observation are given permission to share with any minister or church staff whom they feel may profit from reading this story.

www.ingramcontent.com/pod-product-compliance
Lightning Source LLC
Chambersburg PA
CBHW071902290426

44110CB00013B/1252